For Sara & Campbell

Library of Congress Cataloging-in-Publication Data

Bernstein, Ross.
  The code : football's unwritten rules and its ignore-at-your-own-risk code of honor / Ross Bernstein.
      p. cm.
  Includes bibliographical references.
  ISBN 978-1-60078-175-9
  1. Football—Corrupt practices—United States. 2. Football players—United States—Conduct of life. I. Title.
  GV959.B395 2009
  796.332—dc22

                                                                          2009016701

This book is available in quantity at special discounts for your group or organization. For further information, contact:

Triumph Books
542 South Dearborn Street
Suite 750
Chicago, Illinois 60605
(312) 939-3330
Fax (312) 663-3557
www.triumphbooks.com

Printed in U.S.A.
ISBN: 978-1-60078-175-9
Design by Sue Knopf; page production by Patricia Frey
Photo courtesy of AP Images unless otherwise indicated

Foreword by Jerome Bettis

13-year running back and Pro Bowl selection for the Pittsburgh Steelers

The code of honor is a very important thing in professional football. As a former player, it meant a great deal to me. The code is about respect. It is about how you respect the game, your teammates, and your opponents. It is also about how you are respected, too, which ties into your credibility as a person. I always wanted to play the game the right way, and hopefully I was thought of as someone who was a good person, both on and off the field.

Retaliation is a big part of the game, and you had to be smart about how you went about it. You had to wait for the right opportunity, otherwise you could take a costly penalty and really hurt your team. That is a selfish thing to do. Sometimes you could get a guy back on the next play, other guys have had to wait years. You remember things though, that is for sure. If a guy cheap-shots you or plays dirty, you don't forget stuff like that, especially if he hurt you or tried to hurt you. That is where you draw the line—if a guy tries to do something that could possibly end your career. That is where the game polices itself. You just can't tolerate that kind of thing. No way.

In today's game, with all of the camera angles, you can't afford to do anything stupid. Plus, you can get fined $25,000 to $50,000 after the fact by the league, or worse, you could get suspended for a game. Most fans don't realize this, but in football we get 16 game checks. That is how it works. So if you miss a game due to suspension, you lose 1/16 of your annual salary—which, at this level, is a whole lot of money. That alone has cleaned up a lot of the dirty stuff in football because that hits guys where it hurts the most—in the wallet. Football is unique that way, I think. I mean, in baseball, if a pitcher beans a guy, or in hockey, if a guy punches someone, he might get thrown out of a game—but the punishment and fine is nothing like it is in football with regard to retaliation.

Back in the day, quarterbacks could set up and call plays to get guys that had done something dirty. Well, today you can't do that kind of thing. So you have to be patient and wait for your opportunity. You will let your teammates know that the guy you want to get is on the list, and hopefully someone will help you out if they can get a good shot on him throughout the course of a game. We are all brothers and teammates out there, and we all want to take care of each other and help each other out. You protect them, and they protect you—that is what the code is all about. You never want to do anything illegal or something that will injure a guy, but if you get a chance to get a guy, even if it is borderline between clean and dirty, you take the shot. You've got 10 guys there to back you up. Players need to know that you won't tolerate that kind of stuff, otherwise they will keep doing it to you and anybody else they think will let them get away with it.

You know, there is a lot of karma in this game. If you play like an idiot, then your name is mud. You look at the guys who were known as cheap-shotters, and they are hated in the football afterlife, so to speak. If you were an asshole when you played, you are usually considered an asshole when you are retired. That stuff doesn't change, and players don't forget. That reputation doesn't leave you. It doesn't translate off of the football field. Players see people as who they are, and if you played like a dick, you will be thought of as such for a very long time. That is just the way it goes. You don't ever want to be labeled as that kind of a guy, but you reap what you sow in this game.

Intimidation is a big part of the game, too. My running style had a lot to do with intimidation. I wanted to run over people and hurt them. I was clean about it, but I wanted to send them a message that I was going to dictate the tempo of the game. I wanted to pound on defenses early in games to soften them up. Or I might try to single out one guy in particular to really come after him and expose him. That way he might be afraid to really take me on in the second half when he was tired. When guys are worn out, they will try to make ankle tackles rather than go for your body where they will get a lot of impact. Well, that was exactly what I wanted, because I could make a quick move in those situations and bust those plays for big gains. Even though I was a big guy, I had a lot of speed, and I could use that to my advantage in creating opportunities that might not exist for smaller running backs. I wasn't afraid to go straight at guys right up the middle. That was where I made my living, down in the trenches where it got dirty and ugly. But I could also bust it outside too, which forced guys to stay honest. I think that combination of being a dual threat really intimidated a lot of guys.

Trash talking was a form of intimidation, too. It was a factor with some guys because it could take them off of their games. Everybody tried to trash-talk me, but I never fell for it. I would get up from the bottom of a pile with a big grin on my face, which spoke volumes. I was out there having fun and wasn't about to be thrown off by some guy talking smack. No way.

Guys will do all sorts of tricks to get away with things in football. They always have. Hey, if you can get away with it, why not? If you can draw a penalty for your team and get a first down, that is a big deal. I remember as a kid watching Dennis Rodman draw fouls out on the basketball court, flopping around out there. He was the best at that. Guys would touch him, and he would fly backward. It was hilarious. But he got in there and did the dirty work to help his team any way he could. I will say this, though— there is a big difference in the gamesmanship between a lineman getting a holding call or a receiver getting a pass-interference call versus a guy using steroids. That is just cheating in my book. They create an unfair playing field and should never be tolerated. As a result of guys getting bigger, faster, and stronger than they should be, others could get hurt as a result. So that has no place in the game as far as I am concerned.

One of the more controversial areas of the code deals with sign stealing. There is a right way and a wrong way to go about it, and clearly the Patriots went about it the wrong way with the whole Spygate thing a few years ago. It was a big deal. What they did with regard to videotaping stuff was cheating. There were a lot of pissed-off people when that whole thing went down, including me because we had lost two AFC Championship Games to those guys just prior to all of that. So for me, just the possibility that they may have cheated in some way makes me very upset. Who knows? Did they videotape our signs, too? We were very upset when we found out about all of that stuff because those things affect a lot of people both on and off the field.

There is a clubhouse code, too. You don't talk about your teammates. If your quarterback had a bad game, you don't single him out with the media and say things. That is what eats up locker rooms and can never be tolerated. The same is true with contract stuff. You can't comment on guys' situations or things of that nature because it creates a lot of dissention between the other players. Even if a guy is holding out for whatever reason, you just have to let it go and concentrate on doing your job. You can talk about it in the locker room, but that is it—what is said in there stays in there.

Lastly, another big part of the code was playing hurt. To play at this level, you have to play hurt. We all did it, and that was just the way it was. I was fortunate that I didn't have too many serious injuries in my career and was able to play for 13 seasons. Most running backs only last for a few years in this league, so I take great pride in the fact that I worked hard, trained hard, and kept my body in good playing shape for so long. I always wanted to be out there for my teammates and never wanted to let them down.

Winning the Super Bowl in 2006 was the ultimate. I couldn't have imagined a better way to go out than on top. I feel so blessed to have been able to play this game for as long as I did and for all of the opportunities that it has afforded me in life. Now as a TV analyst, I get to see the game from a whole new perspective, but I still have that same love of the game—and that is what it is all about.

Foreword by Ahmad Rashad

Four-time Pro Bowl wide receiver with the Minnesota Vikings and
Emmy Award–winning television sports journalist

The first word that comes to mind when I think of the honor code is "respect." If you didn't have respect for the game or for your opponents, then you weren't going to last very long as a player in this league. There were personal codes that each player lived by. It was sort of the way you conducted yourself and the kind of person you were. You know, I never had anybody take a cheap shot at me throughout my entire career. Not one. I took pride in that because that said that I was respected by my peers. As a result, I never had to worry about that kind of stuff when I was running a route over the middle or going up against a guy who had a reputation for playing dirty. Even when we played the Raiders, who were notorious cheap-shotters in my day, they just played me straight. Again, it was a respect thing.

You watched enough film to know who the cheap-shot artists were. Those guys had to keep their heads on a swivel, too, because they would eventually get what was coming to them. The game policed itself, definitely. The guys who would clip you or roll up on your knees, they didn't stick around very long for the most part. To me, you play hard and you play clean—none of that other bs. That wasn't my style.

Football is a game of intimidation, and that can come in many forms. When I played up in Minnesota, the cold weather was our biggest intimidator. We would always run out for the warm-ups with this big facade like we weren't cold. Of course, we were freezing. But the other teams didn't know that, not for sure. They would be looking at us out of the corners of their eyes thinking, "How come these guys look so warm? They must be some bad dudes." The cold was more intimidating than any big hitter or anything else because it affected everybody. Opposing players used to hate to have to go up there in December or January, especially the brothers. Oh, they really hated it. And let me tell you, it was cold up there. Real cold. Like inhuman cold. I guarantee you that the first thing teams did when they looked over the schedule every year was to look at when they played us because nobody wanted to go up there in the dead of winter. Nobody. A lot of times I caught passes out there without ever feeling the ball. There was just this heavy thump against my frozen hands. The weather would completely psych out guys from warm-weather teams. We had such a home-field advantage in those days that we would beat teams that we weren't supposed to beat every time in that stuff. Every time. The fans up there loved it. It was a pride thing for them. They would be out there all day tailgating and having fun. We as players just learned to live with it. We knew you could play with numb fingers and frozen feet, which gave us an edge. We had to. Our coach, Bud Grant, was old school. He never allowed us to use heaters on the sideline or even wear gloves or turtlenecks under our jerseys. He wanted us to stay focused and figured that if we were thinking about staying warm then we weren't thinking about football. Opposing players would be sitting on the sideline just looking at us, wondering how the hell we could survive like that. It got to them. It really did. They thought we were superhuman, but the reality was we were just as freezing and miserable as they were. We just couldn't show it.

As a receiver, I tried to do all sorts of things to give myself an honest advantage and get open. Everybody had their own tricks of the trade or veteran moves, as we used to call them. For instance, there were ways to push off without getting called. I don't think that is cheating, either. That is what I would call gamesmanship. Look at the offensive linemen siliconing their jerseys. Is that cheating? I don't think so. After all, the defensive linemen aren't supposed to be grabbing them anyway, right? My favorite trick was being able to utilize my home-field advantage back at old Metropolitan Stadium. Like a lot of stadiums of that era, it was a dual-sport facility that was used by both the Vikings as well as the Minnesota

Twins. I knew exactly where the pitcher's mound was out there, and I knew that if I could back a cornerback over that hump, he would lose his balance a little bit. I used that trick every single week. Guys never picked up on it. It was great. Or if it was a really cold game, I knew to always make my cuts off of the yardage lines because they were painted and you could get traction from where your foot would stick in there. Was that stuff cheating? Hell no.

One of the biggest aspects of the code I think is for guys to play hurt. We all did it—that was just the way it was. Back in our day, there wasn't all of this "probable," "questionable," or "doubtful" stuff either. You either played or you didn't play. That was the only line that mattered. The only question the coach would ask you was, "Can you go?" That was it. He didn't care about how you were feeling. You either played or you didn't, and usually the guys who didn't weren't on the team for very long. We didn't have as many guys on the roster in those days either, so the teams that were the most successful were the ones that were the most resilient. We had guys on our team like defensive end Jim Marshall, who played in 270 consecutive games—an NFL record. Talk about tough. You would have to literally carry that guy off of the field to get him out of the game. These days, if a guy hurts his little finger, he is out for like two or three weeks. It is crazy. That stuff never went on when I played. Never.

When I think of guys like Jim Marshall, I just have to smile. I remember going to training camp every year with the Vikings in this little town of Mankato, about 90 miles south of Minneapolis. Training camp in those days was tough, but it was also a lot of fun. It was where we could bond as teammates and build team chemistry. We could also haze the rookies a little bit, too, which was always good for some laughs. The greatest hazing ritual we could put our rookies through in those days would be to make them drive down to training camp with Jim Marshall. Now, most normal humans would make the trip in about an hour and a half, but Jim would do it in about 45 minutes. He was crazy—absolutely fearless. He would just scare the hell out of those guys. One time he had a carload of rookies with him, and he was flying down some back road doing about 90 mph. Apparently they came upon a sign that said, "Road Out," but instead of slowing down, Marshall sped up and tried to jump it. Well, he didn't quite make it, and he damn near knocked the wheels off of his car. I remember seeing these three young black guys, the rookies who were with him, when they finally made it in to camp. They looked almost white from being so scared to death. They begged us not to have to drive back with him. It was one of the funniest damn things I have ever seen—absolutely hilarious.

Another aspect of the code says that what happens in the locker room stays in the locker room. Things have certainly changed today, though. The locker room is no longer the sacred place it used to be. Not anymore. That was before ESPN's 24-hour coverage and before all of the reporters that they allow in there. Now players can achieve notoriety by doing or saying crazy things to the press. It used to be that the things you said in there truly did stay in there. Now, no way. Plus, there are cell phone videos and all sorts of other things that make it impossible for guys to have a safe haven. It is a whole different world now. I am glad I am not a part of all of that, to tell you the truth. Sure, I miss playing the game, but I don't miss all of that stuff.

I was lucky. I got to play in some big games—conference championships, Super Bowls, and even some Pro Bowls. One of my most memorable, however, came back in December of 1980 when I was with the Vikings and we were playing the Browns at the Met. We were down 23–22 with a couple seconds on the clock. Tommy Kramer just threw up a Hail Mary from about 50 yards out, and I somehow came down with it in the back of the end zone after it bounced off of a couple of other receivers and defenders. It was amazing. Time ran out, and we just started celebrating. The Miracle Catch, it was called. It was a big win, too, because it gave us the Central Division title. You never forget special moments like that with your teammates.

I remember from that point on, whenever we would play in Cleveland in that old raggedy Municipal Stadium, they would get back at us by turning off all of the hot water. It was brutal. We would play there and immediately after the game, guys would sprint to the locker room to get in the showers and get whatever hot water that was left in the pipes. It was nuts. Those were different times, wild times indeed. Let me tell you, I don't miss that stuff. I miss the guys and I miss the games, but not all of the other stuff. It is pretty funny when you look back at it now, though.

I was lucky that I was able to leave the game on my own terms…literally. When I quit after my last game, I never even went to clear out my locker. When I drove away from the facility that day, it was like, "Hey man, that's it, I'm gone." I had prepared for my exit out of football, and I left the game on my terms. Plus I felt like when I left, I left the fans wanting more rather than less. I had been All-Pro the year before, and it wasn't like my game was down at that point where people thought it was time for me to hang it up. It's sad because you see so many guys today that had unfulfilled athletic careers and just won't let go. I had a life outside of football though and was eager to begin the next phase of my life. Football wasn't everything to me. During the season, I even used to come home after games and play tennis. Years later, Bud [Grant] put all my pads and everything in a box and sent it to me. You know what? I have no idea where all that stuff is today.

Preface

Like most sports fans in America, football reigns supreme for me. I live for Sunday afternoons when I can watch my beloved Vikings do battle on the gridiron. My wife even knows when the Vikings have won or not, and she doesn't usually watch the games. She can just hear a lot more swearing, moaning, and things that bounce off of walls. She knows I will be happy if they win and pissed for at least several hours if they lose. Crazy? Absolutely, but it is just something that she has come to accept. You see, my psychotic love affair with this game started when I was a kid. I can still remember watching the Vikes on TV and then heading out to the backyard to play snow football all afternoon with my neighborhood buddies. We just couldn't wait to get out there and beat the hell out of each other.

I grew up in the small southern Minnesota town of Fairmont, which was about an hour south of Mankato, home of the Vikings' training camp. I have so many great memories of packing up the wagoneer family truckster and driving up to "Kato" with my dad and brothers to see my childhood heroes, the vaunted Purple People Eaters—Alan Page, Jim Marshall, and Carl Eller—along with Chuck Foreman, Ahmad Rashad, and of course the quarterback, Fran Tarkenton. I worshipped that guy. In my backyard, I *was* Fran Tarkenton. I am not sure if I ever took off his No. 10 jersey long enough for Mom to actually wash it. I wore that ratty thing so much it actually turned from purple to brown.

I was only six years old when Dallas beat my Vikes in the divisional playoffs in 1975, but I can still remember it like it was yesterday. How crazy is that? I can't even recall a birthday party until I was like 12, yet I remember crap like this. I remember watching the game in our basement and seeing my dad and two brothers going ballistic when Drew Pearson miraculously caught the game-winning touchdown from Roger Staubach after clearly pushing off cornerback Nate Wright. And yes, he did push off. They would call it the Hail Mary. Needless to say, we had *another* name for that catch in our house, and one that wasn't so righteous. The fans went nuts. One drunk lunatic even heaved a whiskey bottle off of the third deck of old Metropolitan Stadium and hit the referee in the head just moments after the big play. Luckily it didn't kill the guy, but if it had, I think a lot of folks up here would have considered it to be justifiable homicide. I even remember hearing afterward about how Fran Tarkenton's dad, whose name was ironically Dallas, tragically dropped dead of a heart attack while watching the game on TV. You just can't make this stuff up.

From those humble beginnings I, like most Vikings fans, became jaded somewhere along the way. Just like they pull babies out of their wombs by their skate blades up here in the land of 10,000 frozen lakes, we are also expected to drink our fair share of the purple Kool-Aid every Sunday from September to January. We are invested. We start the season with such high hopes and expectations, knowing full well what the outcome is going to be. Will this be the year we finally win it all? Maybe? Please? I watch the draft; I listen to the analysts and pundits on talk radio, and I read their blogs; I soak it all in like a sponge. It is such an odd love-hate relationship. My purple hangover gradually fades away during the off-season, and then I come back reinvigorated each August, just in time for training camp.

Yes, we are invested, but not too invested. We have all been there. We have all "wasted" our fair shares of Sundays up here, where we committed four hours of our lives into a sure win over Detroit only to be heartbroken in the end by a returned kick or phantom fumble. We get burned and we learn, some more slowly than others. So now we invest only moderately. Many will listen on the radio as if to minimize the commitment as well as the ensuing collateral damage. It's funny. On Sunday game days, you will see a lot of fans wearing their purple out and about, rather than in front of the tube or at the game. They will have their radios tuned into the action, though, while they are perched in a deer stand, tucked into a duck blind, chilling out in an ice-fishing shanty, or just driving in the car "up north." We all jump on and off that bandwagon from time to time, because we are hesitant to get burned again. Some of us even go mad. Such was the case for my uncle Hank who, after years of suffering, went nuts and started rooting for the Green Bay Packers. Poor bastard.

The one constant through it all is hope. There is always hope. It is like fantasy football. Yes, I am a fantasy football dork. The best day of the year for fantasy freaks is draft day because it represents hope. Everybody has hope at the draft. Everybody, at least on paper, thinks that they've won the golden ticket. Why? Because we are "experts." I will never forget the time my old fraternity brother Rusty drafted Vikings kicker Fuad Reveiz with his precious first-round pick the year *after* he retired. Poor Rusty. We still laugh about that on draft day all these years later. One guy will always ceremoniously draft old Fuad in his honor. Rusty never recovered from that one, trust me. And just FYI—no, I will never draft a Green Bay Packers player on my fantasy team—just out of principle. But I digress. The point is that as Vikings fans, we all have boat loads of hope at the beginning of the year. What happens from there, however, is usually the problem.

Yes, it is an odd life we have, us die-hard Vikings fans. When the Vikes beat the hated Packers or Bears, that is like a drug that will keep us high for days. It is oh-so-sweet. But when the Vikes lose, it is bad. Real bad. Especially if they lose in the final seconds to the cheese-heads. That leaves a mark. It really sucks. You know, through the years I can actually date my life to big games and memorable seasons. Some are good; others are horrible. The four Super Bowl losses still sting…a lot. Oddly, and perhaps somewhat selfishly, I now find myself rooting for Buffalo and Denver to win the AFC championships whenever they make the playoffs. I want them to make it to the Super Bowl so badly. I want them to get there and then lose. Badly. You see, I want somebody else to hold the dubious distinction of Most Super Bowl Losses. Denver was right there with us, having lost four straight between 1977–89, but then they rode John Elway to a pair of titles in '97 and '98. I was so jealous. As such, that leaves just us and Buffalo. So go Bills! Until you make it to the Super Bowl, that is. No hard feelings. I know you understand our pain.

I thought we were going to get another crack at it back in 1999 when Randall Cunningham and Randy Moss brought us oh-so-close to making it back to the big dance. I was there at the NFC Championship Game with my two big bros, smiling and laughing, dishing out gratuitous high-fives to complete strangers. It was amazing. Then, with about two minutes to go in the fourth quarter, Gary Anderson, our very own human bobble-head doll—complete with the old school single bar face mask—came out to ice the game against Atlanta. This guy hadn't missed a single field goal all season. This was money in the bank, as good as it gets in the NFL. So we just drank beer and imagined ourselves sitting on the beach in Miami that next week, playing hooky and soaking up the sun.

You see, we were on a mission—we were going to exorcise some demons and kick the 900-pound monkey's ass that had been sitting on our collective backs for decades. We had it all planned out. We had flights to Florida; we had a hotel; we had a rental car; we had a couple of sweet tee times; and we "knew a guy" who was going to hook us up with tickets. We were set. Then Gary Anderson walked onto the field, lined up, kicked the ball, and missed it wide left. Are you kidding me? I started having flashbacks to my childhood. The Falcons then rallied to tie it up on a Chris-Chandler-to-Terance-Mathis touchdown with just under a minute to go. But we were still in it. There was still hope. After all, we had the league's most potent offense. We would rally. Right? Wrong.

Enter our coach, Denny Green, who decided to take a knee and just let the clock run out. Unbelievable. Atlanta kicker Morten Andersen then put the collective dagger in the backs of Minnesotans everywhere when he connected on a 38-yard field goal in overtime, giving his squad the stunning 30–27 upset. We just sat there speechless, watching the Falcon players do their Dirty Bird dance all over our dreams. I will never forget taking that dreaded walk of shame out of that monstrosity we call the Metrodome back to our car, in utter silence, amidst a sea of deflated purple pride. It was probably 20 degrees below zero, and I was wearing a sweatshirt. I didn't care because I was numb. I was literally too pissed to be cold. I just wanted to go home and cry.

I have often wondered, "Are we cursed?" Am I going to die like that old Cubs fan? You know, that 106-year-old guy they interview every time the Cubs make the playoffs who says he cannot die in peace until he sees his Cubbies finally win a World Series? Sixty years down the road, am I going to be *that* guy? You see, this is the stuff that keeps me awake at night. Oh, and I also stay awake thinking about my team moving to Los Angeles, which scares the crap out of me, too. Look, they hijacked our Lakers to Los Angeles back in 1960, and they could do it again. For the record, did you really think there were lakes in Los Angeles? Anyway, we need a new stadium up here, and nobody wants to pay for it. Sound familiar? If it were up to me, I would just funnel all of the state revenues slated for education, health care, roads, and government services into building a $100 billion dollar stadium…but that is just me.

So unless I win the lottery, I have been reduced to changing my game plan. Now, instead of rooting for Buffalo to win—only to lose—in the Super Bowl, I am rooting for Jacksonville, Oakland, and San Diego to really stink it up. I want them to stink worse than we do so that one of them will have to move to L.A. instead of us. Shallow? Awful? You betcha. Sorry, but a fan's gotta do what a fan's gotta do. I just hope that my Vikes can find a way to win it all sometime soon, because I don't think I can take another 60 years of this. And I certainly don't want to wind up like poor old uncle Hank.

Introduction

Football is, and always has been, a sport steeped in a culture of violence, intimidation, and brutality. Players have learned, however, to navigate through its mazes and labyrinths of physical contact by adhering to an honor code of sportsmanship known simply as the code. As mysterious as it is sacred, the code is an unwritten set of rules that has been handed down from generation to generation. It is usually learned the hard way by the players through good old baptism by fire. If they cheap-shot a guy or disrespect a veteran, they are going to get it. The how, what, why, when, and where are merely details. It can come at any time from anyone anywhere. Rest assured, though—it will come. Retaliation is a strange animal, and it is at the very core of what the code is all about.

As for the genesis of this book, it is the sequel to a pair of national best-sellers of the same name which chronicle the unwritten rules of hockey and baseball. What an amazing five-year adventure this has become. It started with hockey. I was a former college hockey walk-on at the University of Minnesota and thought I understood the game. Boy, was I wrong. In that book, after interviewing more than 100 NHL enforcers, I learned about how their game polices itself and why hockey players don't wear face masks—because everybody has to be accountable for their actions out on the ice. Disrespect someone, whack a guy in the head with your stick, or take liberties with the other team's star player, and you may lose some teeth. The same is true in baseball. If a player celebrates a little too much after a home run, peeks back to steal the catcher's signs, or slides hard with spikes high into second base, then he too will have to be accountable. That may mean getting thrown at up and in, or it may mean getting drilled with a 95-mph fastball in the ribs. Either way, the wheels of the code are set into motion, ensuring justice through intimidation and retaliation.

Like hockey and baseball, football too has its own sacred code of honor—an unwritten, unspoken set of rules that allow the players to police themselves on the gridiron. Retaliation in football, however, is not as transparent. With full face masks on their helmets, players can't just punch someone to settle a score. They can't risk a 15-yard penalty by decking a guy who cheap-shotted their quarterback or, worse yet, went for his knees. So they have learned to be creative—and stealthy, too, which isn't so easy if you are a 350-pound lineman. Under the specter of penalties, fines, and suspensions, players have to use stealth when retaliating against dirty players out on the field. Sure, bench-clearing brawls will occur from time to time, but most of the revenge that goes on is behind the scenes. Patience must be exercised when settling old scores, and the veterans will wait until the time is right to exact the justice they feel fits the crime. While the game has changed immensely over the years, one thing remains the same—the players take care of their own. They know that if they break the rules of the code, then there will be hell to pay. You see, football is all about respect and disrespect, and if a teammate is cheap-shotted, blind-sided, or chopped at the knees, then the wheels of retaliation will be set into motion. Players must be accountable for their actions. The code says so.

Yet the code is not just about head-slaps, verbal taunting, and the many unseen horrors that can occur under the pile. It is also about running up the score late on a team, excessive celebrations, head-hunting after interceptions, bounties, eye-gouging, and rookie initiations. There is a fine line between cheating and gamesmanship, and the players and coaches have always been on the lookout for an edge. The old adage, "If you ain't cheatin', you ain't tryin'," has always applied on the gridiron and includes things such as Stickum, siliconed jerseys, cold showers, and of course steroids. And let's not forget all of the espionage that goes on both on and off the field, as well. Everything from Spygate to dummy playbooks to lip-reading is fair game—unless you get caught, that is. Lastly, the issue of playing hurt is firmly addressed in the book. It's a viral topic that evoked great emotion from the players, especially the ones who feel betrayed by the league with regard to being taken care of in terms of pensions and medical treatment. They are the walking wounded and finally have a platform to be heard.

Football is a game steeped in tradition, with rules dating back to the game's inception more than 100 years ago. While the code has been around since the early days of the game, however, it still remains a very taboo subject shrouded in a veil of secrecy. In fact, many players are downright uncomfortable talking about it on the record. If they did, then that would acknowledge that a code actually exists at all. What a blast it was to meet and interview more than 100 current and former NFL players, coaches, and officials. Some interviews were face to face, while others took place over the phone. Some lasted 15 minutes, while others went on for hours. Each one was unique. Some players opened up and poured their guts out, while others chose to stay off the record. That's cool. I know that the first rule of Fight Club is that you do not talk about Fight Club. The stories and memories that these players share really make the book come to life. It was like a door into another world. What you will discover is nothing short of fascinating. I wanted to examine the roles of intimidation, retribution, and retaliation in the game. I wanted to know how players got even. I wanted to know why they steal signs and how they do it. I wanted to know about steroids. I wanted to know the stories behind the stories and hear what really goes on out there in the huddle.

My book is intended to celebrate the honor and courage behind the players who above all else show respect for the game, their teammates, and their opponents. It is also to celebrate the big hits—or snot bubblers, as some guys call them—that keep us glued to our TV sets each and every Sunday in the fall. I have heard from thousands of men and women over the years who have told me that my previous books were truly enlightening for them. They talked about being able to follow along and eventually be able to understand when and why a hockey fight will take place in certain instances. They now know that there is a genesis to these things and that maybe 10 or 15 little acts of disrespect led up to the eventual fracas. They now have inside information that made the game more fun for them. After my recent book on baseball, readers told me about how they can now understand the poker tells and decipher much of the espionage that occurs on the diamond. They wanted to understand why guys got drilled, and now they know. Now it is football's turn.

What an adventure it was to meet and interview so many truly fascinating characters along the way. So many celebrity charity golf outings, so many beers, so many stories. There was dinner and laughs with Greg Coleman, John Turner, and Joe Senser at the NFL Alumni Association Gala. There was Art Donovan, the old Baltimore Colts tackle who shared some wonderfully filthy stories about what the NFL was like back in the 1950s. There was hanging out with Jerome Bettis on the sideline of a Sunday night game between the Vikings and Bears. I got the inside scoop from a bunch of amazing quarterbacks, including Joe Theismann, Bernie Kosar, Steve Young, Rich Gannon, Earl Morrall, and Fran Tarkenton. What a thrill. The original Tasmanian Devil, John Randle, discussed the art of trash talking. Dan Dierdorf and Mike Ditka talked about the issues now facing the older players, the Gridiron Greats, many of whom are crippled and struggling with health care and disability issues. There were many deep throats, too, including assistant coaches and advance scouts, who enlightened me off the record about the science of sign stealing. And just because I wanted to cover all of my bases, I even interviewed a handful of notorious nasty boys, too, like Conrad Dobler, Bill Romanowski, and Jack Tatum, all of whom have doled out their fair share of cheap shots over the years. I even interviewed an advance scout—you know, the guys who are so "off the record" it was like you didn't even talk to them? I can't mention his name, or he could be fired, but let me tell you that Deep Throat had nothing on this guy. So many different opinions, so many different points of view—it was truly an experience of a lifetime.

I was an all-conference offensive lineman in high school, so I figured I had a pretty good understanding of the game. But after spending a year writing this book, I realized that I had no clue about what really went on in the trenches. None. I was completely blown away by what I discovered. My goal in writing the book was to go behind the scenes and let others in on an unspoken facet of the game that had always intrigued me. I hope to inform, entertain, and educate others in the process. I wanted to cover a broad spectrum of personalities and capture as many stories as I could. So I interviewed guys who played all different positions, came from all walks of life, and were from all different eras. What the players shared with me was insightful, inspiring, and even hilarious. My caveat to you is that I don't claim to be an expert—I'm just a mega-fan with a passion for learning and a passion for the game of football. Sure, the quotes are long, and there are a lot of connections to my home state of Minnesota with the Vikings. No worries—I am not expecting to win a Pulitzer any time soon. Just go with it and have fun. I wanted the players themselves to weave their personal stories throughout the book. This is their voice. I hope you enjoy reading about them half as much as I enjoyed writing about them. Cheers!

1

Just What Exactly is the Code?

The first game of football, then an amalgam of soccer and rugby, was played on November 6, 1869, between Princeton and Rutgers. The game grew from the East Coast and spread west over the ensuing decades, with college and semi-pro teams popping up throughout the United States. Finally in 1920, the American Professional Football Association was formed, with the legendary Jim Thorpe serving as the league's first president. Two years later, the APFA changed its name to the National Football League and nearly 90 years later, it remains the most popular sports league in the country. From those humble beginnings, the game has changed and evolved, with new rules, new training methods, new ownership groups, new stadiums, and new billion-dollar media deals.

The one constant through it all, however, has been the code of honor. Each player sees these unwritten rules differently. Each player has his own personal and professional moral code of ethics on what he will or won't do for himself and his teammates out on the gridiron. Each player has his own personal story. Here are some of those stories.

"Football is a game of intimidation," explained Dan Dierdorf, 13-year NFL offensive tackle. "It is a game of imposing your physical will on the player across from you. Your goal is to dominate that guy. Period. That part of the game of football will never change. Now if a guy across the line tries to hurt you or one of your teammates, then you have to make it known that things like that are not acceptable. There are right ways and wrong ways of doing that, however, and that is what the code is all about. I never once tried to injure the guy across from me. Now, did I try to be such

1

a physical force that he couldn't get up after I hit him? Absolutely. I never wanted to cripple him or send him to the hospital, but I wanted to send him to the bench—and there is a difference. There is a difference between trying to blow out somebody's knee and trying to hit him so hard that he doesn't want to play anymore. Yes, I tried on every play to send the guy across from me to the bench. That was the way I played the game, and I make no apologies for that.

"Look, we hated the guys we played against. There was real animosity there. We were tough, and we got after it. Hell, I played next to Conrad Dobler, which was like playing next to a tornado. There was always a lot of noise, and occasionally there was a flying object that would come your direction. That was how it was. It was like going to battle. We weren't buddies with those guys across from us. I tell you what, the guys of my era, when we see what happens after a game today, where all they guys are standing around hugging and kissing and shaking hands, we can't believe our eyes. We never did any of that. Are you kidding me? When games were over in my day, we left the field and went to the locker room. There was no love fest out at the 50-yard line. Having said that, however, there was a level of respect that was rarely ever violated. It was understood that you could respect your opponent but still strongly dislike him.

"I never tried to show anybody up or anything like that, either. I just wanted to do my job and help my team win football games. Nobody ever showboated in front of an opponent in our day like they do now. If Deacon Jones sacked the quarterback, he didn't dance around and show anybody up. He didn't stand over the top of him and show him up. He just did his job. He acted like he had done it before, which he had many, many times. I never spoke a word out there—that wasn't my style. If a guy trash-talked me, then I tried to knock him on his ass. That was the way the game was played back then."

Putting the team first is one way Karl Mecklenburg defines the code. "Yes, there is absolutely a code," said Mecklenburg, an 12-year NFL linebacker. "To me it was, 'I am not going to injure you on purpose and end your career' and visa versa. As long as you aren't trying to injure anybody, anything would go in my eyes. Everyone is vulnerable on the football field though, and you could get hurt on any given play. I got injured in the Super Bowl when we were playing San Francisco and had to miss most of the game. I got leg-whipped really bad by one of their guards, and he wound up tearing the cartilage in both my knees. It was totally dirty. He had tried some crap with several of my teammates, too. The guy was out of the league the next year because of it—none of the other teams would sign him. They knew he was going to get hurt, that guys would retaliate against him. Once you get labeled as a dirty player like that and are a liability, nobody wants you.

"You see, back in my day, the game used to police itself. Nowadays you don't see it as much. For instance, when I was playing, the wide receivers were the quietest guys on the field. They were in a vulnerable position coming across the middle and so forth. We had some really intimidating defensive backs in Ronnie Lott, Kenny Easley, Dennis Smith, and Steve Atwater, who could enforce their will on those receivers when they wanted to. As a result, there was a level of respect with those guys, where nobody tried to show anybody up out there. Nowadays, you see the receivers showboating around and doing all sorts of disrespectful things. So from an old football player's standpoint, that is sad to see. Back in my day, if a guy danced around and carried on the way some of these guys do today, he would not have been around for very long. We didn't tolerate stuff like that back then. No way.

"When a team is functioning properly and winning, usually all of the players are putting the team first. That, in a nutshell, is another big aspect of the code. If somebody cheap-shots your quarterback, you have his back. If there is an opportunity to call someone out in the press, then you think about the consequences and you don't do it. If you are not getting as many catches as you did the year before, and the team is winning, then you just shut up and do your job. If the outside linebacker gets injured and they move you from inside linebacker to outside linebacker, even though that is not your natural position and it helps the team, then that is great. All of those types of things—that, to me, is the code. It is about putting the team first."

What goes around comes around according to the code. "The code to me was about respecting the history and heritage of the game," said John Randle, 14-year NFL defensive tackle. "The players of the past, our elders, were the ones who made the game what it is today. Because I struggled just to make it into the league, I think that I appreciated every play that I was in there a little bit more, and that was what drove me to work so hard and to be my best. When I put on that uniform and stepped out onto that field, it wasn't just about a paycheck to me. It was such a privilege. I was doing something that I know millions of people wished that they could be doing, and I never took that for granted. What a blessing. So it was all about respect—respect for the game and respect for your opponent.

"Football is a game of karma. You might get away with something out there from time to time, but eventually it will get back to you and bite you. Guys watch so much film, and they don't miss a thing. If you are dirty or if you cheap-shot someone, guys know, and they will talk about it. What goes around comes around in this game. I look at guys like T.O. [Terrell Owens] when he does all of those things to draw attention to himself—like the time he pulled out the Sharpie marker and autographed a ball after he scored a touchdown, or the time he ate the kid's popcorn in the stands—stuff like that comes back on you, I think. I really do. The game is bigger than the players, not the other way around. Same thing with Chad Johnson, changing his name to Ocho Cinco. Yeah, it was funny, ha-ha, but it was disrespecting the game in my eyes. Once again, that karma came back on him, and he didn't have nearly the success on the field after all of that. It was a huge distraction, and it was totally unnecessary. Those antics take away from the game. The bottom line on the code is this: whether a player is putting himself above the game, or if he tries to disrespect or hurt someone out there, then that guy is going to get it. It may not be right then and there, but rest assured, the code says he will get it. And when he does, it is going to be sweet for whoever gets him. Karma is a bitch."

Self-policing is an important aspect of the game. "The code to me was about how the game policed itself and about how the players protected one another," said Steve Young, 15-year NFL quarterback. "Football is a violent game, and when people play outside the rules, it becomes extremely dangerous. You learn over time how to protect yourself and your teammates within the confines of the rules. That self-policing out on the field is really important in my opinion, otherwise nefarious players might take advantage of certain situations. So if you see someone doing something dirty or outside of the rules out on the field, like going for someone's knees, the players will address that pretty aggressively. Because of that, you don't see a whole lot of dirty play. It is a deterrent because players understand that there are serious consequences for their actions. As for me personally, I wouldn't say I ever tried to hurt

Tony Dungy, Longtime Coach, on the Code

"You kind of feel like there's a code of honor, a code of ethics in the league. You want to win. You want to do things the right way."

anyone who cheap-shotted me. I would make sure that he got the proper attention though from my teammates."

Protection is an important aspect of the code. "To me, as an offensive lineman, the code was always about protecting your quarterback at all costs," said Rich Baldinger, 12-year NFL offensive tackle. "You made sure that he stood on his feet at all times, and you would do whatever you had to do in order for that to happen. Whether that was a holding penalty or whatever, you did what you had to do to make sure he was going to be protected. When I was with Kansas City, our quarterback was Steve DeBerg, and he was somebody who you really wanted to go to war with. You would do whatever it took to protect him because you knew he was going to do everything in his power to help his team win. He had such a passion for the game and really redefined the word charisma. His attitude inspired me to play my best and to do whatever it took to keep him safe back there. I never had too many problems though, probably because a lot of guys knew that I used to hang out in Little Italy in New York! Hey, I had 'connections.' What can I say?

"I once fought three different guys in a game against San Diego without my helmet on. I ended up with a sweet black eye; it made me look pretty tough. You just took care of your own out there. Sure, there were dirty players, and you would deal with them accordingly. The guys who could never really play the game and weren't blessed with a lot of talent, they were the dirty ones. The good players were never dirty; they didn't need to be. They respected the game. As far as I was concerned, if guys wanted to play dirty, then I would accommodate them and dish it right back. I certainly wasn't afraid to get into a tussle out there from time to time, especially if it was a dirty player. You had to teach those guys a lesson right away to make sure they understood you weren't going to tolerate it."

Mike Morris shares a similar opinion. "The code was all about taking care of your own," said Morris, 12-year NFL long snapper. "The code was never explained to me; it was just an assumption that if someone would come and get your quarterback, you had to take care of business. If you didn't go help him out and somehow punish the guy for taking a shot at your signal-caller, then you would get in trouble back in practice the next day. If your teammates saw you on film not helping out or doing your part to protect your teammate, you would get reamed. You had to take care of your quarterback's backside. If an opposing player got through the line and dunked him, it was on. We were going to get that guy. My offensive line coach at Minnesota, Johnny Michaels, would brief us on this stuff. He basically told us that if someone took a cheap shot at our quarterback, it was up to us to go and get him. He didn't care how we did it, but it was up to us to send a message to that guy about what was not going to tolerated."

"As players, we policed ourselves both on and off the field," said Jim Marshall, 20-year NFL defensive end. "We had some pretty well-defined rules [that] made sure we did nothing to disrespect the game. If you broke some of those rules, it was going to be you against the rest of the team. You just didn't do anything that was going to hurt the team. That was the bottom line. That included everything from fighting to going out and getting drunk before a game to just being a selfish player. We as teammates took care of each other. There were always ways to get to those people, to keep them in line. Sometimes you could just talk to them, and if that didn't work, then there were some physical things that we could employ. No one player was bigger than the team, and it was up to the veteran players to make sure everybody stayed in line."

There is a line players shouldn't cross. "The code is about respect," said Pete Bercich, six-year NFL linebacker and coach. "Sure, you can hit guys hard, but there is a line you can't cross. Case in point, when Detroit tackle Gosder Cherilus hit Vikings defensive end Jared Allen in the knees in 2008. He was behind the play and didn't have to chop him. No way. It was a legal hit, but it was very, very dirty. It was not a clean hit whatsoever. The game is brutal enough without having to deal with crap like that, in my book. Guys understand that they are going to knock each other's eyes crossed and run each other over, but there is an understanding that they will not cut each other's legs out from underneath them. That is what ends careers. Rolling up on guys' feet is what causes bad injuries and affects their livelihoods. That is where we draw the line. That is a big part of the code. My dad played in the league in the early '60s, and it was a totally different game back then. You didn't play for money in those days—you did so because you loved to play the game. Today it is totally different; it is all about big business."

Bernie Kosar notes the importance of a healthy respect for the game's history. "The code of honor was all about respect, and it meant a great deal to me," said Kosar, 12-year NFL quarterback. "It may sound cocky or selfish, but the respect that you show the game and your teammates has to be above just about everything. It all comes down to respect in every aspect of the game. That is the bottom line. For instance, it is so disrespectful to run up the score at the end of a game when you are way up. The respect of just letting the game end versus racking up your stats was a big thing to me. I never bought into the idea of a team throwing passes when they were up 24–0 with two minutes left in the game. Or when a lineman is engaged with a blocker and another guy purposely comes over and chops his knees, that is highly disrespectful to the player and to the game.

"I will never forget when I first got into the league back in 1985. I was one the youngest quarterbacks to ever start a game and sure, I was nervous and all of that, but I remember being so excited to play the Raiders. They had won some Super Bowls, and it was such an honor to be playing opposite Jim Plunkett and to compete against their great bump-and-run corners Lester Hayes and Mike Haynes. For me to call plays against guys like linebacker Matt Millen or safety Ronnie Lott, I couldn't even believe I was doing it at the time. That really, really got me excited, because I had so much respect for those guys. You know, football is such a humbling game. Even to this day, whenever I see guys like Plunkett or Archie Manning or Terry Bradshaw or Brian Sipe or Billy Kilmer or Sunny Jurgensen, that generation of quarterbacks that was right in front of me, I feel indebted to them for everything that they did for the game. It is almost like if we were in line somewhere, I would insist that they went ahead of me. I just have so much respect for those guys and for what they did to grow the game the right way. That is all code stuff right there, all of it."

"My philosophy was to go out and get to guys before they could get to you," said Ray Hitchcock, two-year NFL offensive guard. "My main focus was to protect my teammates, especially my quarterback. You also wanted to make sure that nobody was taking liberties with your starting running backs or wide receivers, either. You never wanted to lose one of those guys from your starting lineup, so you would try to protect them at all costs. If they were overly aggressive toward them, then you had to get in there and even the score as much as you could. It was a constant battle, but you could never let your guard down."

Developing a personal codes starts early in a playing career. "The honor code in my opinion begins way back when you are a kid, and it evolves through high school, college, and into the pros," said Frank Youso, eight-year NFL offensive tackle in the 1950s. "Along the way, a whole host of people are involved in helping you create it: parents, teachers, coaches, friends, and relatives. They are the ones who help determine what kind of a man you are and what kind of ballplayer you will be. If you associate yourself with good people, you work hard, you have a good heart, and you do the right things, then you will develop a good honor code."

Looking out for your teammates was essential to Earl Morrall. "The honor code was about the guys taking care of one another out there," said Morrall, 21-year NFL quarterback. "If some guy came running in and took a cheap shot or hit somebody late, the next time there was an opportunity, the offensive guys would rally around and make sure they evened the score. We would get his number for sure. If a guy got hurt intentionally on a clip or something from behind, then we were going to make sure that guy got what was coming to him. Guys wouldn't tolerate that stuff. If a guy got hurt from somebody playing dirty, well, then there would be a vendetta to get that guy. Heck, the play could be over with, but somebody would get a running start and level that guy to even the score.

"We had an enforcer on our team, somebody who enjoyed doing that kind of stuff. Our guy was Jim Martin, a linebacker who used to be a frogman in the war. He was one tough customer. You didn't want to mess with him, no sir. We just wanted to make sure that opposing defenses understood what was going to be tolerated. We didn't want to injure the guy—maybe just shake up his brain a little bit. You just wanted to deliver a blow that sent a clear message. There were some mean guys out there who were going to take a shot if they could, so you had to be wary whenever you were out there. You couldn't relax until that whistle was blown, and even then you had to still watch out for a few seconds after. That was the way it was in the early days, though. Today you can't do that type of thing. Things have definitely changed, that is for sure."

The code has changed over the years. "The code isn't as prevalent today as it was years ago," said Ernie Accorsi, longtime NFL general manager.

"The old timers will tell you that the players took care of everything out on the field. That, of course, was before the days of unions and common agents. Even though there was a great unity among the players, they took care of their own and weren't afraid to go after guys who broke the code. Overall, it is a respect thing. It used to be that if you took a cheap shot at a player, then you had better look out, because someone was coming to get you. And they would, too. That went on through the '70s, but things change. There is a lot more pressure on officials to call penalties and even fine and suspend nowadays. The old timers much prefer the way the game used to police itself, but things change. I remember an incident years ago where a great defensive end got really upset during a championship game. With the game out of reach, the opposing team's quarterback called a timeout to try to score one more touchdown and run up the score. He couldn't get revenge during that game, so he wound up flattening that quarterback in the ensuing Pro Bowl a few weeks later, sending him to the hospital.

"I don't know if it is because [players] are afraid of fines and suspensions or what, but you don't see a lot of that kind of stuff anymore. I think another aspect of it is that when guys retaliate in football, it can be absolutely devastating. I mean in baseball you can drill a guy or in hockey you can punch a guy, but in football if you hit a guy full speed, you can really injure him. So that is a part of it, too. When guys that big collide, it can be extremely dangerous. The code has changed. It really has. I remember one time during a game with New York where our punter, Jeff Feagles, was standing around after a punt. The play was over and then all of a sudden Philadelphia linebacker Jeremiah Trotter came over and just wiped him out. Feagles wasn't expecting it; he was just defenseless. He could have gotten killed, it was that bad. I was in the press box and everybody is saying 'We've got to get him,' but nobody got him. I was disappointed. I really was. I can tell you that if that happened back in the '60s, he would not have finished the game. Somebody would have gotten him for that cheap shot. Without a doubt."

Sean Payton notes changes in the code. "The biggest code for me is treating quarterbacks not with kid gloves, but within the boundaries of the rules," said Payton, longtime NFL coach. "Nowadays the league is so good about protecting that position, which I think is great. There definitely used to be an old code about how opposing defenses would try to knock the quarterback out of the game, especially on interceptions and that type

Steve Sabol, President of NFL Films, on the Code

"Yes, there is a code in football, and it is significant. The game has changed over the years though. It really has, and so has the code. In the early days, so many things were legal: the crack-back, the head-slap, spearing, you name it. If the rules of today were in effect in the 1960s, half of the players in the Hall of Fame would have been fined more than what they ever earned. The hits are bigger today, but the game is much more sanitized than it was in those days. Television has changed everything. Nothing escapes the CAT-scan scrutiny of TV. Nothing. All of those dirty little tricks are now caught and dealt with immediately. Everything is exposed nowadays. When we started, we had an end-zone camera and a top camera. We didn't even have field cameras. Now we have isolated cameras on every player. It is amazing. So to a great extent, it is the advent of television that has cleaned up the game. Players know that they can't get away with stuff anymore, which I believe is great for the game. Retaliation used to be a huge part of the game. Back in the '50s and '60s, if a player did something dirty or illegal to your teammate, the players would all gather in the huddle and call a 'booty play' where they would all go after that guy. They would basically sacrifice a play just to get that one guy. It was crazy stuff. Now because of TV, we don't see that type of thing anymore. Guys know that they will be penalized, fined, and suspended, so it has essentially been eliminated.

"I remember one time back in the '70s when we at NFL Films put out a tape about the 'Greatest Hits.' There was some concern that the game was becoming too violent, and people were worried about us glorifying and celebrating all of this gratuitous violence. Well, George Halas came right out, and his exact words were, 'This game is built on the premise that a good player becomes less good when he is hit so hard that he doesn't want to be hit again.' That was powerful. We had Halas miked for a game one time between his Bears and the Lions. His favorite expression by far was, 'Lay the bastard out!' He must have said it 10 times throughout the course of that game. He didn't mean to cheap-shot anybody. He just wanted his guys to hit the Lions as hard as they could.

"Big hits are one of the biggest premises of this game. I mean this is a tough, violent, fierce, physical sport. And that is okay. In fact, that is a big part of the appeal. Now that does not mean being dirty. Yes, there is an unspoken code that exists in this game, and it is all about respect. Sure the players want to knock the shit out of each other, but they will do so cleanly and honestly. I don't know of any player in all my years of doing this where he has said he wanted to intentionally hurt someone. These are men who are trying to make a living. Nobody wants to deprive another man of the opportunity to make a living by doing something dishonest or illegal."

of thing. I think that 15 to 20 years ago, if a team took out the other team's quarterback, then there was going to be retaliation on theirs. That was just how it was in those days, but things have changed. The 'what-goes-around-comes-around' mentality is not like it used to be, not with all of the fines and suspensions that we have today. If a guy takes a stupid penalty to get back at a guy, he can get punished by the league after the fact, and it could cost him literally millions of dollars."

"The code was about protecting your teammates," said Stu Voigt, 11-year NFL tight end. "The bigger guys protected the little guys. We didn't tolerate cheap shots from anybody. That was so important. Whether it was on the bottom of a pile or on an interception or after a play, we just weren't going to stand for it. Whenever we played the Bears, for instance, we knew that they were going to try to intimidate us by being aggressive and by trash talking. With Dick Butkus leading the way, they were the Monsters of the Midway in those days. So we stuck together and made sure that we didn't take any crap from those guys. We never wanted to hurt a guy or injure him, but if he did something dirty, he was going to get hit hard. Bud [Grant] would not tolerate late hits or unsportsmanlike conduct penalties. No way. We were a championship-caliber team back in the '70s when I played, and that stuff was not allowed. So if you were going to get a guy back for something, you really had to choose your spots. You know, we just played for the love of the game back in our day. We had jobs in the off-season, for goodness sake. I signed for $6,500 and then got $15,000 for my first year. That was decent money in those days. Nowadays guys get fined more in a week than we made in several seasons. We just had a lot of fun in those days, and we raised a lot of hell. If I could go back and do it all over again, you bet your ass I would in a heartbeat."

The code is a learning process. "The code for me started way before I ever got into the NFL," said Pete Najarian, three-year NFL linebacker. "It first started back in high school, and then it moved into college and then evolved in the NFL. It was a learning process of what was right and what was wrong. As a linebacker, I loved to hit guys out there. I was aggressive, sure, and I got my share of 15-yard penalties. But I never intended to injure anybody out there, and that is at the core of the code for me. It is about playing hard but playing with respect for your opponents."

The code has to be enforced. "The level of respect for one another and for the game is basically what the code is all about," said Joe Theismann,

15-year NFL quarterback. "You are not going to do something to embarrass us. You are not going to do something to embarrass yourself. You are not going to do something to embarrass the game. We are going to take care of you and make sure that you understand that there is this code of honor that can't be broken. When you talk about the code, or the unwritten rules, there had to be enforcers who dealt with retaliation. On the police force, it is the blue line. With the mob, it was omertà. In baseball, it is 'you throw at my guy, and I will throw at your guy.' There are different codes in different aspects of society, but they all basically boil down to respect. There are no enforcers in football today. Now it is every man for himself, and that to me is sad."

The game is about more than the individual players. "Integrity and respect are the first two words that come to mind when I think of the code," said Bob Lurtsema, 11-year NFL defensive end. "I always felt like the code of honor meant that it should be an honor to play in the National Football League. I mean, we thought the fans were getting ripped off by paying good money to buy tickets just to watch us have fun. We loved playing football, and most of us would have done it for nothing. As players, we had a bond together. We were family. That is not an exaggeration or a cliché; it was what was real and what was exciting about being a professional football player back in those days. Nowadays many of the players have a totally different mindset. It is more like, 'Hey, you fans are lucky I am here, now pay me my money.' It is all about me, me, me. When I see a player today make a big play like a sack or an interception, and he runs toward the end zone pounding his chest because he knows the TV cameras might have a better shot of him that way, it really saddens me. That is not what this game is all about.

"We would never do that kind of garbage in our day. We would have either gotten pounded on by our opponents or cut by our coaches. Either way, we wouldn't be playing for very long. Embarrassing the player who you just beat by showboating around on the field is very disrespectful in my opinion, and that is a big part of the code, too. I don't like the taunting stuff any more than I like to see guys taking cheap shots or playing dirty— all hallmarks of the code. This game is for the fans, and we can never forget that. We appreciated what the fans were allowing us to do, to earn a living playing a game, and I think we have gotten away from that. Back in our day, 90 percent of the players would go out in the parking lot after games to hang out with the fans. We would drink a few beers, throw a ball around with the kids, and tell stories. It was wonderful. The players can never forget why they are out there. Sure, winning games is the bottom line, but they are ultimately out there for the fans."

"For me the code was about playing hard and playing aggressive but never intentionally hurting somebody," said Brent Jones, 11-year NFL tight end. "You would never want to end a guy's career, but you could certainly send him a message if he was playing dirty or being disrespectful. Guys who were cheap-shotters and who circumvented the rules, sometimes those guys needed to be reminded of the code, and we would just have to do that from time to time. You would just have to deal with the individual battles and frustrations as best you could and try to resolve them within the confines of the rules. Occasionally though, you had to get creative in how you would get things done. I remember one time playing in a game where this one linebacker kept holding me all game. The refs wouldn't call anything, so I took matters into my own hands and got one of my offensive linemen, Kevin Gogan, to help me out. Kevin was a respected player but could be mean and nasty when he needed to be. Anyway, he went over to that linebacker and basically told him that if he didn't stop holding me that he was going to go for his knees. Now, he didn't do it, but it got the linebacker to think twice about holding me."

Players earn respect through their conduct. "The code is about respect," said Doug Sutherland, 12-year NFL defensive tackle. "It is about respecting the game and about respecting your opponent. I remember one time during a goal-line stand, I was in a pile and my knee was being bent backwards. The offensive guard I had been battling against all afternoon grabbed me and pulled me back, literally saving me from an injury. He didn't have to, but he saw me in a vulnerable position and helped me out. We still battled against each other for the rest of the game, but I looked at him differently from that point on. I certainly wasn't going to do anything chippy or after the whistle, that was for sure. You earn respect in this game, and his actions really earned mine. It was just like that with certain players. Take a guy like Walter Payton. You would never dream about taking a cheap shot at a guy like him because he was such a class individual. He was so well respected around the league and an overall great guy. If you did something to a guy like that, it would come back to bite you one way or another."

"I never played with any mean-spiritedness or anything like that," said Dave Osborn, 12-year NFL running back. "I had a lot of respect for the game and didn't want to resort to being undisciplined or any thing like that. If a guy cheap-shotted me, that was just a part of the game, I wasn't going to risk getting a penalty by doing something foolish and cheap-shotting him back. When I played, you went 100 percent and you took your best shot every play of the game. I tried to play just as hard on the last play of the game as I did on the first. That was my mentality. The best way to retaliate in my book was to outplay your opponent and beat them fair and square."

Not playing dirty is essential to the code. "The code to me is all about not taking unnecessary cheap shots or playing dirty," said Matt Birk, 12-year NFL center. "When a player is in a vulnerable, susceptible position, our code says that you have to back off. Sure, you can hit a guy hard, but you can't intentionally try to hurt or injure him. If you do, then that is when you will get retaliated against. You know, we watch a lot of film in the NFL, way more than any other sport, I would imagine. I mean, we watch everybody and study all of their tendencies. If a guy plays dirty or does something that violates the code, we see it and make a note of it for the next time we play them. If a guy takes an unnecessary shot at a running back when he is on the ground, or if he twists his leg or does something that is above and beyond what is called for, we will get back at that guy. We try to send messages either verbally or nonverbally early in games as to what is and isn't going to be tolerated. As an offensive lineman, you are responsible for your position guys, the quarterbacks, running backs, and receivers. So it is our job to make sure that nobody messes with them. If they do, then we will take matters into our own hands to make sure that justice is served."

E.J. Henderson agrees. "The code to me is a sort of moral code or how guys play as far as being dirty," said the Vikings linebacker. "That includes stuff like hitting guys below the knees, fighting under the pile, or just being disrespectful. Anything that a guy does that might be career-threatening, that is not really football to me. I will try to hit guys hard, but I will pull up on them if I think I might injure them. That stuff isn't necessary. Some guys play the cheap-shot game, but that to me is a waste of time and energy. To me, that is not what the game is all about. I would also add that what happens on the field stays on the field. Sure, things will happen in the heat of battle, but we are all brothers out there and need to be respectful of one another. That is so important to me."

* * *

Other players simply didn't see it the same way.

"There was no code in my day," explained Fran Tarkenton, 18-year NFL quarterback. "It bothers me when all of these macho guys want to talk about the physicality of the game and about retaliating and all of that garbage. In my 18 years in the league, we never got back at anybody. Nobody was set up to have their legs chopped up or anything else like that. I never saw it. Did I get some cheap shots every now and then? Hell yes, but I didn't just get back at those guys. That's not how I played. I was too busy trying to win ballgames to worry about who I was going to retaliate against for something. Sure, there were some dirty players in our day, but it wasn't prevalent. Take a guy like Conrad Dobler. I had always heard that he was dirty and about how the defensive linemen always complained about him. Yet I never heard of anybody ever going after him or setting up a play to chop his knees or anything like that. I think a lot of those stories are created by the media. I don't know. All I can tell you is that I didn't play that way."

"When I took the field to play football, it was like going to battle, and in many regards, there was no code of honor for me," said Bill Romanowski, 16-year NFL linebacker. "I was going to do whatever it took to win. I wanted to beat my opponent down, and I was willing to do anything and everything to achieve that. That was my mentality. It wasn't until I was done playing that I realized that there could have been a different way to do it. I always had great respect for the game and for the people who have made it what it is. But there was such a great fear that I had that I was going to lose my job that I would do anything out on the field to win and to keep my job. I wanted to play as hard as I could to beat down my opponent. I just wanted to win. That was all."

2

Revenge and Retaliation

R evenge and retaliation are at the very core of what the code is all about. There are all sorts of ways for players to get payback—some are obvious, and others are things you may not have known about. Getting even has always been part of the game though, especially in the early days of the league when players didn't wear face masks. Just like in hockey, with no face masks, the players had to be accountable for their actions out on the field. Fist fights and phantom cold-cocks were a regular part of the game in those days. With only a couple of referees and no TV coverage, guys could just about get away with murder.

Face masks first started appearing in the 1940s as crude rubber concoctions that were fashioned to the leather helmets. Plastic helmets became all the rage in the 1950s, and plastic face masks soon followed. It was a subjective choice though, and not all players wanted to wear them. Wide receiver Tommy McDonald was the last non-kicker to play in the NFL without a face mask, and he retired from the Browns in 1968. Punters Pat Studstill of the Rams and Bobby Joe Green of the Bears were the last players in the NFL to not wear facemasks, and both retired in the early '70s.

For the most part, the vast majority of players wore masks by the mid-1950s, and as such, the rules of retaliation began to change. It didn't take long for players to figure out that the most egregious offense they could commit was to go after his opponent's knees. That more than anything else became the biggest fear for all players. Because once your knees got torn up, that could be end your career. This was before the days of MRIs and arthroscopic surgery for torn ACLs. When your knees were gone, that could mean your livelihood was gone, too. So players learned to retaliate with varying degrees of punishment. Maybe it was a blow to the neck, a clip, a blind-side hit on your quarterback, or whatever. The bottom line, back then as well as now, was that players will not tolerate being disrespected or cheap-shotted out on the field and will always find a way to settle the score. Always. Every player is unique though, and how they choose to handle each situation is what makes this aspect of the game so interesting.

Things started to change with regard to how the league dealt with fighting and retaliation in 1960 when Pete Rozelle was named as the new commissioner of the NFL. Rozelle wanted to grow the game and saw the power of television as a means to achieve that. However, he knew that in order to do that, he was going to have to clean up the game's rough-around-the-edges image. He knew it was going to take time, but he was determined to put football on par with baseball in terms of popularity with the fans. One person who witnessed the transformation first-hand from the very beginning was Fred Zamberletti, who has served as a trainer with the Minnesota Vikings since the team's inception in 1961. "Zambo" has seen it all on the gridiron during the past half century, and he is still going strong.

"Back in the '50s and '60s, the game was much more violent," Zambo recalled. "There used to be fights in nearly every game. It used to be that you could block guys below the waist or from behind. It was brutal. Clips, crack-back blocks, clotheslines, head-slapping, I have seen it all over the years. I have helped a lot of guys off of the field in my day, that is for sure."

There was one incident in particular that would prove to be a hallmark moment in the transformation of the league's image regarding the tolerance of fighting. "The rule about fighting on the field got put into place because of a preseason game between the Vikings and Chargers out in San Diego," Zambo recalled. "San Diego quarterback John Hadl threw deep, and safety Paul Krause deflected the ball into the air, where fellow defensive back Karl Kassulke caught it on about the 6-yard line for an interception. Right after the interception, Vikings defensive end Carl Eller ran over and leveled Hadl behind the play with a vicious forearm shiver. Hadl flew backward to the ground and looked hurt. The San Diego bench immediately emptied, and a huge brawl ensued. One of the San Diego players, Rick Redman, charged across the field and hit Eller from behind, sending him sprawling and knocking off his helmet into the air. Well, all hell broke loose from there. Guys were swinging helmets. It was crazy. Carl was one tough character and wasn't going to take that, so he wound up chasing a couple of guys clear off the field. When order was restored finally, Eller was kicked out of the game. Afterward, Commissioner Rozelle fined every single player that stepped onto the field. It was unprecedented, and it was a pretty clear message that fighting was not going to be tolerated by the league. That was a defining moment in the league's history, I think. It was significant. You don't see the retaliation in the game today like it used to be. Today the game is under such scrutiny with all the TV and the video replay. Guys can get fined for questionable hits that are reviewed days later by the league office, so that has cleaned up a lot of the unnecessary roughness and dirty play. Things have come a long way over the past 50 years, that is for sure."

As for Eller, he saw the hit as an opportunity to take out the quarterback, not as a cheap shot. "That was a legal block," Eller said. "The ball changed hands on that play, and I was downfield. I was a blocker when we intercepted the ball, and [Hadl] was a tackler. I've got nothing against Hadl; I was blocking him."

Retaliation is a very personal thing. How each player chooses to get even is quite fascinating. Each position has its own code on how these things are handled on a case by case basis. Players can't afford to take costly 15-yard penalties that will hurt their teams, and they certainly can't afford to get ejected from a game for settling a score. There are individual penalties, or selfish penalties, and there are team penalties. If a player gets back at somebody at an inopportune time and kills a big drive late in a game and really hurts his team in the process, that is considered selfish and disrespectful. On the other hand, if a guy gets back at a player who has taken liberties with his quarterback or deliberately tried to injure somebody, then that penalty is oftentimes considered a "team penalty," or an honorable one.

"My teammate, running back Chuck Evans, got cheap-shotted from behind by a guy after the whistle, an absolute potshot that damn near took

Conrad Dobler, 10-Year NFL Guard, on Retaliation

"We kept a little black book of names, absolutely, of guys who cheap-shotted our teammates. We had a list, particularly of guys who were in our conference—the Cowboys, Eagles, or Giants—who we knew we could get back the next time we saw them. I loved to get guys, hell yes. The beauty of playing offensive line was that once the ball was past the line of scrimmage, I could go out and hunt and destroy. The defensive guys were constantly chasing the ball carrier, whereas we were out there looking to nail guys. I would love getting back at dirty players like that, to chase them down and ear-hole them when they least expected it. Hell yes.

"I remember playing Miami on Thanksgiving Day one year. It was our third game in 10 days, and we were spent. Anyway, one of their rookie linebackers, A.J. Duhe, started mouthing off. So I said in the huddle that we needed to take care of him. Sure enough, the next play our center, Tom Banks, went over and speared him. Then when Duhe was getting up, I went over and speared him again right in the ribs for good measure. Now I never meant for Tom to go out and get him on the next play I meant let's any one of us get a shot at him when the opportunity presents itself. He just happened to be in the right place at the right time. As for me, I saw him getting up and the whistle hadn't yet blown, so I figured I would get a piece of that son of a bitch, too. I wanted to send a message that we weren't going to tolerate that shit. No way. Payback is a bitch.

"Another time when I was playing in Buffalo, a guy from New Orleans came at me on the first play of the game and knocked me on my ass. He then said a few things to me that I didn't appreciate. So the very next play, when he tried to get by me with a rip move, I pinned his arm under mine and just dropped. As I did, his arm snapped. Did I mean to break his arm? No. I wanted to hurt him, to teach him a lesson, sure. I never wanted to injure somebody to the point where they couldn't earn a living, though. But the guy challenged me, and I retaliated. Sometimes that stuff happens, and that is just football. Look, I played a rough, tough game the way it was supposed to be played. The whole dirty thing came from my opponents. And why did my opponents do that? Because I kicked their f---ing ass.

"You know, NFL Films always shows this one particular play to show how dirty I am, where I am stepping on the head of a Giant's defensive lineman. If you look closely at the footage, however, what you don't see is that this guy was going for my knees. That was the reason I stepped on his head—not to be dirty, but because he had just tried to take my knees out. Hey, I have always said, 'If you are man enough to give a cheap shot, then you had better be man enough to take one.' Believe me, I took my fair share of cheap shots. I have had seven artificial knee transplants to prove it.

"The best retaliation story on me was by Rams defensive tackle Merlin Olsen. I hated that son of a bitch. I remember the time he held me up by my shoulder pads only to have Jack Youngblood come down and take my knees out. I turned around and kicked him square in the face. They intentionally tried to end my career, right then and there. Merlin and I used to battle back and forth every time we faced each other. Well, when he retired, he got into acting and he landed the role of Father Murphy on NBC about this clean-cut guy who runs an orphanage. Yeah right! Anyway, in one episode there is this graveyard scene where if you look closely, you can see one of the tombstones reads, 'Conrad Dobler. Gone, But Not Forgiven.' I thought that was hilarious. Here we are, years after retirement, and I am still on old Merlin's f---ing mind. Hey, I never held a grudge, but he clearly needs to get over it."

his head off," said Mike Morris, 12-year NFL long snapper. "So I just ran right over and nailed the guy as hard as I could in retaliation. I of course got a penalty, but I didn't care. Our coach Dennis Green bitched at me for getting a 15-yarder, but I just couldn't let that guy do that to my teammate and get away with it. I just felt like it was the right thing to do, to teach that dink a lesson. My teammates all agreed and patted me on the back afterward. They had my back. That's how you earn the respect of your teammates from doing stuff like that, and in so doing, you know that they would do the same for you. Shit like that just can't be tolerated. If they know they can get away with it, they will do it all day."

"If you were going to retaliate and get a guy, you had to choose your spots," said Doug Sutherland, 12-year NFL defensive tackle. "You couldn't just be selfish about it because of the ensuing penalty that would hurt your team. One time we were playing Miami, and they had just scored a touchdown on a goal-line play. After the play, their receiver, Paul Warfield, leveled our safety, Paul Krause, on a cheap shot. I saw it happen and immediately ran over and elbowed him in the back of the head, decking him. I got a penalty for it, but it wasn't that bad of a situation to take one in. They had just scored a touchdown, and the 15-yard penalty would be assessed on the kickoff, which would result in a touchback in the end zone. The worst-case scenario was that we got the ball on the 20-yard line. That was a good time to get revenge in my eyes, and my teammates agreed."

"If you didn't stick up for your teammates, they wouldn't respect you," added Bob Stein, seven-year NFL linebacker. "I remember playing in a game against the Raiders one time and seeing Ben Davidson cheap-shot our quarterback, Len Dawson. [Davidson] dove on him, helmet first, and then kind of pile-drived him. Our star wide receiver, Otis Taylor, came running in and went right after Davidson. A huge brawl erupted, and it got pretty ugly. You have to stick up for your quarterback; that is the foundation of the code. If the opposition goes after your team leader, you have to take a stand. You simply can't let them get away with it, or they will keep doing it over and over."

Sometimes getting back at a guy was less about payback and more about earning respect from your teammates. Such was the case with Paul Wiggin, a former player and head coach.

"I got kicked out of a game as a rookie with Cleveland back in 1957 when I retaliated against a guy who had cheap-shotted me," Wiggin said. "I hauled off and hit him right in the jaw and knocked him to the dirt. Despite the fact that I got ejected, I immediately gained the respect of my teammates for what I did. I had been a goody-goody from Stanford up until that point, and in one punch I had instantly garnered their admiration. You can't teach toughness. You either have it or you don't, and luckily for me I had it—at least on that particular play anyway. So from that I learned a valuable lesson about getting even and settling scores. You have to choose your spots, and you have to be smart about it.

"Years later, I remember playing against John Henry Johnson, the Hall of Fame Steelers running back, who was one of the most notorious cheap-shotters in NFL history. This guy was so mean and nasty that players hated to go up against him. He cut my chin on at least two occasions and tried like hell to do so on a few others. As much as I hated that no-good s.o.b.

Stu Voigt, 11-Year NFL Tight End, on Retaliation

"Retaliation was a big part of the code, absolutely. You had to protect your teammates, no matter what. The guys on defense were the ones usually doing the dirty work though, getting most of the payback and taking care of the vendettas. It was funny too, because we used to razz our defensive guys quite a bit about not being the brightest bulbs on the tree. There was an old joke that basically said that whereas the offense's playbook was about 5 inches thick, the defense's playbook consisted of a single sheet of paper with a picture of a football on it that said, 'Okay guys, go get it!'"

and as much as I wanted to get him, the opportunity just never presented itself. Sure, I got a couple of good licks on him, but I was never able to really get him without the possibility of taking a stupid penalty. Believe me, I would have loved to have really nailed that guy, but it just wasn't in the cards. If I could have gotten away with it, I would have taken a cheap shot on him. It just never happened. I still think about it all these years later. Anyway, I just dealt with it. I waited and waited for that one opportunity to eventually get that guy, but it never came. That is just how it is in football—you have to be patient and you have to be lucky. There is a time and place for everything, and you can't let your emotions get the better of you."

Sometimes you just have to be patient and wait for the right moment. Such was the case for Chiefs Hall of Fame linebacker Bobby Bell.

"I remember playing in a game, and there was a rookie running back from San Diego who disrespected me," Bell said. "He came running out on a flat pattern out of the backfield, behind the play, and as he came by he threw me an elbow. I just said, 'Hey man, it's cool, the play's over. No need to throw any bones.' Well, he did it again a short while later, the same thing. So I just watched him and kind of took notes on this kid. Three weeks later, we played the Chargers again, and the first time they threw him the ball out of the backfield on my side, I just laid him out flat. It was a perfectly clean hit, but I really nailed him. Wham! He just laid there, and they eventually had to help him off the field. He was all right, but he had to sit out the rest of the game. After the game when we were getting on our team bus, the kid came over to me and said, 'Hey man, why did you try to kill me out there?' I just smiled and said, 'Do you remember the last time we played back in Kansas City when you elbowed me not once but twice? Well, I was just showing you how to do it properly, son, that's all. I may be an old man, but you need to show me some respect.' I just smiled and got on the bus. I think he learned his lesson."

Matt Blair, a 12-year linebacker with the Vikings, had a similar situation where he also had to wait for that perfect moment to get even.

"I remember getting whacked one time when I was a rookie while I was standing around near a pile," Blair recalled. "I didn't even see it coming. It was raining out, and all of a sudden I went flying across the turf and ended up in a puddle. It was crazy. The guy who did it was sort of a known cheap-shotter, and that was his thing. Well, about three months later, I had a chance to get that guy on an interception when he wasn't expecting it. It was clean but vicious. I got him right across the jaw, and it really messed him up. I later wound up talking to him at the Pro Bowl when he came over to talk to me. I was kind of worried but just smiled after he thanked me for helping him lose 15 pounds after they had to wire his jaw shut. We were cool after that."

For known cheap-shotters, guys are seemingly always on the lookout for that rare opportunity that may present itself just once or twice a game. Dirty players give guys extra incentive.

"Nobody had a problem with guys who hit hard or who were mean and nasty," said Bob Lurtsema, 11-year NFL defensive end. "It was the dirty players that we detested. We had a few notorious cheap-shotters in my day. Take a guy like Cardinals guard Conrad Dobler. He was the dirtiest player I have ever played against. I remember when I was with Minnesota and we were playing the Cardinals one time. I was playing left end, and Doug Sutherland was playing next to me at left tackle. Well, Dobler had cheap-shotted Sutherland earlier in the game, and he was looking to get back at Dobler. His opportunity came midway through the game when Dobler pulled to his right and got caught up in traffic. Sutherland, who was rushing through that same gap, came upon Dobler as he was lying on the ground. Instead of jumping over him though, he planted his foot right in Dobler's crotch. He was a hurting mess. It was ugly. Was it intentional? I don't know. Who knows—if that is another player, maybe he pulls up and shows him some respect? Not with that guy, though. Subconsciously Sutherland probably figured that was going to be the best time to get him, so he did. I don't know. I do know this though—there is a lot of karma in this game, and what goes around eventually comes around."

Karma. The players swear by it. They know that eventually the dirty players get what is coming to them, one way or another. Quarterback Joe Kapp was a firm believer in karma. Kapp was tough—so tough that he was once on the cover of *Sports Illustrated* with the caption, "The Toughest Chicano." As a quarterback, Kapp would retaliate against dirty players by running them over on his way out of bounds. He detested cheap-shotters but knew that he had to be disciplined as far as keeping his emotions in check. Instead, Kapp would channel that pent up energy and harness it in the form of momentum.

John Randle, 14-Year NFL Defensive Tackle, on Retaliation

"If somebody cheap-shots your quarterback, then it is up to you to decide whether or not you want to get even. I wouldn't try to be cheap or dirty, or even take a penalty—I would just be on the lookout for when an opportunity presented itself. If I could nail a guy who was known as a cheap player, then I would go out of my way to do so. That is football. If an opposing player 'accidentally' rolled up on our quarterback's leg, then I might 'accidentally' do the same to theirs. You never want to injure a guy, but you have to take care of your own. What goes around comes around in this league, and that is what the code is all about. If they want to play dirty, then maybe we might want to do the same. It all depends on the situation, but you just can't tolerate players taking cheap shots at your star players. If they do it once and get away with it, then they will just keep doing it. You have to send a message. That is how the game polices itself.

"We had ways of getting dirty players, too. We would set up plays to get cheap-shotters on certain stunts and stuff like that. Maybe you would ear-hole him to stun him, and then someone would come around and nail him from the other side. You do that two, three times in a game, and they will think twice about chop-blocking you. When I was with Minnesota, Henry Thomas and I would do that shit all the time. It was awesome. We would do grab-stunts to spin guys around, and we would just make them pay. It was awesome. I am getting excited just thinking about it. Then if you get to him and he gives up a sack, that just made it even sweeter because you knew he would feel like shit. You could then rub that in and do even more talking to him, knowing that guy was going to get called out on TV as well as later on film in front of the whole team the next day. That would usually shut him up."

"The greatest get-back I ever saw came when I was playing up in the Canadian Football League with British Columbia back in the early 1960s," Kapp said. "A guy by the name of Angelo Mosca, a defensive tackle from Hamilton, had the dirtiest play I ever saw in all my years of pro football. He cheap-shotted my teammate, Willie Fleming, during a Grey Cup game one time when he was out-of-bounds by a good three yards. It was a blatant late hit that many thought was a deliberate attempt to knock our star running back out of the game. The poor guy wasn't even expecting it, and he really got walloped. It was a momentum-swinger, and we lost the game. Well, we didn't have an opportunity to get him back that game, but we were watching films the following season during practice one day of a game between Hamilton and Toronto. In that game, we saw a guy line up

Vince Workman, Eight-Year NFL Running Back, on Retaliation

"Some guys reacted to cheap shots right away. Not me. If a guy cheap-shotted me, I would keep it in the back of my mind. I would get his number. I was one of those guys who was always sort of searching for that number out on the field, waiting for that one opportunity to get him back when the time was right. Maybe when he wasn't paying attention, then that would be your chance to take your shot at him. It may not necessarily be a cheap shot either, but just a good clean hit that would teach him a lesson. Guys will commonly refer to that as the cleats-up-in-the-air shot. For me, as a running back, I wasn't in a very good position to retaliate very often. So my linemen would help to protect me and take care of a lot of that stuff. They were always there for me, pulling people off of the pile, making sure nobody got in an extra shot on me. That is how you know if your teammates like you or not. If they protect you, they like you. And if they don't like you, they will let you get cheap-shotted. Luckily, I had good teammates who liked me and had my back out there."

for a punt across from Mosca. He then took one step back and proceeded to kick that mean s.o.b. right in the face. It was the craziest thing I have ever seen. If his head would have come off, it would have gone for a field goal. We saw this and couldn't believe our eyes. We re-ran it over and over and actually saluted the guy by giving him a standing ovation. It was wonderful. Dirty players eventually get what is coming to them, and that is what the code is all about in my opinion. We got even the next year when we beat Hamilton for the Grey Cup title. And I tell you what, we all used that hit as an extra incentive to beat those guys, too. I made sure of it."

Quarterbacks are the most vulnerable players on the field and are usually the No. 1 target of would-be cheap-shotters. It is difficult for them to retaliate nowadays, but back in the day when quarterbacks could call their own plays in the huddle, they could orchestrate all sorts of mayhem. One of the most feared and respected signal-callers of all time is Redskins Hall of Fame quarterback Joe Theismann, who led by example and took no prisoners for 12 seasons there. For Theismann, it was all business.

"I took great pride in standing up for my teammates. That was what the code was all about," Theismann said. "Hey, if a guy laid a dirty hit on me, or if a defensive back went after the knees of one of my wide receivers, or if a defensive lineman tried to take out one of our offensive linemen, there was no question, somewhere in that next quarter, those guys would be targeted. We were going to get him. We had to send a message that stuff like that was not going to be tolerated. That was just the way it was. We would set it up in the huddle. I would call the play where maybe we would run a sweep to the side of the guy we wanted to get. The tackle would then stand the guy up, and the receiver or whoever would just fly in and level the guy's ass.

"Now, it would depend on how nasty that particular person was as to whether or not he would really lay into him. Every team had its own enforcers. We had guys like Charlie Brown and Roy Jefferson, who were really tough. Charlie was notorious for taking guys out with his forearm. He was an intimidating guy. Remember, I played football when you really could beat the living crap out of one another. The dollars weren't anywhere near what they are today. The owners didn't have the investment in the players that they have today. So there were a lot of variables that were part of the game back then that aren't in place today. If you got hurt, you got hurt. You had to protect yourself because the officials weren't going to do so. It wasn't their job to do that; it was my job to take care of myself. That was the way it was. And if you did have to get somebody, then it wasn't personal either. It was business. You just had to send a message that you simply weren't going to tolerate them either intimidating or cheap-shotting your guys. As the quarterback, it was my role to help facilitate that type of thing, and I took pride in that.

"The game was much different when I played. We didn't socialize with one another or go to each other's golf tournaments in those days. I didn't golf or hang out with Roger Staubach or Dan Fouts or Joe Montana or Bob Griese or any of those guys. Nowadays, everybody is a friend of everybody. That is not bad, but it is very different than how things used to be. For me, I am still of a mindset that it is us versus the world, to be honest. It was you versus them. Period. I wanted to win and was willing to do whatever it took to help my teammates win. I wasn't interested in being buddies with everybody. I wanted to win. Sure, I was friends with those guys in the off-season, but during the regular season, it was all business."

Revenge was personal for 12-year NFL quarterback Bernie Kosar, who would retaliate by going right after guys who had cheap-shotted him. He wanted to embarrass them. First things first though, as sometimes he had to make sure he could even get up.

"To be honest, when I would get hit hard, I mean really lit up, I wasn't thinking about getting back at anybody," Kosar said. "The first thing I was thinking about whether I was alive or not. Am I dead? Sometimes you have to just stop and look around. I am not kidding. It is crazy being hit that hard, especially if you don't see it coming. It is like being in a train crash. You don't even know which way is up. When you come to your senses, then you can decide how and when you want to get a guy back for a cheap shot. Certain guys were known for doing stuff like that more so than others, like Eagles safety Andre Waters. He was one of those guys who would go for your knees and take you out when you weren't looking. He definitely played with an edge. I liked the aggressiveness of the game, so I would come right back and throw right at him. That was my ultimate revenge, to beat him deep and just burn his ass."

For another quarterback, Rich Gannon, a 17-year NFL veteran, the penalties and fines far outweighed the desire to get back at somebody.

"I think there is a certain amount of sticking up for you buddy in the trenches and protecting your quarterback, but you had to be so careful out there when it came to retaliating or you could get fined $10,000 pretty quickly," Gannon said. "A heat-of-the-moment brawl could end up with an ejection or a suspension, which could lead to a trip to New York to meet with the commissioner, which would ultimately lead to a fine. The bottom line with retaliation is that you just can't take a 15-yard penalty for getting back at a guy. I mean they have more than 20 cameras at some games now, so if you do something, you are going to get caught—maybe not right away, but eventually, when they review the tape after the fact. So you have to be patient and take your shots if and when they present themselves.

"Times have changed, though. If you watch the old NFL Films, you would see that a player wasn't down until he was down. Guys would get their fingers stepped on, they would get kicked or jumped, and they would usually get hit once they were down. Nowadays, that stuff doesn't happen. They have really cleaned that stuff up. The officiating is very different now, too, with regards to how the rules are enforced. There used to be a gray area as to what was a personal foul, whereas now it is pretty clear cut. Now they have a rules committee and a competition committee, so things are much different. Trust me, I have been in a lot of locker rooms during my 17 years in the NFL, and I don't remember too many instances where guys sat around talking about how they were going to get other guys back."

Bill Romanowski, 16-Year Linebacker, on Retaliation

"Retaliation is a big part of the game. I did it. We all did it. Sure, I would grab somebody's throat or punch them or try to poke their eye out. You do all sorts of crazy things in the heat of battle. If my hand got up under a guy's facemask, I would just grab whatever I could grab and squeeze whatever I could squeeze. That was my mentality out there. I wanted to get past that guy and get the guy with the ball. That was my job, and I would do just about anything to do it. Guys would cheap-shot me back, sure. But if my focus was on getting someone back, I would really lose track of what I had to do out there to be the best football player I could be. I knew that if I spent my time retaliating against guys, I would be defeated, so I just let that stuff go."

Once in a while, players would have to get clever on how they got back at guys. For 12-year defensive end Don Joyce, a notorious tough guy who played back in the '50s, it was all about timing and creativity.

"If there was some smart-ass who was cheap-shotting our guys, he would become a marked man and we would get him," Joyce recalled. "We would actually look for ways to get those guys. There was a guy like that, a really dirty player, who was with Detroit, and we got him pretty good one time. It was a cold day, so we all had our big overcoats on, or capes as we called them, and we figured that if we could get this guy out-of-bounds by our bench, then we would take care of him. Sure enough, midway through the game he came by the sideline, and one of our guys clotheslined him and knocked him a few yards out-of-bounds. We then gathered around him and really worked him over. We just sort of hid behind our big capes, using them like a shield. Of course back in the '50s, there were no TV cameras to worry about, either. So we got him pretty good, and we taught him a lesson. That was how it was in those days—anything would go. There weren't a whole lot of rules regarding cheap shots, and it could get pretty rough out there."

For Joyce, backing down was never an option, regardless of the outcome.

"You know, I am probably the NFL's all-time leader in career fights and for getting thrown out of games," Joyce added. "And like any good criminal, I can always say that I didn't start a one of them! I wasn't a dirty player. I was just tough and was always ready to stand up for my teammates. Guys would come at me and challenge me, and I would

Ray Hitchcock, Two-Year NFL Offensive Guard, on Retaliation

"Dirty players are despised. If a guy cheap-shotted me, I would go after him immediately and even the score. I would find a way to get him on the very next play, and if he hurt me, then I was going to do the same to him. You had to let it be known that you weren't going to tolerate stuff like that or you would get abused all day long and eventually be out of a job. I got ear-holed one time so hard that I lined up on the wrong hash the next play. It was a completely cheap shot. I was so out of it I didn't even know where I was. The most dangerous and despised thing a player can do is to go for someone's knees. Sometimes in the heat of battle, guys will do stupid things, and none is more stupid than this. The high-low was a tactic that a lot of teams would employ, where one guy would stand a guy up and engage him, and then have another guy come and cut him at the knees. We have all had it happen to us at one time or another, and it can be scary. Those are career-enders. Another dirty little trick guys will do will be to go for your throat, because it is exposed and you can cause a lot of damage. A quick shot to the neck or throat will stun you and can literally take your breath away. The biggest cheap-shotter I ever played against was Eagles safety Andre 'Dirty' Waters, who tried to take my teammate Art Monk's head off one time. Bill Romanowski was another one that you had to watch out for. That was their thing. They had to overcompensate for a lack of talent by playing dirty."

never back down. That just wasn't my nature. I remember one time back in 1952, I was playing for the Chicago Cardinals and we were playing the Washington Redskins at old Comiskey Park in Chicago. Washington lined up for a field goal with Bill Dudley kicking and quarterback Sammy Baugh as his the holder. Baugh was a 16-year veteran and future Hall of Famer, but he was known as a very tough player. Anyway, the kick was short, and my teammate Don Paul caught it and ran it out. Meanwhile, I was playing defensive end and had tried to block the kick. I missed it and was lying on the ground. I heard the roar of the crowd and realized what was going on. I then turned and saw Baugh circling back to make an angle at Paul, as he was going to run by. So I stalked him and lined him up. Sure enough, just as he was going to tackle Paul, I blind-sided him and drove him clear out-of-bounds.

"We both finally came to a rolling stop near the Redskins bench, at which point he reached up and grabbed my nose, breaking it. We didn't wear facemasks in those days. As soon as he grabbed on and started squeezing, I grabbed his hand and did the same, ultimately breaking it along with a couple of his fingers. Neither of us would let go—it was pretty crazy now that I think about it. The Redskins players eventually came over and shook me off of him. Baugh then got up and stomped on me, for one last good measure. Needless to say, we both got thrown out of the game. Well, later on as I walked back to our team dressing room, I saw Sammy there waiting for me. He said, 'We are going to get a fine from the league commissioner Bert Bell.' In those days, the fines for getting ejected were $25. 'I will call Mr. Bell,' he said, 'and tell him that it was my fault and that I started the fight.' He then told me that he was sorry for kicking me and that he was going to pay my fine for me. Stunned, I thanked him and went on my way. Little did I know that because of his broken hand, he would never play again. I felt pretty bad about it, but I had no idea that would be the ultimate outcome of our tussle together. Sammy was a real class act. He earned my respect that day, that was for sure."

While the players know that what happens out on the field is all business, occasionally things can get personal. As such, once in a while the need to retaliate becomes overwhelming, even if the game is over.

"I will never forget the time when I was playing with the 49ers back in the '60s and our tight end John David Crow got Rams defensive end Deacon Jones on a vicious crack-back block," said Howard Mudd, seven-year NFL offensive guard and 36-year NFL coach. "Deacon was so upset that after the game he chased him all the way into our locker room. The game was at old Kezar Stadium, and both teams went through the same tunnel to get to the locker rooms. It was pretty crazy. Deacon was one tough customer; you didn't want to mess with that guy."

"We were playing the Redskins one time, and one of their running backs grabbed my privates while we were under a pile," added 11-year linebacker Mike Walter. "I was really pissed but just blew it off and didn't think too much about it. Later in the game, the same guy wound up sticking his entire hand inside my facemask and just started groping at my eye. He scratched it all up, and it ultimately swelled shut. It was really bad. I was so upset. Anyway, after the game, I ran across the field and down into their locker room. I started calling him out, challenging him. My eye was all beat up, and I was down there ready to take on the world. Well, the next thing I knew, the entire Redskins offensive line came over and escorted me out of the room."

Dealing with cheap-shot artists and dirty players is a subject that is extremely personal. Each player has his own way of dealing with those issues. One of the most popular forms of retaliation is to hit a guy when he is just standing around after a play. Guys who have let up and are hovering over a pile, assuming the play is dead, have big targets on their backs—especially if they are considered dirty players.

"I remember one time seeing a guy take a late hit on one of my teammates after the whistle," said longtime center Matt Birk. "He had let up, and this guy just drilled him from behind in the back, knocking him over. When you are not expecting to get hit and don't prepare yourself for impact, that is when you can really get hurt. Well, the next series I was engaged with him and once the whistle blew, I just kept finishing him and finishing him, eventually driving him right over the pile. He had let up on the play but I didn't and wound up just pancaking him on his back. I told him in so many words that I was getting him back for what he had done to my teammate and that this was how it was going to be from now on. I got a penalty for it, but I didn't care. My teammates didn't either because they knew that I was protecting one of our own guys. Sometimes you have to send a message to dicks like that, otherwise they will pull that crap over and over again. You can't do that kind of thing very often, because the penalties can really hurt your team, but in that instance it was okay."

Players have tried all sorts of dirty tactics over the years in an effort to gain an advantage over their opponent. They will push the envelope until they either get caught by the refs or until they get retaliated against themselves. Either way, it is a constant cat-and-mouse game of riding fine line between cheating and gamesmanship. One of the greatest tactics used by defensive linemen back in the '60s and '70s was the head slap. Although it has since been outlawed, players will occasionally ear-hole a guy in an attempt temporarily stun him.

Deacon Jones, otherwise known as the "secretary of defense," was the master of the head slap. "I copied it from Rosey Grier," Jones acknowledged. "You needed quickness and quick feet to make it awesome. When you come off that ball and your takeoff is as fast as mine was and then you've got a Sonny Liston right hand upside somebody's head, that's going to cause a lot of pain. That's going to cause eyes to blink and close. I wanted linemen to concentrate on trying to stop my hands because he could not get outside quick enough to stop my outside move. With a blow upside the

Mick Tingelhoff, 17-Year NFL Center, on Retaliation

"You had to play the game with respect, or you wouldn't last very long out there. If I took a cheap shot at somebody, I knew damn well that somebody on the other side of the ball was going to take a shot at me. That was just how the game was played back then. You played it hard and you played it fast, but you played it straight. Even if you got away with a cheap shot or something like that, everybody would see it on film the next week anyway—which was even worse. We all shared the same film after the game, so if you saw a guy do something dirty, you knew that everybody would be out to get him. That was the code—the players taking care of each other out there."

head, his eyes were going to close, and my next move was an arm over and back inside as hard and as fast as I could. It was totally unstoppable. That's why the league outlawed it because you can't block it. They didn't want the quarterback to get hurt. They took the hit to the head completely out of play, and in my mind that was not a bad idea. Guys had started using it as a weapon. They would ball their fists up and just start swinging at people."

Former Chiefs linebacker Bob Stein remembered the move well. "Deacon Jones, Claude Humphrey, and Carl Eller, those guys were all masters at head-slapping," recalled Stein. "They had it down to a science. They would whack you on the side of the head, on your ear hole, and your head would be ringing for the next five minutes. Talk about getting your bell rung. You could do a lot of damage to a guy by doing that, but it used to be legal."

Other dirty tactics that players will pull out of their bag of tricks include throwing chalk from the white lines into their opponent's eyes, or just plain ol' eye-gouging, which was perhaps second on the list of most egregious offenses, behind only chop-blocking. Guys simply wouldn't tolerate some idiot toying with their vision.

"One time I got poked in the eye on purpose by a defensive lineman, and my contact actually shattered in my eye," recalled John Alt, a 13-year NFL offensive tackle with the Chiefs. "It was really painful and just pissed me off. So I went after his knees to send him a message. I learned pretty quickly that if you didn't retaliate right away and let it be known that you were not going to allow people to push you around, you wouldn't last very long in this league. Needless to say, he never tried that crap on me again."

Otis Sistrunk, Seven-Year NFL Defensive Tackle, on Retaliation

"I used to talk to the guy lined up across from me before the start of every game, and I would ask him how he wanted to play—dirty or straight. They usually chose the latter, but sometimes guys would do things to try to hurt you, and when that happened, you had to take care of yourself out there. I was tough and I hit hard, but I never tried to intentionally hurt anybody in all my years in the NFL. Some teams had contracts put out on quarterbacks in my day, but I never paid any attention to that stuff. I just tried to play hard and play the game with respect. I figured if I did that, then everything would take care of itself. You had to choose your spots, too. I mean if a guy did something dirty, you couldn't just get him back—you had to wait until the right time, like maybe on an interception or something. That was when you could really blind-side a guy to get back at him. Sometimes you just had to do what you had to do."

Going after somebody's knees is simply unacceptable. The chop-block, which actually used to be legal, is now outlawed. There is even a term the players will use when referring to someone who chopped them, saying they tried to "career" them. The lengths players will go to retaliate against anyone who goes after their knees is nothing short of remarkable.

"One of the dirtiest players of my era was Eagles center Jimmy Ringo, who was a known cheap-shotter," recalled Bob Lurtsema, 11-year NFL defensive end. "I lost my cool one time and actually kicked him in the face after he repeatedly chop-blocked me in my knees. I wasn't proud of that, but I had just had enough and completely lost it."

"If a guy ever rolled up on my knees, I was going to go after him and get him, period," said Rich Baldinger, 12-year NFL offensive tackle. "I would want to brawl with the guy and make him fight me man to man. My goal would be to humiliate him, because there is no place for that in football. A career injury is a lifelong injury as far as I was concerned, because I saw a lot of guys who were hobbled their entire lives due to cheap shots. So I had no respect for guys who did dirty stuff like that—none. Cheap-shotting was for guys who were not very good athletes and for guys who were lazy. Hey, I was probably one of the worst athletes who ever played in the NFL, but I made up for it with hard work and a healthy dose of respect for my opponents."

"I remember back in the early '80s when Raiders defensive end Howie Long chased down 49ers coach Bob McKittrick in the tunnel after a game because he was so pissed about being chopped," added Howard Mudd, seven-year NFL offensive guard and 36-year NFL coach. "Howie was convinced that McKittrick had told his players to do it, and instead of going after the players, he went straight to the source. Needless to say, it wasn't long thereafter that chop-blocking from behind became outlawed."

For 14-year offensive tackle Keith Fahnhorst, chop-blocking was occasionally used as a retaliatory measure to settle down an opponent who was playing chippy.

"I remember playing Atlanta one time back in the early '80s when I was with San Francisco," said Fahnhorst. "Their defensive coordinator at the time was Jerry Glanville, who had his cornerbacks flying around taking a lot of cheap shots. So we started going after their guys hard, especially their interior linemen. We would have our center stand up the nose guard and then have the back side tackle just cut him. I don't remember anybody ever getting hurt, but it certainly scared the hell out of those guys. Once word got out that we were going after them, then things settled down and we got back to playing football."

Glanville, who never shied away from having his boys push the proverbial envelope, knew where to draw the line—and chop-blocking was off limits.

"No. 1, if you as a coach encourage guys to go after player's knees, then you should be kicked out of the league," said Glanville, a longtime NFL coach. "No. 2, if a player goes after another player's knees and intentionally tries to hurt him, he too should be kicked out of the league. The single worst thing you can do to a player in the National Football League is to go after his knees. It just can't be tolerated because it is a career-ender. Jets tackle Joe Klecko would go crazy if anybody rolled up on him. If it happened, he would forget about where the ball was and immediately try to kill that guy. He ruled the roost when it came to stuff like that, and because of that, nobody went after his knees."

Like Klecko, other players established reputations for going off on guys who they felt were disrespecting them. Such was the case for Mean Joe Green, who detested being held by opposing offensive linemen.

"Mean Joe Greene was a coordinator for me when I was coaching with the Dolphins," recalled longtime NFL coach Tom Olivadotti. "I remember him telling me one time about how he never allowed opposing linemen to hold him. He passed that along to our players and was really adamant about it. He said that if a guy ever held him, he made sure to get back at him one way or another. He would give him a warning, and then he would make him pay. He just made sure that the guy across from him knew that under no circumstances would he accept him holding him. If they did it, he would get them somehow, someway. He felt very strongly about the players being able to police themselves. He knew the umpires weren't going to call everything, so he took it into his own hands to make sure he was being treated fairly. He did not want to be disrespected out there and was willing to go the extra mile to make sure guys played him straight."

One of the best ways for an offensive lineman to get a guy who tries to chop him is to pancake him. Getting pancaked is sure ESPN highlight reel material, which is oftentimes extremely humiliating to the player and his fragile ego.

"There was always a way to get those guys," recalled longtime NFL coach Tom Olivadotti. "For example, if there was a guy who was a cut blocker, they would send two guys after him to drive him backwards and pancake him—really drive him back and bring him down hard. You could do it, but you were sacrificing an awful lot to get revenge on the guy. You had to hope like hell you didn't get burned on the play, but hopefully it would make a point to the guy for the rest of the game. If he knew that was what he was going to get every time he chopped him, he might think twice about it before doing it again."

For running backs, one of the biggest things they hated was when defensive players would push off of them when they were getting up from the ground.

"God, I absolutely hated that," said Darrell Thompson, former running back for Green Bay. "You would always hear the refs say, 'Okay guys, make sure you push off the ground,' because they will lay on you to tire you out and then push off of your body to get up. It totally sucked. So whenever some big fat ass would push off on me, I would just knock his arm away so that he would fall over. It was hilarious. They would get all pissed, but I didn't care. I didn't want to get punked out there."

However, there are some things that players will do that go beyond disrespectful, such as spitting on someone's face. Many can remember the 1997 *Monday Night Football* game when Broncos linebacker Bill Romanowski spit in 49ers wide receiver J.J. Stokes' face. The cameras caught it plain as day, and Romanowski was fined $7,500. For some

Pete Bercich, Six-Year NFL Linebacker and Coach, on Retaliation

"If you have a dirty player on your team, a lot of times his own teammates will take care of him. The policing goes that way, too. They don't want a teammate who is giving them a bad name and who is enticing the opposition to play dirty toward them. That is the thing about football—if a guy cheap-shots someone, the odds of that guy retaliating on the guy who hit him are minimal. Instead he will just get somebody else, and the whole thing escalates. So if there is a guy playing cheap, the veterans will usually sit him down and tell him to shape up. Dirty players reap what they sow, and what goes around comes around in this league. If a guy gets labeled as a dirty player, it is all over. His own teammates won't want to be around him, and they certainly won't be inclined to back him up if and when he gets into trouble out there. Those guys are just a cancer.

"Take a guy like Kevin Mawae, a really good center, a real Christian guy. He is one of the dirtiest players you will ever see. He dives at guys' feet, hitting them in the back of the legs, that sort of thing. It is not just players, either. It could be entire team units. Let's say the league sees a number of players at a certain position doing dirty things. Take Denver, for instance, and their offensive line. They were notorious for cutting and rolling, where they would hit the ground and then roll up on guys' legs to try to bring them down. They will bring the coach out to New York to sit him down and ask him what he is teaching. They aren't afraid to get into the coach's pocket, too.

"Every single play is filmed and reviewed in the NFL. Every one. And they have a dedicated staff that sits there and looks at everything to make sure guys don't get away with any cheap shots. They will fine guys after the fact for plays that they don't even get penalties for. They are constantly policing the players, making sure they play the game fairly. That is a case of how money and technology have improved the game and made it more safe for the players. They had to crack down on all of the dirty hits. If fans are chucking down $100 per ticket to watch a game, their team's quarterback or star player had better be starting. Football is a business, and the league knows what it has to do to keep the seats full."

athletes, incidents like that can be public-relations nightmares. Such was the case for Baltimore Orioles' slugger Roberto Alomar, who became public enemy No. 1 when he spat on umpire John Hirschbeck just a year earlier in 1996. For Romanowski, however, who lived and played on the edge, it only enhanced his reputation as the bad boy the fans loved to hate.

Milt Sunde, 11-Year Guard, on Trust

"I remember one time playing in a game against the Giants back in the mid-'60s. We had smaller rosters in those days and as such, the offensive and defensive starters all played on special teams, too. Well, you would get pretty tired out doing all of that, especially after playing on a long drive or something. Well, one particular play as we were about to punt, I looked across the line and saw the guy opposite me was pretty tired. He said, 'Why don't you and me take it easy this play?' To which I said, 'That sounds just fine to me.' I was tired of getting beat up out there and figured I could just catch my breath as I ran down field. Just then, as the punter let the ball go, that guy across from me came at me and made like he was going to block me. I just sort of relaxed, expecting him to release by me and head down field. I saw him come at me with a big smile on his face, and just as I was about to turn and head down field, he hauled off and whacked me with a left hook right across the chops that sent me to my knees. He set me up but good, and I bought it hook, line, and sinker. I learned my lesson after that one—never trust anybody out on the football field who is not wearing the same color jersey you are."

Despite the fact that he relished that hard-earned reputation, Romanowski later admitted that he wished he could take that one back.

"That was something that I am not very proud of," he said. "It was the first and only time I ever did something like that, and I wish I could take it back. My emotions got the better of me, and I did something stupid."

Many other players have spat on their opponents and gotten away with it, though. Some of them even reveled in it. Billy Ray Smith Sr., a defensive end who played with Los Angeles, Pittsburgh, and Baltimore from 1957–70, allegedly used to chew tobacco during games and spit on the fingers of opposing linemen to provoke false starts.

Even Hall of Famer Mean Joe Greene got away with it as an intimidation tactic, as described in a 1975 *Sports Illustrated* article. "Then there was the time Mean Joe Greene spit on Bears linebacker Dick Butkus. The Bears were humiliating the Steelers. Butkus was blitzing at will, taking long running starts and smashing into the Steeler center just as he snapped the ball, and Greene couldn't stand it any longer. The Steeler offense was on the field. Greene had no business out there, but when Butkus passed within 10 feet of the Steeler bench, Greene bolted out at him, yelling challenges, and drew back and spit full in Butkus's face. 'Butkus didn't look intimidated,' says Steeler Defensive Captain Andy Russell, 'but there was Greene obviously wanting to fight him, and fully capable of it, and you could see Butkus thinking, 'This wouldn't be the intelligent thing to do.' 'So Butkus turned and walked back into the security of the carnage on the field. When Russell ran into Butkus in the off-season and asked him how he could let a guy spit in his face without retaliating, Butkus said, 'I was too busy making All-Pro.' Greene—who was himself named All-Pro for the fourth time, and NFL Defensive Player of the Year for the second time, last season—is perhaps the only man alive who could make Butkus come off sounding rather prim."

For 17-year veteran quarterback Rich Gannon, spitting on someone was just plain stupid and selfish. "I remember one time when I was with Oakland and we were playing Pittsburgh," Gannon recalled. "Oakland, of course, has always had a notorious reputation for being tough and intimidating. Well, one of our defensive ends spit on the face of the Steelers punter during that game, and it cost us a 15-yard penalty and ultimately the game. He, of course, got fined by the league, but it was totally uncalled for. I mean, there is a difference between playing hard and being physical, and being dumb. Spitting on a guy's face is just plain dumb. You can't put your team at risk in order to get somebody back or to get revenge. It just can't happen. That is completely selfish. Football is a team game, and stuff like that cannot be tolerated. Plus, it was completely disrespectful to spit on a guy like that. That was a bad, bad scene. You cannot win in this league with selfish players. No way."

Maybe the only thing more cheap and dirty than spitting on somebody is biting them—which has been known to take place from time to time over the years, especially under the pile during a fumble. One player who had been a purported victim of a dental debauchery was 12-year defensive tackle Doug Sutherland, who wanted to finally come clean regarding an infamous episode with his longtime arch nemesis.

"I had many battles over the years with Conrad Dobler," Sutherland said. "He was a notorious cheap-shotter. Yeah, he was dirty, too, but I want to officially set the record straight on something that has been bugging me for years. The story of him biting me one time under a pile is officially an urban myth. He never did bite me, but it got reported that way by the media, and they just ran with it. I just went with it, too, because it made for a good story, I suppose. Well, we can officially set the record straight now. The poor guy has suffered enough and doesn't need that on his conscience, too!"

For many players, the best form of retaliation was to simply do nothing at all. For them, it was all about staying focused and doing whatever they could to win the ball game. For eight-year NFL running back Chuck Foreman, it was all about using cheap shots as a form of motivation. He was a firm believer in the motto, "Don't get mad—get even."

"I remember playing the Rams one time, and I got into a situation where I got stood up and couldn't go any farther," Foreman recalled. "I was in an awkward position, and there was no where for me to go. So I just told the guys who had a hold of me, 'Okay fellas, I am done, take it easy,' meaning let's all back off and make sure no one gets hurt. Their linebacker, and I won't mention his name, said "F--- you!' and took me straight to the ground, hard, with my leg all twisted up. I got hurt and wound up missing three games, which really upset me. From that moment, I made my up mind that whenever I played against him in the future, he would regret every play. Sure enough, I made that guy pay. I made him look like a fool every time we played the Rams. That was my retaliation. That was a blatant cheap shot as far as I was concerned, and the biggest violation of the code that there is. I could have ended my career on that play. There is no excuse for that. But as much as I wanted to get that guy back, I never resorted to doing anything dirty. I just used it as motivation to make him look stupid out on the field. He made it personal."

Keith Millard, an eight-year NFL defensive tackle, felt similarly. "I was never a big believer in going out of my way to 'get' somebody," Millard said. "I have been injured plenty of times myself and understand how frustrating it can be, so I never wanted to put anybody else through that. Any coward can go out of their way to try to maim somebody and to end their career. The guys who do that garbage, who try to intimidate people by doing that kind of stuff, they have no respect from their peers whatsoever. They have no character and are looked upon like a cancer. They usually have very little talent and have to rely on playing dirty to keep their job. The guys who stand over a pile, roll up on you, or cut you from behind, they have no business playing this game as far as I am concerned.

"For me, the way I dealt with guys like that was to keep my intensity way up, keep my mouth shut, stay focused, and simply outplay them. I

Toughness

Cleveland Browns Hall of Fame fullback Marion Motley was about as tough as they came back in the 1940s. Once during a game against New York, Motley rumbled 50 yards for a touchdown while carrying defender Harmon Rowe on his back for the final 20 yards, all while repeatedly being punched in the face. Afterward, a photographer asked Motley to smile for a picture, to which he apparently replied, "I can't. My teeth were knocked out!"

---

wanted to just keep coming and keep coming and ultimately make them look bad. That was the best revenge for me. Eventually they would fall apart. There was nothing worse than being made to look bad, whether on TV for the fans to see or in the training room for your teammates to see. Sometimes it was tough not to retaliate, but you had to be disciplined out there. You can't just take a stupid penalty, because it is usually the guy who reacts to being cheap-shotted who gets caught.

"I remember playing the 49ers one time. Their offensive linemen were notorious for leg-whipping and high-low chop-blocking, which was how they intimidated guys. They would do anything to protect their quarterback, Joe Montana, and to get their running back, Roger Craig, through the line. They might have gotten a good shot on me or got me off my feet, but I tried to never get caught up in that stuff and just stayed focused. I never wanted to get into a fight out there or get into a trash-talking war, either. That stuff took me out of what I did best, so I ignored it. As soon as you let a guy know that he could get into your head, either via trash talking or by cheap-shotting you, he would keep doing it over and over. So unless it was something very obvious, I tried not to let my opponents know that they were bothering me."

Hall of Fame coach Bud Grant felt very strongly about retaliation and even threatened to make his players put their money where their mouths were when they took matters into their own hands.

"I played in an era when we didn't wear face masks, so retaliation was a big part of the game," said Grant. "If you did something dirty to somebody, you more than likely were going to get punched in the face. That was just part of the game. The players policed themselves in that regard. Cheap shots were part of the game, too, and you learned pretty quickly how to take care of yourself as well as your teammates out there.

Nowadays, retaliation is totally different. They are wearing body army with nearly indestructible helmets. You could take a baseball bat and hit a guy over the head as hard as you could, and it wouldn't hurt him. I always told my players when I was coaching that the dumbest thing they could do in a game was to get into a fight. What are they going to do? Kick somebody? Grab them and wrestle around? They are not going to hurt them. More than likely, they will break their hand while trying to punch someone in the facemask. That is just stupidity. Ultimately what happens is that they hurt the team by getting a 15-yard penalty, and maybe worse, they get thrown out of the game. To me, all that fighting on the football field proved was how dumb you were. If they wanted to let the other guy punch them first, that was fine by me. If they could let the other guy take a penalty and get thrown out, that was actually good for our team. But as soon as they retaliated, then they were just as dumb as the other guy. Plus, I used to tell my guys that if they got thrown out of a game and missed a half, that was half a game's salary. I never had to follow up on that threat, thank goodness."

John Gagliardi, the winningest college football coach of all time from St. John's University in Minnesota, took anti-retaliation to an extreme.

"One of the few drills that we run up here at St. John's—we are not big on drills—is what we call the 'walk-away' drill," he explained. "We have players pair off against one another, and one guy will take a fake cheap shot or late hit on his partner, and his partner will in turn just walk away. We really do. We don't want our players A) cheap-shotting, or B) retaliating, so we actually practice this. Some coaches believe that in order to be an aggressive team that you have to take a lot of penalties. As for me, my philosophy is the exact opposite of that. I firmly believe that the fewer penalties you have, the better our chances of winning are. Hey, it has worked out pretty good for us so far."

Retaliation: Going after the Quarterback on an Interception

One of the most popular ways for players to retaliate is to go after the quarterback immediately following an interception. If you are on offense and you hear the defensive players start screaming "Oskie!" or "Bingo!" you had better watch out. Or as the players will tell you, that is the time to keep your head on a swivel, because somebody is going to be coming for you. The defensive players live for these moments, when they can finally take a shot at the signal-caller, or perhaps even flip an unsuspecting offensive lineman upside down. While this form of retaliation has been around for as long as the game has been played, there are certainly right and wrong ways of going about it. For the defensive players, the opportunity to drill a guy who had been pissing them off all game was oftentimes too good to pass up. Like with all forms of retaliation, however, this too was all about respect.

"Interceptions were the best time to retaliate," said Karl Mecklenburg, 12-year NFL linebacker. "Most offensive players don't know how to look out for someone coming after them. So we would just clean up on whoever you choose. Of course, you are going to choose somebody that you have seen take liberties with your guys. Yes, interceptions were times to settle some scores, absolutely. Take a guy like John Alt, the offensive tackle from Kansas City. He was a good, clean player. He played hard, but he did it the right way. I respected him a lot. As a result, if there was an interception when we were out there together, I might get in his way and make sure he doesn't tackle our guy. But I would never try to light him up or take his head off. Other guys, however, who were cheap-shotters, I would go out of my way to find those guys. Respect is a two-way street in football. If you give it, more than likely you will get it back.

"I would also add that all retaliation aside, we used those moments, such as interceptions, to go after the other team's best player. If their best guy was a quarterback or running back or whoever, we would try to get as many helmets on that guy as possible. We wouldn't be dirty about it or injure the guy; we just wanted to get in our hits to try to soften him up.

"It gets pretty crazy out there for those few moments right after the interception, and things can get ugly. There was an offensive lineman who played for San Diego back in my day, Harry Swain, who was really chippy and someone you always had to be on the lookout for. He was known for getting those little extra hits on guys, or for hitting them from behind, or for coming in late to clean you up when you were standing around the pile. Well, during a game with those guys one time, I went looking for him following an interception. I wanted to get him back for having hit me late earlier in the game. So I peeled back and just drilled him. It was a brutal hit, and he didn't see it coming at all. The first thing to hit the ground was his head. It was a great shot and totally legal. As I got up, feeling pretty good about myself, I suddenly realized that it wasn't Harry—it was another offensive linemen, Courtney Hall. I felt terrible about it. One of his teammates, an offensive tackle who had gotten hurt earlier in the game, saw it and came running on to the field afterward to fight me. Well, we got into it, and he ultimately got fined and suspended. Now I really felt bad. Anyway, the next time we played San Diego, I was pretty worried because I had three of their starting offensive linemen that all wanted to kill me out there. Needless to say, I had my head on a swivel that entire afternoon, and luckily I got out of there in one piece."

For eight-year veteran defensive tackle Keith Millard, taking out the quarterback was a tactic that was practiced and revered. "In my day, if a quarterback threw an interception, we were coached to go light him up," said the former league defensive MVP. "You could do whatever you wanted to get him off of the ground. That was open season. They were live meat when they threw a pick, and everyone knew it. Even if you really went after a guy, you wouldn't be considered a coward for doing it because everybody was fair game in that situation. It was your chance for redemption, and your eyes would get real big when the boys would yell 'Interception!' Hey, those guys are wearing shoulder pads, too, and we are all vulnerable to injuries. I never tried to hurt a quarterback, but I definitely tried to hit him as hard as I could. As a defensive player, you wanted to hit that guy and do everything you could to take him out of his game. If you could intimidate him by getting after him, you could get inside his head. If he is worrying about you and about whether or not he is going to get hit, then you have succeeded. You can take him out of his rhythm and get him to throw early or to run out of the pocket. If you could hit him on a clean, strong, legal hit that took him off of the field, then that was okay in my book. If you could get a good hit up high on him and wrap up his arms and tackle him that way, on his shoulder, that was all right in my book. Or if you could get your helmet on his helmet and get him a little dizzy, that was all right, too. In Minnesota, we played on that awful turf in the Metrodome, which was rock hard, so if you could get a quarterback and drive him into that stuff, you would definitely make him feel it. You never wanted to roll up on his knees or anything—that is a career-ending move that is totally unnecessary. You just wanted to get a good hit on him and let him know you were there and that you were planning on being there all day."

For many defensive tackles, it was personal. This was their big chance to light somebody up, and they were not going to squander it.

"If you got a chance to tee off on an offensive lineman who had been holding you all day, man, that was awesome," said John Randle, 14-year NFL defensive tackle. "Or if there was a dirty player you had been wanting to get back at, as defensive linemen, we lived for interceptions. That was a free pass to just go out there and get someone. It was usually a race to get to the quarterback and to try to nail him. But if you couldn't get him, then a running back or a receiver would suffice. It was like a shot of adrenaline— you just went head-hunting. To see a receiver or offensive guard trying to make a tackle out there, it was like a fish out of water. So we would time it just right to blind-side them when they least expected it. Pow! I would knock the shit out of them and say. 'Hey, payback is a bitch, son!'"

It didn't matter if you were buddies with the guy, either.

"I was good friends with quarterback Dick Shiner. We were teammates together in New York," recalled 11-year defensive end Bob Lurtsema. "Years later, we wound up playing against each other in a game one time, and I took his ass out after he tossed an interception. I just leveled him. He didn't even see me coming. He was laying there on the ground, and as I was getting up he said, 'Lurts, you of all people, you son of a bitch!' I just smiled and said 'Dick, it's just a part of the game. I'm sorry!' He just smiled back and said, 'Part of the game, my ass, you f---er!' It wasn't personal; it was just business. I didn't want to hurt him or anything, but I laid into him pretty good with a clean hit. He understood, and it was all right. Had it been somebody else who took him out in that situation, he might have gone after him. But once he opened his eyes and saw who it was, he just smiled."

Former Buccaneers linebacker Peter Najarian was known for being a hard hitter, yet he never wanted to cross that line in the heat of the moment when the ball changed possessions.

"I never wanted to be *that* guy," he said. "As a linebacker, sure, we are told to go get the quarterback in those situations, but that was not my style at all. To me, that stuff in some way violates the code. It might be my own personal code, but it goes against what I believe in, so I didn't do that stuff. Sure, I would hit hard and do anything to help my team win, but I wasn't going to play dirty or cheap-shot guys along the way. Quarterbacks are extremely vulnerable out there. Their shoulder pads are a joke. They are really small so that they can throw the ball with a wide range of motion. As a result, you will see guys try to wrap them up and drive them into the ground shoulder first to injure them or knock them out of the game. They don't wear big chin straps or mouth pieces, either. I never viewed the quarterback as the guy to go after on an oskie, ever. Sure, I would block him and take him out, but nothing cheap. I might look for other guys, who we would refer to as nose pickers—the guys standing around picking their noses and not paying attention.

"Let me be clear—I did try to hit quarterbacks hard, say in a sack situation or if they were scrambling. Absolutely. But again, I didn't want to be cheap. I wanted to play them straight up. That was my style. One time when I was playing in the World Football League up in Sacramento, I lost my cool and got called for it. There was this one quarterback who always tried to tiptoe down the sideline just as he was about to go out of bounds to get that extra yard. I warned him about doing it and sure enough, later in the game he did it again right in front of our bench. So I just annihilated the guy [and] really blasted him. Needless to say, there were yellow flags flying before my body even hit the ground. The funny part about it was that when I looked up, the first person I saw was my dad, who was standing right behind our bench. He immediately looked at me and reached for his back pocket, as if to signal me that he wanted to throw a late-hit flag on me, as well. I just started laughing. I was totally busted. I was like, 'Good lord! It's your own son! What are you doing calling a flag?' To this day, my dad and I still laugh about that. All I can say is that my message was heard loud and clear, because that quarterback never tiptoed down the sideline like that again."

Former San Francisco linebacker Jim Fahnhorst felt very strongly about the opposition trying to take liberties with his team's meal ticket.

"If a guy gets a clean hit on your quarterback, that is all right,' Fahnhorst said. "But if he cheap-shots him or wraps him up and tries to hurt him, then we were going to knock the crap out of the guy. Even now, you see defensive guys doing that little extra roll, when they are down on the ground, to try to take out his ankles or knees. You see that, and it is so transparent to me. The guy is trying to roll up on him and injure him. In our day, that guy would have gotten drilled. We wouldn't tolerate that kind of stuff."

Offensive linemen, for the most part, take great pride in keeping their quarterback safe. Mess with their signal-caller, especially if he is a Hall of Famer, and they are going to get you back. You can bank on it.

"If a guy cheap-shotted our quarterback, we would make sure to get him, especially if it was Joe Montana," recalled 13-year offensive tackle John Alt. "Joe was an untouchable out there with regard to that kind of stuff, and it was our job to protect him at all costs. Our entire offensive line would discuss it and figure out a way to take care of business. If it happened during a game between a divisional opponent, we would meet privately that week during practice and determine the best course of action to get back at him. You just couldn't tolerate that kind of stuff."

For some offensive linemen, however, it was all about trying to make the tackle while not getting "highlight-reeled."

"As a lineman, you had to really be on the lookout whenever there was an interception," said former Broncos offensive tackle Jon Melander. "The defensive players are taught to go after unsuspecting goons like myself in those situations. That is their free shot to go out and get somebody, and they live for that stuff. One year when I was with Denver and we were playing the Raiders, our quarterback John Elway threw an interception, and I immediately started to run after the cornerback to try to force him out-of-bounds. Well, sure enough, as I was running over there, defensive end Nolan Harrison lined me up and just leveled me. I never saw him coming. The first thing to hit the ground was the top of my helmet, and it wasn't pretty. It was totally legal, and I learned a pretty good lesson out of it. The thing that I worried about most after I got up was not if I was injured or not, but if it was caught on film. Nobody wants to be on the

Tom Olivadotti, Longtime NFL Coach, on Retaliation Following an Interception

"I had my own rule on this when I was coaching in Miami—if one of our guys got an interception and then got tackled by the quarterback, he was going to get fined," Olivadotti said. "I never followed through on it, but they knew that they were going to catch hell if that ever happened, and it never did. Louis Oliver set the record for the longest interception return for a touchdown, it was like 104 yards, and the only person left to tackle him down inside the red zone was the quarterback. He later said to me, 'All I could think about was your damn fine,' so it worked. Guys didn't want the humiliation of seeing themselves being taken down by the quarterback on film the next week either, which was a big deterrent for them, too."

highlight reel come Monday morning for that kind of stuff. That razzing from your teammates is way worse than the hit itself."

Big hits on the quarterback can swing the momentum in a game. But they can also be used as motivation by the other team for payback. Such was the case back in 1976 during a game between the Vikings and Steelers.

"I remember playing Pittsburgh on a Monday night and just leveling [Steelers quarterback] Terry Bradshaw after he threw an interception," said defensive tackle Doug Sutherland. "I saw my opportunity to put him on his back, and I took it. I came in full speed and just let him have it right square in the ribs. He didn't see me coming. I launched him right in the air, and he must have flown at least seven yards backward. It was crazy. He was not a small guy, either. It was just a one-in-a-million hit. I thought I had killed him. It was a clean hit though, and my teammates all congratulated me. I didn't want to hurt him, but it was a free shot at their main guy, and I took it. He had to be helped off the field and was clearly sore for the rest of the game. We wound up beating them that night, so it was an effective hit."

The next year, the two teams met in the Super Bowl, where Bradshaw used that big hit as a rallying point for his teammates.

"I remember that hit," said Vikings center Jeff Siemon. "It wasn't dirty, but Bradshaw was definitely upset. Well, the next season we met up with those same Steelers in the Super Bowl, and sure enough, they beat us. Bradshaw was a cocky player, and he certainly let us know how he felt about that hit the season before. All he had to do was point to the scoreboard, and that was retaliation enough."

As for the coaches, they all have their own unique spin on quarterback retaliation following a pick.

"My philosophy as a defensive line coach was that we needed to put a calling card on the quarterback early in the game," said longtime coach Paul Wiggin. "I wanted our guys to play clean, though, and I would have never told them to try to take a quarterback out of a game. No way. I remember one time when I was coaching in Minnesota, and we were playing Houston. Warren Moon was their quarterback in those days, and he was one of the best in the business. Well, my thought was that if you didn't let a guy like Warren Moon know that you were serious about stopping him early in the game, then he was going to throw for 300-plus yards and beat you. We had Keith Millard and Chris Doleman on our line that year, and those guys were tough. The defensive linemen are the tempo-setters in my opinion, and I knew that if I could get those guys fired up, then that was like throwing a bucket of blood in front of a shark. Those guys hit Moon early and often that game and sent a clear message. They sacked him seven times for a net loss of 40 yards and had him off balance all game. He wound up throwing for like 70 total yards the entire game, which was incredible. We didn't do anything dirty or take him out of the game or anything like that, either. We just came after him early and often and got him off of his game. We let him know that it was going to be a long day and that we didn't want him getting too comfortable back in the pocket. Even if they weren't able to sack him, I wanted those guys to tap him on the shoulder and let him know they were there. We wanted him to know that we were there on every play and that we were going to keep coming and coming. You could make a quarterback skittish if you were able to knock him down and get inside his head enough. That was a tactic, and it was legal. That type of intimidation can only be executed if you have the players who can pull it off, and they were good. That is a mentality, to be able to play that tough and to be that relentless."

"It is pretty funny to see what [quarterbacks] do whenever there is an interception, because they know that everybody and their sister is coming for them," said longtime coach Jerry Glanville. "They are all pretty pathetic, if you ask me, flailing around trying to tackle somebody. They are terrible. Now they just time it out so that they can stay back there and not even come close to making a tackle. It is pretty pathetic. They are definitely a target back there though, and guys will go after them in those situations. Teams with star quarterbacks would rather they just stay away rather than risk getting hurt. I remember one time when I was coaching with the Lions and our linebacker, Paul Naumoff, went after Jets quarterback Joe Namath after an interception. He nailed him on a pretty good hit. Well, sure enough, about half of the Jet's roster immediately went after Naumoff and damn near killed the guy. Both benches cleared, and it got pretty ugly."

For the quarterbacks, it is a double-whammy. Not only are they upset about throwing an interception and killing a drive, they also have to be on the lookout for the 11 guys who are all out head-hunting for them. For 12-year quarterback Bernie Kosar, throwing INTs was like torture.

"I absolutely hated to throw interceptions," said Kosar. "In fact, I tried so hard not to throw picks that at one point I had a record for the least amount of them thrown per percentage. Once in a while, when I threw one, I just wanted [the defense] to kill me because I didn't want to face the reality of what I had just done. I remember one time actually considering impaling myself on the first-and-10 marker because I was so mad about throwing an interception at the end of a game. I was so into wanting to win, and for me to feel like I was letting my teammates and the fans down, was almost too much to take. Facing the music for making mistakes like that out on the field was one of the worst feelings in the world. I almost obsessed about not throwing them, and when I did I would really get down on myself. I would go back and study film and try to find a reason why it happened. I was so hard on myself. Even if I got run over by a defensive lineman, I almost figured that I deserved it for what I had done. It was like I didn't care at that point. I was just so obsessed with the whole thing. I would physically get sick about it. I hated throwing them more than almost anything in life in those days. I really did. I know that doesn't sound good, but I was a real perfectionist and never wanted to let my team down."

"When you throw an interception, as a quarterback, you have to be on the lookout because everybody is coming for you," added Rich Gannon. "The first thing the defensive guys are taught is to go find the quarterback and to try to nail him. One of the worst hits I ever took was on an interception when Bill Romanowski hit me on the sideline. I never saw him coming, and he got a hard shot on me that knocked me on my back really hard. I was hurt and had to get treatment for several weeks. I was stiff and sore, and it bothered me for quite some time. It was a clean hit though, and there was nothing I could do about it. As a quarterback, you just have to keep your head on a swivel and watch out for guys like that. That was why I hated to throw interceptions. Not only was it bad enough that you turned the ball over, but then you knew that you were going to get nailed on top of it. I played against and with Romanowski, and it was definitely better to play with him than against him. He was tough. He was someone who you hated to play against, but you loved him as a teammate because he would do anything for you."

So many quarterbacks were going down in the Canadian Football League that the league changed the rules to protect them.

"We have a rule up here in Canada when that happens," said 15-year CFL quarterback Anthony Calvillo of interceptions. "If you throw one and you are nowhere near the play, then the defensive lineman can't block you or hit you. The rule came about because so many quarterbacks were getting lit up after interceptions and getting injured. So this protects us a little bit. The referees will even yell out to the players, 'You can't touch him! You can't touch him!' I will sort of act like a safety in those situations and act like the last line of defense where I stay out of the action unless I am the last guy to beat. If I do go after the guy, I will try to strip the ball or force him out-of-bounds. Your instinct tells you to get up there and go after the guy because you are upset about throwing the pick, but you have to be smart about it. The defense is so jacked up at that point, and they are all looking for you to take you out. They will gang-tackle you, too, and try to wrap up your arms so that when you get driven down you will land on your shoulders. They are coached to take out the quarterback. That is their job. It is brutal, but that is just the reality of playing this position."

Some quarterbacks were so tough that you simply didn't want to mess with them. According to legendary Baltimore Colts defensive tackle Art Donovan, back in the '50s and '60s, there was a handful of quarterbacks who fell into that category. "Back in my day, you would go after every quarterback in the league after an interception except for three guys— Johnny Unitas, Norm Van Brocklin, and Bobby Layne. Those guys were as tough as nails. You didn't want to mess with those guys, believe you me."

One more guy who could be added to that list was 12-year NFL and CFL quarterback Joe Kapp. "Whenever I threw an interception, I was so pissed off that I was usually one of the first guys to race over and tackle him," Kapp said. "In fact, the best hit I ever got on a guy came in the 1969 NFL Championship Game between Minnesota and Cleveland, when I knocked Jim Houston out cold. It was like 5 degrees out at old Metropolitan Stadium, just colder than hell. He was probably too busy worrying about staying warm rather than watching for me, because I really nailed him. Yup, a pussy quarterback knocked out a Pro Bowl defensive end. That felt pretty good. We won that game, 27–7, and I earned some respect out on the field that day, that was for sure."

While the offensive linemen feel responsible for protecting their passer, the job of keeping the quarterback safe ultimately falls upon the referee.

"Whenever there was an interception, it was our job as referees to do whatever we could to protect the quarterback," recalled 25-year NFL referee Dick Hantak. "We had to make sure that nobody went after him, because they are extremely vulnerable at that point. In fact, I have actually yelled at quarterbacks on several occasions during an interception to watch out and to get out of the way of a player coming at him from his blindside. The defense would get a big boost of adrenaline when they got an interception, and the first thing some of those linemen would do would be to go straight for the quarterback. So that was always one of my greatest worries. We had to be the eyes in the back of their heads sometimes, we really did."

"It is the referee's job to protect the quarterback," added 22-year NFL referee Bernie Kukar. "Wherever the quarterback goes, that is where the referee goes. He is the protector of the quarterback. So if a guy tries to cheap-shot him on an interception, the referee will see it and act accordingly. In the old days, guys used to go after them a lot more than they do now. Now there are rules to protect them more, unless they are involved in making the tackle. If they hang back and don't go after the ball carrier, then they can't be roughed up. Again, the referee's main focus is to follow the quarterback. That is the biggest investment most teams will have, and they want to make sure we protect that investment. The owners are the ones who dictate these things, and that was very clearly stated to us."

Retaliation: Under the Pile

Many linemen will tell you straight up that the pile is without a doubt the most dangerous place to be during a football game. If you are standing near it, gawking, you can get lit up like a Christmas tree. To "pile" someone is a term used when a player absolutely levels somebody who is standing around the ball carrier and his ensemble of tacklers, waiting for the ref to blow the whistle. Guys will come running in, pretending to either dive for a phantom fumble or get in on a tackle that has already come to rest, and just blow somebody up. The unsuspecting sap who gets nailed then flies ass-backward into or over the top of the pile, creating even more carnage for the players below. It makes for an awful mess and falls into the gray area in the grand scheme of cheap-shotting versus gamesmanship.

But what happens above the pile only pales in comparison to what horrors actually take place underneath it. What really goes on under the pile has long been considered urban myth. You see, much like Vegas, what happens under the pile stays under the pile—until now, that is. Under the pile is where the really gruesome stuff takes place. This is the stuff your mother warned you about and was the main reason she wouldn't let you play football in the first place. It is hard to believe that even with 75,000 fans sitting and watching, such mayhem can occur in broad daylight. It is not a place for the faint of heart.

"There is some really nasty stuff that goes on under the pile," said former assistant coach Dean Dalton. "Eye gouging, nostril and cheek gouging, you name it. It can get ugly. And don't forget about the guys who will go for the nads. They are the worst. I mean fans don't realize just how vulnerable players' private parts are out there. Sure, they wear huge shoulder pads, helmets and thigh pads, but they don't wear nut-cups. So if you don't watch yourself, you could come out of the bottom of a pile singing soprano in a heartbeat. It is one scary place to be, under there, that is for sure."

"And I will add this. Just like quarterbacks have to be careful for defensive linemen after throwing interceptions, the defensive linemen have to be careful for offensive linemen when they are standing near the pile. If they are just standing around and maybe taking a breather while the play is just winding down and before a whistle has blown, that is an extremely dangerous place to be. Smart offensive linemen will sprint over and label them into the pile while sort of pretending to get pushed or maybe pretending to dive into the pile in an attempt to jump on a loose ball. So cheap stuff like that goes both ways."

For eight-year defensive tackle Keith Millard, sometimes there was a pot of gold at the end of the rainbow. "I have seen all sorts of crazy things over the years," Millard confessed. "Guys get their eyes gouged or their mouths ripped open from hands coming up in their face masks. They get punched and elbowed in the ribs and even get grabbed in the nuts. It was not a pleasant place to be. As a defensive lineman, if you ever got into a pile with a quarterback, that was just a huge bonus. You could intimidate him and try to get in his head, or maybe push off of him as you were getting up to let him know that you were coming back for him. There were all sorts of little mind tricks you would try to do. You wanted to wear those guys out and get to them wherever you could. Everything goes under pile. Everything."

If you are a quarterback, you did not want to wind up down there. It is a tough call, too, because if there is a fumble, your first reaction is to go get it. However, the veteran signal-callers know better than to just dive in and risk not being able to live to fight another day.

"You do not want to be under that pile. That is a horrible place to be—especially for a tall, skinny, slow kid," quipped 12-year NFL quarterback Bernie Kosar. "Guys will do anything to get the ball. Hell, I have had bite marks around my groin, believe it or not. Guys will spike you in the elbow or hand to try to mess up your ability to be able to grip or throw the ball. It is brutal. All sorts of crazy things go down under there."

"The bottom of the pile is not a good place to be," added 17-year NFL quarterback Rich Gannon. "Guys will do anything to get the ball under there. It is insane. I have had guys twist my ankle the opposite direction and grab my arm and start bending. You get a couple of 300-pound lineman screaming at you and trying to smash your face in the ground, and it gets pretty intense. Eventually you just have to let go of it unless you want to get seriously hurt under there. I will never forget one time when I was with Kansas City and we were playing Detroit on Thanksgiving Day. Right before halftime, they kicked off with a squib-kick. My teammate, Greg Manusky, who was an up-lineman in the wedge, caught the ball and started running with it. Well, he got hammered, and the ball popped out. The ball was rolling around, and everybody dove for it. Greg got one hand on the ball but had his other hand under a body. A Lions player had possession of it, but Greg wasn't going to just give it to him. So he screamed to one of his teammates next to him on the pile to grab the guy's nuts and squeeze. His teammate just looked at him, so he yelled it again, at which point he obliged and started squeezing. Sure enough, the ball squirted out, and by the time the officials got everybody cleared off, there was Greg holding the ball with that one free hand."

Everybody, no matter what position they played, has a story about something that happened to them under the pile. It is a sort of football rite of passage. But sometimes things can get downright dangerous—even deadly.

"One time back in 1961 when I was with the Vikings we were playing up in Green Bay," recalled eight-year offensive tackle Frank Youso, "I wound up getting hit so hard while I was tackling a guy off an interception that my entire face mask got crushed into my face. What made it worse was that I wound up at the bottom of the pile, with about 10 guys on top of me. I couldn't move and could barely breathe. I started to panic and was hollering for everybody to get off. Well, nobody heard me, and by this

Bill Romanowski, 16-Year Linebacker, on What Goes On Under the Pile

"I was under a pile one time during a game against the Giants and was trying to rip the ball out of Dave Megget's hand. All I could get was a finger though, so I just yanked it as hard as I could and cracked it like a chicken bone. It just snapped. Then I heard him scream. He was a tough player though and even came back into the game with his fingers wrapped together. My mentality in dealing with running backs or receivers under the pile was to try to A) get the ball and recover the fumble, and B) limit that guy's ability to be able to hold on to the ball or catch the ball for the rest of the game. I knew that he was going to have a tougher time doing his job for the rest of his game, and I was willing to do whatever it took to help my team win. I saw it as an opportunity, and I took it. Everything is fair game under the pile. I once had my cheek nearly ripped off by Dave Widell. He reached up under my face mask and dug his nails into my cheek and just started ripping. I still have a big scar from that one. I have seen him since then and we have joked about it, but I still think he is a dirty son of a bitch. It wasn't personal—it was just football under the pile, I suppose."

point I was desperate. So I looked up and saw a big Packer rear end right in front of my face, so I rammed my finger right in there as far as I could, and the pile broke up in about 3 seconds. It was actually a lot worse once I got up, too. I had suffered skull fractures in five places and had to be hauled off to the hospital."

For veteran long-snapper Mike Morris, it was all about keeping his head above water—literally.

"The scariest pile incident for me by far was during a game in Cleveland," Morris said. "It had been raining like hell, and there were big pools of water out on the field from where the linemen had dug it all up. Well, I dove for a fumble and wound up at the bottom of a pile with about 10 huge guys on top of me. I wound up face-first in a deep puddle and was literally drowning. It was the scariest thing I have ever been through. Water was completely up past my ears and I couldn't move a muscle. I was already breathing hard from the play, and then I really started to panic. I was swallowing water. It was insane. Luckily some guys started moving around for whatever reason, and I was able to just get my head turned enough to get a breath of air through my nose. I just kept thinking about what they

Jim Fahnhorst, Seven-Year NFL Linebacker, on What Goes on Under the Pile

"My philosophy was pretty simple: if you wound up with the ball under there, hold on tight and cover your nuts, because anything goes under the pile."

were going to say on *SportsCenter*: 'Lineman drowns on 20-yard line.' That was some seriously crazy shit."

"It is crazy down there," added veteran center Matt Birk. "The refs will actually jump on top of the pile and sort of slither their way down into a crack to see who indeed really has the ball. They do it quickly too, because the ball changes hands under there a lot more than people would think. Guys will do all sorts of nasty stuff to you to get the ball. It ain't pretty. They will grab any body part that they can reach under there and start pulling or twisting in order to get you to drop the ball. I was under a pile in a game against the Giants one time where I got totally pinned and couldn't move my arms or legs, not even an inch. There was a fumble, and a bunch of linemen wound up jumping on me. It was brutal. And it took forever to clear guys off it, too. I am totally claustrophobic, but I just stayed calm so I wouldn't freak out. I was so happy when I finally saw daylight. I thought I was going to die under there. I really did."

The sight of a 5'6" 150-pound referee slithering down into a pile of 6'7" 300-pound giants is one of the more bizarre things you will see on any given Sunday. That is their job though, and they do it with pride.

"There is so much stuff that goes on under there," Kukar said. "We try to get in there as quickly as we can to determine just who has the ball, but it can change hands four or five times before we can see anything. We will make the determination as to who has what we call the major portion of the football. It can be tough. I will just call out 'He's got it!' and then everybody lets go. Sometimes we will yell, 'Defense has the ball!' but the offense comes out with the ball. Well, they had the ball, at least when we got in there and made the call. There is a lot of grabbing, twisting, scratching, and clawing going on, along with a whole bunch of screaming and hollering. As officials, we have to climb in that mass of bodies and try to get to the bottom of it. It is not a very fun place to be."

"When there is a fumble and there is a tremendous pile-up, it is survival of the fittest," added 23-year NFL referee Jerry Markbreit. "Whoever has the ball when the official gets down to it gets it. It could have changed hands in there three or four times, but that is just football. We try to climb down in there and see who has it, and as soon as we confirm who has it, the play is over. Whoever gets it, gets it. That has always been our stance on that issue."

"I would just try to get as many people out of the way as I could so that I could get a view of who had the ball," said 25-year NFL referee Dick Hantak. "There are bodies everywhere, and the ball can change hands under there several times. It is so hard to see what is going on underneath there from our vantage point. Guys are grabbing and pushing and pulling and doing whatever they can to get that ball. We try to get in there as soon as we can to see who had the ball originally before it starts changing hands. We try to be as fair as we can, but sometimes it is an almost impossible task to figure out who may have had the ball in their possession before being stripped of it under there."

Retaliation: Running Up the Score

Running up the score, or piling it on, is a method of retaliation that evokes a lot of raw emotion from the players and coaches. Like in baseball, where a team is supposed to shut it down, perhaps with a seven-run lead in the eighth inning, so too are football teams supposed to shut it down if they are up by 21 in the fourth quarter. That magic number is extremely subjective, though, and makes for some vile confrontations following a blowout. Teams have long memories and don't forget being embarrassed on national television. They will use those bad losses as incentive and motivation for their next meeting, guaranteed.

"I remember a game back in 1983 against the Broncos at Arrowhead Stadium," said 12-year offensive tackle Richard Baldinger. "It was an awful day, 28 degrees below zero with windchill. I think there were like 9,000 fans in the entire stadium, it was so brutal. We were up pretty big, and with 47 seconds left in the game, our coach, John Mackovic, called a timeout so that we could score another touchdown. The next season when we went to Denver to play those guys, they ran up the score and shoved it down our throats. I think they crushed us like a hundred to nothing. It was a beating. They used that game as motivation and really kicked our asses out there. They were flying around out there and just rubbing our noses in it. There is a lot of karma in football, and what goes around comes around. Hey, I don't blame them. We probably deserved it. What you don't know is all of the behind-the-scenes stuff. Maybe our coach had a bone to pick with their coach. Who knows? Regardless, we went home with our tails between our legs after that one."

Coaches can go both ways on a blowout. If one coach has a personal grudge against another coach, he may try to bury him and publicly humiliate him. This will warrant the gratuitous wave vs. handshake following the game at midfield. Or out of respect, that coach may try to shut it down. In so doing, he may pull all of his starters and simply run the ball. This can be tricky though, because the second-stringers all want to show their stuff and don't want to be handcuffed out there.

"There is a code amongst the coaches too I think, and running up the score is all up to them," said Pete Bercich, former linebacker and coach. "As players, we are going to go all out on every play. If the coaches want to shut it down, they will pull the starters out of the game, or they will call in certain plays, like running versus passing, to make sure the score doesn't get run up. But there could be some bad blood from a previous game, or maybe a coach has an issue with another coach from a previous job and he wants to settle an old score. You never know. Overall though, it is never a good idea to bury a team too badly because they will remember it and use it as motivation to beat you even worse the next time you face them. Or as a coach, they might be applying for a job with that coach across the field the next year or two as well, so maybe they think of that stuff, too. It is a pretty small coaching fraternity, and these guys all know each other for the most part."

"A lot of the old-school coaches had no problem running up the score on their nemeses," added 12-year long snapper Mike Morris. "These guys all know each other and have coached with and against each other for years. Maybe one of them had gotten fired from a previous coaching staff that they had been part of and had an axe to grind. You never know. Maybe someone said something in the papers about so-and-so. These guys are so ultra-competitive and will try to teach each other lessons all the time. The fans might think they are being disrespectful and unsportsmanlike, but stuff like that usually has a history that goes deep and involves some bad blood somewhere along the line."

"It is an unwritten rule that you don't hammer somebody when you already have the game in hand," said longtime coach Jerry Glanville.

John Gagliardi, Winningest College Football Coach of All Time, St. John's University, Minnesota, on Running Up the Score

"We have tried a bunch of different things over the years, from taking a knee to punting on first down. Nothing would really work because your opponents would feel disrespected or embarrassed either way. So we eventually decided to play the deep, deep reserves. If we suited up 170 guys for a game, we would try to get them all in the game. We don't have a junior varsity, and we don't cut kids who try out, either. So I don't know what more you can do, to tell you the truth. If your opponent can't stop your fifth- or sixth-string players, then that is a whole other issue. I think some of the high schools have a mercy-rule nowadays, like the 10-run rule in baseball. Maybe that is the answer?"

"Unlike in college, there is no ranking system that matters with regards to points; you are not trying to move up in the polls. Well, I got in trouble one time with the commissioner when we ran it up on a team. We were up by 50 points midway through the third quarter, and I told my coordinator not to throw another pass for the rest of the game. I didn't want to run it up even more, and more importantly, I was trying not to get the coach on the other sideline fired. Well, the commissioner got upset, not because we had run it up, but because we were trying not to score late in the game. There is a code between the coaches and believe me, what goes around comes around in this business, so you didn't want to make any enemies out there. That is why you will even see teams with a big lead just take a knee inside the 5-yard line at the end of a game, rather than score any more points."

"Running up the score never bothered me a bit, whether we got beat 30 to nothing or 40 to nothing," countered longtime coach Bud Grant. "As long as they put in their back-ups, then it was up to us to stop them. The backups want to show that they can play, so they are going to play. I was never offended by any of that stuff when I was coaching. I didn't take it personal or anything."

Another sign of respect is for a coach to simply eat the ball in the final seconds of a game, rather than run up the score. This too can be controversial if the other team feels disrespected.

"I remember one time we were just getting killed," said 15-year CFL quarterback Anthony Calvillo. "There was about 3 minutes left in the game, and they had the ball. Instead of running it, though, they just took a

Marc Trestman, Five-Time NFL Offensive Coordinator, on Running Up the Score

"When I was the coordinator in Arizona we were playing Dallas in the first game of the 1998 season. They were up 30–0 late in the game and their head coach, Chan Gailey, kicked a field goal on us. That was total bullshit in my mind, an absolute disrespect for the game and for the people who play it. You know, you get what you deserve in this business. Everybody loves the NFL, but the NFL loves nobody. There is no unconditional love in the NFL. None. If you disrespect it, if you don't work hard, if you don't prepare, or if you don't do the right things, then the game will chew you up and spit you out. Disrespect the game and you in turn will be disrespected. It may not be right then and there, but karma has a way of catching up to you in this business. Make no mistake about it. What goes around comes around. I would never run up the score on another team—that is not my style. In fact, I am the opposite. I have had my quarterback take a knee on the 1-yard line many times in blowouts over the years. I never want to show up another team and disrespect them. Never. That stuff comes back to haunt you in this league. Why give a team a reason to get up to play you? That makes no sense to me."

knee. For me, I thought that was so insulting. It was just a slap in the face. They were basically saying, 'You can't stop us so we are going to show pity on you.' That was extremely disrespectful in my eyes. I understand that they didn't want to run it up, but they could have given the ball to a backup running back and given him some reps or something. It was ridiculous. I remember stuff like that, and you use it for motivation down the road."

Some players felt like it was the job of the opposition to simply stop them. According to Joe Theismann, "My philosophy on that was, 'Hey, if you don't want me to run up the score, then stop me!'"

"My philosophy is pretty simple—stop them," added offensive guard Ray Hitchcock. "I was playing for the University of Minnesota back in the early '80s, and Nebraska put up 84 points on us, so I have been there. It sucks. I guess as long as teams stop passing, just run off tackle, and maybe put in their reserves, that is all you can ask."

Others, meanwhile, loved to pour it on. Such was the case for 16-year linebacker Bill Romanowski. "To me, that was okay. It was just sticking the dagger in because you never know when a team could come back on you. To me, you don't beat a team—you bury them. That was my mentality, to go for the kill."

Retaliation: Going After the Kicker

It used to be legal for guys to go after the opposing team's kicker. In fact, it was quite an effective tactic used by many teams during the '70s and '80s in order to limit the opposition's ability to kick field goals and kick off down field. Seeing kickers get tossed around like rag dolls brought much amusement and delight to players and fans alike, but it certainly wreaked havoc on teams when they were left unable to kick a game-winning field goal. Eventually, what teams would do was to retaliate only when necessary, meaning we won't touch your kicker as long as you don't touch ours.

"When I first got into the league, you could go after the kicker on the kickoff," Glanville said. "You would have a guy wait for him and then let him have it while he was jogging down the field and everybody else's attention was focused on the guy with the ball fifty yards away. In fact, back in the early '70s, kickers would have a personal protector who would hang out back there with them to prevent anybody from taking a cheap shot on them. Well, one time when I was with Detroit, we went after Saints kicker Morten Andersen and turned him upside down. It was bad, too. I mean, he wound up breaking some ribs and some fingers. They booed us for about an hour, and we deserved it. We definitely broke the code on that one. Eventually it just became really taboo to hit a kicker, so you just didn't do it. If you did, then you knew that your kicker was going to get it even worse. So somewhere along the line, we just stopped doing it."

Each team had a designated guy whose job it was to seek and destroy the kicker. It was a dirty job, but somebody had to do it.

"On special teams, it was my job to take out the kicker on kickoffs," recalled Raiders defensive tackle Otis Sistrunk. "I was like 270 pounds, and he was much smaller, but it was my job to get that guy. I would whack him around, and he would get tossed all over the field, even doing flips sometimes. I felt bad about it, but that was my job."

Teams didn't want their kickers to become liabilities, so they started to protect them by whatever means necessary.

"Back in the '70s when I played, it was not uncommon to retaliate against a team by going after their kicker," said Vikings tight end Stu Voigt. "I remember one time when Bears tackle George Seals beat our kicker, Fred Cox, to the sidelines and really let him have it. He just nailed him and bloodied him up pretty good. Ed White then went after Seals in retaliation the next game, and they really got into it. I think Ed might have kicked

Stu Voigt, 11-Year Tight End, on Kicker Retaliation

"As far as kickers went, most of them from my era [the '70s] were not athletes. They were specialists," said 11-year tight end Stu Voigt. "It's like Alex Karras, the defensive tackle with the Detroit Lions, used to say when he was describing his frustrations with the game. In essence, he said, 'You battle for 59 minutes, and then this little guy with a clean uniform [Dolphins kicker Garo Yepremian] comes in to kick a game-winning field goal, to which afterward he says, "Hooray, I keekie you a touchdown!"'"

him in the nuts. It was pretty ugly. They both got kicked out of the game, but Ed was standing up for our guy—which was all right by us. Eventually our coaches had Freddy just kick the ball and then turn 90 degrees and literally run straight to the sidelines."

Fred Cox, a 15-year kicker, remembers the incident well. "I remember Seals decking me on a vicious late hit after a kickoff. The whistle had already blown, and everybody was walking over to the sideline. You see, Metropolitan Stadium had both benches on the same side of the field in those days, and we used to walk by one another as we were coming off the field. Well, he jogged by and forearmed me out of the blue, breaking my nose in the process. I only wore a single bar on my helmet so I could see better, and I had my entire face exposed. It was a horrible cheap shot."

Cox was not the typical kicker of his era, however, and he prided himself on being tough. "Everybody wanted to hit the kicker in my day. It was a tactic. Guys would wait and wait and then come after you, trying to knock you out of the game. They figured if they could take you out, then your team wouldn't be able to go for any field goals late in the game. The way I retaliated against guys who cheap-shotted me, though, was to forearm them in the face. I made no bones about it. It was self preservation. You only had to get that reputation once, then guys would leave you alone. Besides Seals, nobody ever bothered me. You see, I was drafted in the NFL as a running back, not as a kicker. In fact, the first five years that I was in the league, my job was to serve as the wedge-buster on kickoffs. Unlike most kickers, I was actually pretty tough. As a result, guys didn't mess with me the way they did a lot of other kickers. I prided myself on making more tackles on kickoffs than any other kicker in the league. I didn't want to just hang around back behind the play. I wanted to get in there and hit somebody. That is what football is all about in my eyes."

Retaliation: Bounties

Perhaps the most controversial form of retaliation is that of the dreaded bounty. To have one put on your head is both a curse as well as an honor. Bounties used to be all the rage back in the '50s, '60s and '70s, but they have since become taboo. Today, even the mention of word will get you a very expensive date with the league commissioner. To hear the old guys talk about them as a way to earn an extra few bucks, though, is just classic. Don Joyce was a real beauty. He was one of the toughest defensive ends ever to put on cleats in the NFL. His stories of what it was like to play with the pigskin back in the '50s are priceless. Here is one of his classics about the time he had a bounty put on his head.

"I remember when I was with the Colts, and we were playing the Rams in 1954," Joyce recalled. "We had just kicked off, and I was racing down the field. Well, the Rams were known to go after kickers in those days, and one of their guys started smacking around our kicker behind the play. Well, I saw him do this and blindsided him, knocking him over. I then headed down field to get back into the play. Another Ram saw me do this, a guy by the name of Les Richter, and he kneed me from behind at the 50-yard line, knocking me over. I got up, and he did it again. Finally, I got up and grabbed his face mask. His helmet popped right off, and I used it as a boxing glove, drilling him right in the face.

"I found out later that they needed 37 stitches to close him back up—all the way from his forehead down to his cheek. I was kicked out of the game, of course, but I felt strongly about A) standing up for my teammate, and B) standing up for myself after being cheap-shotted not once but twice. Anyway, I got a call from the league commissioner a few days later, Bert Bell, and he told me he was going to fine me $500, which was a huge amount of money in those days. I told him my side of the story, about how the guy had hit me from behind, and asked him if I could plead my case. Knowing nobody on the Rams would testify on my behalf, I asked if I could send him the film of the game to show him why I did what I did. He agreed. So I went to my coach, Weeb Ewbank, and asked him if I could see the film. He said sure. The only problem was that due to costs, he said that we didn't bring our own camera guy to the game and were going to be using the copy taken by the Rams. The teams shared films in those days. Luckily, we had a PR guy who knew the camera man for the Rams and was able to go and get the film before anyone could doctor it and cut out that play, which was what we all suspected they would do.

"Sure enough, we got the film and it showed me retaliating only after being knocked down a couple of times from behind. I sent it to Mr. Bell, and he called me a few days later, telling me that I had been vindicated. He then told me that he had rescinded my $500 fine and was instead giving it to Richter, who was still in the hospital at that point. I told him that he had probably suffered enough, and he dropped the fine from him, too. Ironically, that incident later became a cover story for *Life Magazine* with the caption 'Savagery on Sunday.' Years later, I found out from one of the old Rams players that they had placed a $1,000 bounty on my head. Luckily for me, nobody was ever able to cash in on that over the ensuing years!"

Some players actually liked having bounties put on them, feeling that it made them even tougher and more feared.

"George Wilson was one of the dirtiest players who ever played in the league," said Colts tackle Art Donovan. "He played for the Bears and went on to coach the Lions. Well, he hated our linebacker in Baltimore, Bill Pellington, so much so that he put a bounty on him. Everybody knew about it, too. It wasn't even a secret. Pellington didn't care, though. Hell, he was as tough as they came. A Detroit fullback by the name of Tracy broke Pellington's arm in the first game of the '57 season, forcing him out for the year. The next year, they let Pellington put a steel cast on his arm, wrapped in foam rubber. Needless to say, Billy got a lot of revenge with that thing, using it as a weapon to terrorize everybody in his path."

For others, bounties were all about making a few extra bucks.

"Sure, we had bounties back in my day in the '50s and '60s," said former player and coach Paul Wiggin. "We called them 'incentives' in those days, though. In fact, I was one of the judges on my team who kept track of things during the season. We would get paid for things such as making a tackle inside the 20-yard line on a kickoff or holding a guy to a return of less than five yards on a punt or if you got a sack, fumble recovery, interception, key block, scored a touchdown, made a huge hit, or whatever. Certain players had a number value, too, like if you took out a big name like Y.A. Tittle. I think he was worth $200, which was a lot of dough in those days. Hell, we evaluated everything and came up with this system, which was a real incentive program for the players. We didn't make very much money back then, so any extra money you could make on the job was a big deal. This of course was illegal, and it eventually got banned by the league commissioner."

For the special teamers, the extra money that they earned on bounties helped to pay the bills.

"We had bounties running all the time on kickoffs in the '60s," Cox said. "There were bonuses to be paid for hitting certain people, making tackles, or downing balls. We called them 'special teams bonuses,' and they were designed to help out some of the guys who weren't starters so they could earn a few extra bucks. Eventually the league cracked down on it though, and that was the end of it."

"There were always guys on special teams doing stuff like that," added former Packers running back Vince Workman. "I think it broke up the monotony of not playing all the time for those guys. You would always hear them talking about getting $50 or $100 for the guy who downed the ball or the guy who got the tackle inside the 20-yard line or stuff like that. Or maybe they would all throw in $20 into a pot, and someone would win it for making a big play or something. It wasn't like they would get $1,000 if they took a guy out of the game or something like that. It was more of an incentive to just do their job—a bonus, if you will. And it wasn't like the coaches were involved, either. It was just the veteran guys trying to motivate the younger guys. It was all good."

Some bounties weren't even about the money.

Recalled nine-year NFL cornerback John Turner, "When I was with the Vikings, our special teams coach, Les Steckel, had an award he would hand out that was even better than a bounty. Les was a former Marine, a really tough guy, and he would hand out what he called the 'bayonet award.' To earn it, you would have to knock somebody out of the game almost to the point where they would have to be carried out on a stretcher. It wasn't for a dirty hit or anything like that—it was just for a big hit that would really lay a guy out. You didn't win any money or anything for it, either. It was just a trophy that he would hand out in practice to the guy who was able to pull off a big hit like that in a game. It was a pride thing."

Certain coaches even used bounties as a sort of tactic to start fights.

"A bounty could be used as a sort of tactic, especially for dirty players," said longtime coach Tom Olivadotti. "I remember one time there was a really good player on an opposing team who was kind of a hothead. The coaches knew that he would get into fights from time to time, so they

Joe Theismann, 15-Year Quarterback, on Bounties

"I used to have a bounty on my head, and I was proud of it. I think it got up to $1,000, which I thought was pretty flattering. The higher the bounty, the more respect you got. To me, if they didn't have a bounty on you, that just meant that you weren't good enough for anybody to give a darn about."

sent in a no-name player to goad him into a fight, and sure enough, he bit on it and wound up throwing some punches, which ultimately got him ejected from the game. They would gladly trade a no-name for one of their opposition's top players, so it worked out. It is not something you could do very often, but in that instance it worked."

One of the most notorious bounties ever witnessed in an NFL game occurred back in 1986 at Soldier Field during a game between the Bears and Packers. Longtime referee Jerry Markbreit was there and shared his recollections of what went down that afternoon.

"I was involved right smack dab in the middle of the most notorious bounty incident in NFL history. I was refereeing the game when Packers tackle Charles Martin grabbed Bears quarterback Jim McMahon following an interception, turned him upside down and stuffed him head-first into the ground. It was crazy. I mean this was least 15 seconds after the play was over, too. He really stuffed him. In fact, the word 'stuff' is now in the official rule book, and it came from me, because that is what I announced over the P.A. system at the stadium: 'Personal Foul, unnecessary roughness—he stuffed the quarterback into the ground.' It was an almost surreal scene; it really was. Martin had a 'hit list' towel with the numbers of a bunch of Bears written on it, including McMahon, [running back] Walter Payton, [wide receiver] Willie Gault and [center] Jay Hilgenberg.

"I remember Martin then hovering over McMahon on one knee, taunting him, when finally Bears' offensive tackle Jimbo Covert came barreling in from about 20 yards away at full speed and just decked him square in the back. It might have been the latest hit ever recorded in NFL history. At that moment, I reached down to grab my penalty flag out of my pocket to call a personal foul call on Covert, but realized, of course, that I had already thrown it when Martin had hit McMahon. Then I thought about it for a second and realized that if I offset this penalty, there would be hell to pay. So I didn't do anything. I rationalized it by assuming Covert was protecting his teammate, figuring that Martin was going to go after him again. My line judge came in and did flag it, however, and then all hell broke loose. Bears coach Mike Ditka, who I always kiddingly refer to as 'reserved and mild mannered,' came flying out onto the field. He hollers at me, 'Hey Markbreit, I see two flags down, what the hell is that supposed to mean?' I told him that there were offsetting penalties, to which he replied, 'You have got to be kidding me. How can they be offset when my guy isn't even breathing? There has to be a penalty!' I said, 'Mike, you know the rules.' Irate, he then yells back, 'I am going to give you the Ditka rule. If you want to get home for dinner tonight, you had better not offset these fouls!'

"At that moment, Charles Martin was up on his feet, and so I went over and grabbed his arm. I told him that he was ejected and started leading him toward the sideline. He then pulled away from me vehemently and said, 'I am not going anywhere with you!' I then said to him 'Look pal, if you don't come with me right now, I am going to let the Bears kill you!' 'Okay,' he says. 'Take me to the sidelines.' So I walked him over to his coach, Forrest Gregg, and said 'Coach, this guy is out of the game. Get him out of here immediately.' Gregg then looks at me dumbfounded and says, 'Why, what did he do?' My jaw nearly fell off at that point. Meanwhile, Ditka is out on the field at this point, talking to McMahon. I walk over to him, and he says to me, 'Jerry, I want to apologize for threatening you. I just want you to know that whether you offset the foul or not, we are going to do everything we can to get you home for dinner.'

"Well, I wound up having my line judge pick up his flag after all, and I decided to not offset it. I just didn't feel like it warranted an offset, so I went with my gut. I kicked the guy out of the game, and it became the first time in league history that anybody had ever been ejected for something other than a fight. He also wound up getting suspended for two games by commissioner Rozelle, which was the longest suspension for an on-field incident in history. Anyway, in an otherwise meaningless game, this incident turned to be the biggest call of my entire 43-year officiating career."

While most fans would assume that bounties are long gone in the NFL, former Ravens coach Brian Billick shed some light on the subject in 2008 during an interview with ESPN's Dan Patrick. In it, Billick confirmed the existence of bounties when he spoke about a recent incident involving

Ravens linebacker Terrell Suggs, who had made headlines when he said he and his teammates placed a bounty on Steelers Rashard Mendenhall and Hines Ward. Billick said that he didn't have a problem with the bounty but rather the fact that Suggs never should have made the bounty public. "So-called 'bounties' by players [are] a commonplace occurrence in any locker room and similar to the bravado displayed on most schoolyards," wrote Billick on his WNST.net blog. "Players are constantly motivating each other by putting a certain amount of money in a pool and the cash going to the player that 'knocks' so-and-so out of a game, or gets an interception for a TD, or pancakes a defender on a running play. This is standard operating procedure in virtually every locker room in the NFL. What is worth commenting on is how stupid it is to talk about it afterward. Locker room talk should be just that."

The league's response came from NFL spokesman Greg Aiello, who reiterated, "The rule is clear. Clubs, players, and all club employees are prohibited from offering or paying bonuses to a player for his or his team's performance against a particular team, a particular opposing player or players, or a particular group of an opposing team, or for on-field misconduct, such as personal fouls to or injuries inflicted on opposing players."

Some players, meanwhile, actually wore bounties like badges of honor.

"Raiders coach John Madden once put a bounty on my head, and that really pissed me off," added 10-year guard Conrad Dobler. "He apparently offered $100 to any guy who could take me out. I wasn't pissed about the bounty. I sort of took that as an honor. I was just pissed that he only offered a measly $100. Hell, I thought I was worth at least 10 times that much!"

3

Intimidation

Like revenge and retaliation, intimidation is also a huge part of the code. Intimidation on the gridiron comes in many forms, ranging from physical acts of violence to verbal taunting or trash talking to just plain ol' mean and nasty toughness. For starters, players can evoke fear in their opponents and intimidate them by employing any one of the aforementioned tactics. However, physical violence—or at least the specter of physical violence—is by far the most intimidating to opposing players. What players fear the most are guys who have no fear or respect for the game and will do just about anything to win. When they see guys chop-blocking, leg-whipping, crack-back blocking, and even flying into a wedge on a kickoff feet first to spike a guy—they know that guy is either nuts or on a death wish. Either way, he is extremely frightening.

According to former Green Bay running back Darrell Thompson, "The scariest dudes are the ones who have no regard for their own bodies—guys like Chuck Cecil, Ronnie Lott, and Kenny Easley who would just blow people up. They would try to propel their bodies through your body, which was really scary. You had to be accountable for those guys at all times. You really did. They were game-changers."

Certain players used intimidation as a tactic to get into the heads of their opponents. They would do and say just about anything to get the guy across from them to think more about him than about doing his job. The threat of physical violence was enough for many players to back off and play it straight. One of the most feared hitters of his day was Raiders safety Jack Tatum, otherwise known as The Assassin. Tatum had earned a reputation, so players didn't try to mess with him. He was clear with them, though. He was going to play them straight up until they disrespected him. That was when the gloves would come off.

"I grew up tough back in New Jersey, and I brought that toughness with me to the NFL," Tatum said. "I didn't worry too much about guys cheap-shotting me because what goes around comes around in this league. I wanted to hit guys hard but clean, and I tried to make my tackles head-up. I never tried to cheap-shot guys by going for their knees or anything like that. That stuff is totally uncalled for. Whenever wide receivers would go after my knees, trying to block me downfield, that is when I would get upset and try to make them pay. I would try to punish them. I didn't forget stuff like that, and I was pretty good at making sure those things didn't happen too often. My theory was that if a guy came close to me, he was going to get hit. Period. If a guy ran a route over the middle and I was covering him, then he was in a position where I could really let him have it. I wanted to hit hard, and if that meant that guys had to be accountable for me, then that was all right. I enjoyed being intimidating that way, absolutely. Teams knew what to expect when they came up against the Raiders in my day, without a doubt. We had a saying in those days. We wanted 'to get inside an opponent's head for 60 minutes on Sunday.' And we usually did."

Toughness for some players had nothing to do with size. For them, it was all about attitude. Such was the case for Chiefs Hall of Fame linebacker Bobby Bell.

"I didn't weigh but 220 pounds soaking wet, but I could bring it," Bell boasted. "I loved to play hard-nosed football, and I loved to hit guys. But I never cheap-shotted anybody. That just wasn't my style. I tell you what—I wanted to be thought of [by] other great players as the toughest player they ever played against. To me, if they didn't say my name if asked that question, then I don't feel like I did my job. If I played against a rookie, he had better bring his lunch because I was going to play him the same way I played against a Hall of Famer. I went all out, every play, every game. If you didn't do that, then that is when you would get hurt. That was my philosophy."

For other players, intimidation was just a state of mind.

Conrad Dobler, 10-Year Guard, on Intimidation

"Sure, I tried to use intimidation as a tactic. Absolutely. My old offensive linemate in St. Louis, Dan Dierdorf, used to describe my style as, 'It was like 10 of us playing a football game, and then there is Dobler, who is in a barroom brawl with the guy across from him.' Hey, that was my style. If you could take your opponent out of his game plan and make him more concerned about you than he was about his responsibilities out on the field, then that was mission accomplished. If guys spent their time trying to beat up on me rather than on our ball carrier, that was fantastic. I would take that abuse, sure, because it was helping my team.

"Look, I had a reputation, and I tried to use that to my advantage. I played with an edge and certainly wouldn't take any bullshit from any defensive linemen. I used to just attack those guys. That was my strategy. I was going to use whatever means necessary to beat my opponent out there. That was how I was wired. I would try to distract him, attack him personally, and just abuse him any way I could. It was war when I went out there. I wanted to help my team win—that was the bottom line. For instance, if a defensive lineman jumped up in the air to try to deflect a pass, I would see that as an opportunity. When guys did that to me, I would go right after them and nail them right in the solar plexus, which would bring their hands down immediately. I didn't want them tipping any balls from my quarterback, so I was going to do whatever I could to prevent that from happening. That was my job.

"Opposing coaches used to do most of the dirty work for me. It was unbelievable. They would talk with their defensive linemen before we played and warn them about my rough style of play and get them all riled up. I was already in their heads way ahead of time. It was wonderful. They were ready for me. It was now an ego thing with them, because they weren't about to take any shit from me. Meanwhile, I would go out and do my job, and because they were so worried about me and about what I may or may not try to do to them, they weren't focusing on doing their jobs. What a wonderful sight, to block a guy who is so in tune to beating my brains out, and then to see my running back run right past him and into the end zone. So their own coaches would basically take them out of the game. It was crazy.

"I didn't care what my opponents thought of me. I only cared about my teammates. That was my mentality. You know, back in my day when the coaches voted for which players they thought should be in the Pro Bowl, I made it three straight years. Sure, they hated me, but they thought I was a very good player, the best at my position. Then when they changed the voting to where the players voted, and the defensive linemen voted for the offensive linemen, and vice versa, I never made it again. It became a popularity contest at that point, and I didn't stand a chance. I didn't care though, because for me it was all about sacrificing for your team."

"When I played, I felt like I was an artist," confessed Vikings Hall of Fame defensive end Carl Eller. "Football is a mental game, and I was a craftsman who had great skill and technique. The culmination of all those things made me a great player. Professional football was a real test of all my skills, and I looked at playing as a performance. In other words, when I would do things like putting on a pass rush or stopping a double-team or making a tackle behind the play, I had to push and test myself to the limit to do those kinds of things that were just barely humanly possible. I had to be quick off the ball, and I had to beat the opponent to the ball. Sometimes I had to beat two guys, and sometimes I would have to hold one guy off with one arm and try to grab the quarterback with the other, all while trying to maintain my leverage and watching out for the back who was coming to cut me at my knees. You had to do all that in a split second, and I took great pride in being able to do it well. I really felt like playing professional football was an art."

Intimidation could come from a player believing psychologically that he had an edge over his opponents. Such was the case for 10-year safety Joey Browner, who knew his hands were simply stronger than anybody else's out there, which gave him a mental edge.

"Intimidation for me was going 1,000 percent out there," Browner said. "I wanted to make big hits that would change the game. I wanted opposing offenses to have to account for me out there and to know that if they came my way, I was going to make them pay a price for that. I wanted to check my opponent's man-card. I wanted to see if he had any mettle, to see what he was made of. I wanted to know how good he was because I was going to be coming at him with everything I had.

"I think the secret to my success out there was having strong hands. I had really strong hands and worked extremely hard on that. That was 99.9 percent of my game. That was why I got into studying martial arts, particularly jiu jitsu. It helped me a great deal in football, to increase my mobility, timing, dexterity, and overall strength. It was all about the relationships between power, energy, time, and space. It also taught me a great deal about how to fall the right way and how to avoid injury. I studied the human body and applied that to the art of tackling. It was really fascinating stuff. Strong hands was the key, though. Everything stopped and started right there for me. In fact, I was the originator of what they now call the horse-collar tackle, which will forever be a part of my football legacy I suppose. I used to tackle guys a lot from behind by their shoulder pads. The one that sort of coined the phrase came from when I brought down Broncos receiver Gerald Willhite during a tackle that broke his leg while he was trying to run into the end zone. The league finally outlawed it in 2008, but I guess I will forever be linked to it."

Defensive players have always tried to get inside the heads of opposing quarterbacks by trying to intimidate them. For 12-year quarterback Bernie Kosar, it was all about ignoring that noise and just focusing on the job at hand.

"There were a lot of guys who tried to intimidate you out there, either by playing dirty or by trash talking," Kosar said. "I could never be on the lookout for those guys though because that would take you off of your game. I was so focused [that] I didn't pay any attention to those guys. None. The losers are the guys who pay attention to them. You have to block that out. I could only focus on looking downfield to try to read coverage. If I had worried about all of that other stuff, I would have failed. It requires so much discipline and thought to focus and complete a throw in the National Football League— that was all I could pay attention to. If I got nailed after I threw it, so be it. That just came with the job. I wanted to complete passes and help my team win. That was all I cared about. I didn't care about the Bill Romanowskis or the Andre Waters of the world, regardless of what they were saying or doing out there. Those guys want you to think about them and about what they are saying so that you can't focus on your receiver's route. That tunnel vision was a positive in football but maybe a personality defect in life. Who knows. The bottom line is that you can't let all of that other stuff bother you. You just have to completely tune it out. That was hard for me because I loved to chat with those guys out there on the line of scrimmage. I was a competitor and loved to dish it out just as much as I would take it."

Sometimes intimidation toward quarterbacks will come as a result of a cheap shot.

"Trust me, I hate when my teammates cheap-shot someone because I am the one that is most likely to get retaliated against," explained 15-year CFL quarterback Anthony Calvillo. "One time one of my teammates cheap-shotted an opposing quarterback on a late hit and took him out. It was ugly. Well, sure enough, the next series all I heard was a bunch of angry defensive linemen telling me how they were going to kill me. They just kept telling me over and over that if their guy could get taken out, then

Bill Romanowski, 16-Year Linebacker, on Intimidation

"When you play linebacker in the NFL, your job is to be violent, to strike people as hard as you possibly can. To do that, there is a level of intimidation that is necessary to do your job. Can you knock someone out of a game? Do you gang-tackle? Do you go after the quarterback on an interception? That is just the way it is. If guys know what you are capable of, they will either fear you or respect you. Either way, you had to do your job out there. I hope that I was an intimidating force out there. I certainly tried to be. That was my game. I wanted players to know that if they ran by me, I was going to do whatever it took to take them down, hard. That was my job.

"Being a hard hitter was really intimidating, in my eyes. One of the best hits I ever had was back in 1997, when I shattered Kerry Collins' jaw in a preseason game in about 10 different places. Hits like that are what fired up your teammates. That is why I got paid as much as I did to play football. I would get raises, more money, [and] new contracts when I did that type of thing. So I kept doing that type of thing, hitting players as hard as I could. That was my job. Everybody said it was a dirty hit, but I never got called for a penalty on it. I did get fined after the fact because he got hurt. If he didn't get hurt, it wouldn't have been an issue. Whatever.

"I remember one time in a playoff game against the Jets, I leveled their tight end, Anthony Becht. He was out on the flat, behind the play, and I just knocked the crap out of him. He got so upset that he came after me during the game. In the process, he went offside three times and got a holding penalty. Needless to say, we won the game. I enjoyed being an agitator out there. That was my role.

"I want to be clear about injuries, though. There was never a part of me that wanted to hurt someone badly enough to where they would struggle in any way or so that they couldn't play the game. That was never my mindset. But I would *happily* love to hit a quarterback or running back or wide receiver so hard that they had to be carried off the field. As long as they were able to return the following week and not be injured, that was the best scenario. Again, that was my job—to knock people out of football games."

they were going to take me out. It is a motivating factor for those guys, and it is something that can get in your head because you never know if one of them will hit you late or roll up on your leg or something. You try not to let that stuff affect you, but it can be pretty intimidating."

For many players, intimidation is not just what they do or say. It is who they are. Their whole persona reflects their style of play, right down to how they dress and how they act—both on and off the field.

"Intimidation is a huge part of the game," said former Buccaneers linebacker Pete Najarian. "Each guy has his own way of preparing himself mentally for battle, and intimidation is a big part of that. For instance, whenever you see guys like Ray Lewis doing their dances and screaming and hollering when they first hit the field, that isn't as much for TV as it is to let the other team know that they are loose and crazy and ready to go. It can be extremely intimidating to see that type of thing from the other sideline, believe me. Even the way you carry yourself out there can mean a lot. For instance, when I was at the University of Minnesota, I played under Lou Holtz, who hated long hair and all of that kind of stuff. Well, I was a sort of a Brian Bosworth type of player in my own eyes but had to conform to my coach's wishes in order to play. Later when I got into the NFL, I was able to let my hair go long, grow a fu manchu and goatee, and really be myself. That gave me confidence. When guys saw me, they thought I was a little bit crazy, which was exactly what I wanted them to think. Even if you weren't intimidating to everybody, you would make them think twice about you and about what you were capable of doing out there. You do judge a book by its cover, and I certainly tried to use that to my advantage to gain a little edge."

Sometimes it is the little things that will give a player a boost of confidence. For 14-year defensive tackle John Randle, it was his trademark war paint. That was his edge, his signature—until 1999 anyway when the NFL (or "No Fun League" as Randle calls it) banned him from donning the paint, citing it "wasn't sportsmanlike" to wear.

"The war paint was about having fun, getting ready, and getting excited about playing the game of football in a military style," Randle said. "I would smear on the paint and rub it into different spots, and I think it reflected my emotions. It was a combination of *Braveheart*, different military movies where guys get ready for combat with the war paint, and also from watching Jesse 'The Body' Ventura in the movie *Predator*. All of those things got me fired up to go into battle!"

Another aspect of toughness and intimidation had to do with a certain fear factor that was created around a player's reputation. Back in the days before video footage, players earned a reputation based on hearsay and rumors. If you were good, you might be thought of as great. Occasionally, a rare and almost-superhuman player would emerge out of nowhere and take the sports world by storm. Such was the case for Bears fullback

Bronko Nagurski in the '30s when he appeared out of International Falls, Minnesota, and was portrayed by the newspaper men like a modern day Paul Bunyan. The Bronk was tough, no doubt about it. In fact, he may have evoked more fear into would-be tacklers than anybody in NFL history. The tall tales about Bronk are now the thing of legend.

Bears' owner George Halas once recalled a game against Washington at Wrigley Field, where Nagurski barreled up the middle, sent two linebackers flying in different directions, trampled two defensive backs, ran through the end zone and bounced off the goal post, finally bulldozing into the brick wall that bordered the dugout used by the Chicago Cubs and even cracking it. "That last guy hit me awful hard," the dazed Nagurski said upon reaching the sidelines. One tall tale had him falling out-of-bounds during a game once and toppling a policeman's horse standing along the sideline. Another had the Bronk missing a wild tackle and shearing the fender off a Model T Ford that was parked near the sidelines. "I have said it a thousand times, Nagurski was the greatest player I ever saw, and I saw a lot of them in my lifetime," said famed running back Red Grange. "Running into him was like getting an electric shock. If you tried to tackle him anywhere above the ankles, you were liable to get killed."

"My greatest thrill in football was the day Bronko announced his retirement," said Green Bay Hall of Fame fullback Clarke Hinkle. "There's no question he was the most bruising fullback football has ever seen. I know because I've still got the bruises!"

Team Intimidation as a Result of a Unique Home-Field Advantage

Intimidation could also come from a team's reputation, such as the dynasty Steelers or 49ers teams of the '70s and '80s. These teams evoked fear within their opponents. Or it could mean having to face the Raiders in the Black Hole in Oakland where their fans gave them a tremendous home-field advantage.

Said defensive tackle Otis Sistrunk, "When I was with the Raiders, we took a lot of pride in being feared. We were tough, and we could back it up. That silver and black just signified toughness. We had a saying, 'No Prisoners,' and that was how we played. Everybody thought we were dirty and this and that, but we really weren't. Sure, we had some hard hitters, but our reputation got out of hand for that kind of stuff. Even Jack Tatum's hit on Darryl Stingley back in 1978, a lot of people thought that was dirty, but it was clean. It was rough and it had a bad outcome, but it wasn't a cheap shot. We never wanted to hurt people; we just wanted to play hard and win. Even head-slapping—I never did it to hurt someone. I did it to punish my opponent and to make him respect me for the rest of the game."

Intimidation could also come in the form of an amazing home-field advantage, such as playing in Miami in September when it is 110 degrees on the field with 100 percent humidity. The Dolphins trained in it and were prepared for it. The Broncos were also well-equipped to play at Mile High Stadium, where there was much less oxygen in the air than in Buffalo or Cleveland. We have all seen the classic camera shots of players from visiting teams breathing heavily into their oxygen masks on the sidelines. And players could be intimidated when playing at Lambeau Field or at old Metropolitan Stadium in January against the Packers or Vikings, respectively. Cold weather and the elements have long been considered some of the most intimidating aspects of the game. The players who lived and practiced in those cold weather locales thrived on it, knowing that the players from the southern cities would be scared half to death when they got off the plane and felt the arctic blast.

"I remember playing at the old Met Stadium when it was like 20 below zero," said former Vikings tight end Stu Voigt. "It would get just colder than hell out there. And the ground was nothing more than frozen dirt painted green to look like grass. It was awful. You couldn't even get traction on that stuff with cleats, so guys would try soccer shoes and broomball shoes—anything to get some traction. We would come out in short-sleeved perforated jerseys. We would wear short-sleeved tee shirts under them, and that was it. The equipment guys didn't even put out long-sleeved shirts for us. Hell no. No long underwear or turtlenecks or anything like that, either. No way. We had to look tough. That was one of the ways we intimidated opposing teams that had to come up here in the dead of winter. Truth be told, we were all colder than shit. It was humorous to see the Rams and Cowboys come up with their layers and layers of warm clothes and their big heaters on the sidelines. But Bud [Grant] would never let us have anything like that. Hell no. That stuff was for pussies as far as he was concerned. So we just dealt with it and acted like the cold didn't bother us, like we were super-human. Little did they know [that] deep down we were jealous as hell."

"Look, it was real simple to me," explained Vikings coach Bud Grant. "When it is really hot, you can play. The reverse is also true. When it is really cold, you can play. I played in college in Minnesota outdoors, I played in the NFL outdoors, and I played in the CFL up in Canada outdoors. Yes, it was cold, but we played. That was the end of the conversation. It was just a state of mind, that's all. I never wanted my players to worry about what warm clothing they were going to wear or anything like that. I wanted them to concentrate on the game going on in front of them, not worrying about how cold they were. We used to practice outdoors too, which really helped as far as the guys getting used to the elements. It was no big deal to me. The people who made the biggest deal out of it were the sports writers from out of town. They used to love to write about the cold and about all of that stuff. I thought that was great because it didn't matter to our guys. It only mattered to the visiting team who was going to read that stuff and then worry about the cold."

"You know, the things that bothered me the most about moving from Met Stadium to the Metrodome back in '82 was that it took a lot of coaching out of the equation. Outside I could use the elements to my advantage—things like the wind, sun, rain, snow, or a even a frozen field. That all went away when we moved indoors, along with any psychological advantage it gave our players when we were playing teams like Dallas or Los Angeles, who feared coming up to Minnesota in December or January."

One of the most notorious cold weather games of all time was the 1967 NFL Championship Game between Green Bay and Dallas, otherwise known as the Ice Bowl. With game-time temperatures hovering around 15 degrees below zero and windchills approaching minus-50 degrees, the players had to get creative about staying warm.

"That was the most difficult game of my life. It was just terrible, it was so cold," explained Packers guard Fuzzy Thurston. "I was hurt too, but I just kept pushing myself. I didn't want to let my teammates down. I wanted to win that game for the city of Green Bay. A sportswriter once asked me what I took to prepare for the big game, and my response was, 'About ten vodkas.'"

Whenever cold weather was thrown into the mix, coaches would panic and search for all sorts of ways to motivate their guys to get psyched up to play. It usually didn't take very long for game plans to get chucked out the window.

"I remember when I was with the Cardinals and we were preparing for a big home game with the Redskins," recalled 10-year guard Conrad Dobler. "Our coach, Don Coryell, hated their coach, George Allen, who was known to go to great lengths to gain an advantage. Anyway, it was a record cold spell at the time, and the temperature wasn't going to be above freezing for the game. He had us practicing outside all week to get acclimated. He then decides to give us this big pep talk to get us fired up to play in the cold. He starts by telling us about when they built the Alaskan Pipeline and about how the native Eskimos could work much longer hours in the cold than the workers from the lower 48 states. He said all kinds of tests were done on them to see why they could work so long in the bitter cold with such little rest or even protective clothing. The tests came back inconclusive, and it was determined that it was all psychological, a simple case of mind over matter. The workers from the lower 48 states, however, would psych themselves out by thinking too much about the cold. As a result, they couldn't work very long without taking breaks to warm up. He then drew the correlation about how we were going to be mentally ready for the cold, whereas the Redskins would be psyched out. "You're used to it," he said. "And that is why you are going to kick their asses!" Meanwhile, Dan Dierdorf was sitting next to me, and we were both cracking up over this whole thing. Dan then raised his hand and asked Don, real serious, 'Don, what you have said makes sense. But what happens if I get into my stance tomorrow and look across that line into the facemask of the defensive lineman across from me and I see an Eskimo?' Everybody burst out laughing—everybody except Don. He then got real serious and almost worried and said, 'I wouldn't put it past Allen for a minute, that no good cheatin' son of a bitch!'"

Trash Talking

Verbal taunting or making threats to the opposition has always been part of the game, but trash talking is a relatively new phenomenon. Some players hate it, while others absolutely revel in it. One of the first guys who became known for it was Chiefs linebacker Bobby Bell, who saw the evolution of trash talking from the early '60s into the '70s to today's versions, which are more personal and mean-spirited. For Bell, however, it was all about having fun.

"Trash talking in my day was called *jive talking* or *chalk talk* across the line of scrimmage," explained Bell. "It wasn't as nasty in those days, though. I just tried to have fun with guys. I might ask around to try to find out the name of a guy's girlfriend that I was going up against and then really surprise him by asking, 'Hey man, how's Sue?' And then he'll be like, 'What! Do you know Sue?' And then I would be like, 'Hell yes, man. *Everybody* knows Sue.' That would really get that guy thinking, and while he was wondering what the hell Sue was up to, I was running past him on my way to the quarterback.

"I used to love to get in guys' heads. That was the best. Once you sacked a quarterback, it was like he was going to be on the lookout for you. I remember sacking Joe Namath and then just yelling his name 'Joe! Hey Joe!' all the time from across the line to let him know that I was coming back for more. After a while, he would see me and just melt. Whenever I would rush him and get to him, I would whisper to him 'Joe, don't you ever dodge me, man.' Or maybe I would let up on him and not hit him when I had the chance to. Then I would say 'Joe, man, you owe me one.' Then I would smile. I knew he had some bad wheels, and I didn't ever want to hurt him or anything. I had respect for guys like Joe. He was a class act. I wanted to play against the best though, and he was the best. That is what the code is all about to me—my best against your best, but in a clean and respectful way. You have to remember when I played in the '60s, it was the AFL against the NFL, and it was war. When Joe led the Jets to the Super Bowl title, that was huge for us. Hell, it was as if we had won the Super Bowl, that was how big of a deal that was. So there was no way I wanted to hurt that guy. He was on my side, the AFL. Sure, we competed against one another on Sundays, and we battled as rivals, but overall we were family."

John Randle, a high-octane defensive tackle who played from 1990–2003, took trash talking to an entirely different level. For Randle, trash talking was his way of intimidating opponents from the very first snap until the final whistle. He took what used to be a gimmick and made it into an art form all its own. With his eccentric facepainting and never-quit motor, Randle was one of the most feared sack artists of his day.

Randle had an ongoing rivalry with Packers quarterback Brett Favre, whom he sacked more than any other quarterback. The two loved to talk back and forth across the line of scrimmage, taunting one another. To play off the rivalry with Favre, Randle starred in a hilarious Nike commercial, which featured him sewing a miniature version of Favre's No. 4 jersey and then putting it on a live chicken. The commercial showed Randle chasing

Steve Sabol, President of NFL Films, on Trash Talking

"Dexter Manley—there was nothing he wouldn't say to inflame an opponent. We had Randy Cross miked for a game one time, and he was playing next to Bubba Parris. Bubba, who was a very religious man, is down on the line for the very first snap of the game, and you can hear him say very kindly to Dexter across the line of scrimmage, 'I hope you have a good game, and may God bless the ground that we are going to compete on.' Dexter then answers with a reply so vile, I don't think we can even mention it. Needless to say, that was something we could not put on NFL Films highlights, either!"

the chicken around his backyard and ended with him cooking the chicken on his BBQ. Ironically, People for the Ethical Treatment of Animals (PETA) started protesting Nike, which is supposedly why the commercial stopped airing. Randle's trash talking was catapulted into the national spotlight after that.

"I talked a lot of smack out there. That was my thing," Randle said. "I wanted to do whatever I thought possible to help my team win. That was all I cared about out there. I would go as hard as I could on every play, and I wanted to do things to get under the other team's skin. I wanted to agitate them and get them thinking about me rather than doing their job. I pushed the envelope, definitely. Guys would get so pissed at me. It was crazy. They would punch me in the balls, pull back on my jersey, pull my face mask to one side, poke me in the eyes, and go for my knees. I saw it all. Guys would high-low me, where two offensive lineman would team up on me to try to take me down. That is a dirty move, but I used to get that all the time.

"Trash talking to me was a tactic. It was something I took a lot of pride in, actually. I used to take a lot of time researching my opponents. That offensive lineman across from me on that given Sunday afternoon was going to be my victim. I wanted to intimidate him and drive him nuts. I would read media guides and go on the Internet to find out whatever personal information I could about him. I wanted to just piss him off and get him angry. I would talk about his family, about his girlfriend, and maybe tell him if I thought he was getting fat. I would try everything I could to see what got under his skin. It was hilarious. Those big linemen would try to ignore me, but I would wear them down eventually and get them to just focus on me. That was when I would really go after them, and once I got past them and got a sack or a big hit, I would start rubbing it in. I would remind his teammates that I was working him over and that he was letting them down. I would just try to get in his head and mess with him. Before long, he would try to hurt me or injure me by doing something dirty or on a block downfield. That was all right by me. I could take it. Eventually he was going to miss a key block or do something that would allow either myself or one of my teammates to capitalize on that. It was a game. What a rush. God, I miss that stuff.

"One of my favorite guys to f--- with was Tampa Bay quarterback Trent Dilfer. I used to talk to him all the time and really mess with him. He would scream at me to shut up and to shut my damn mouth. Every time I would get near him, I would tell him I was coming back for him and that he was slowing down. Well, I was trying to sack him after he threw a ball on one play, and while I was laying on the ground next to him, he jumped on me and started punching me. As a result, the ref grabbed him off and ejected him. In fact, he became the first quarterback ever thrown out of an NFL game. It was amazing. I had succeeded in getting the starting quarterback thrown out of the game without even touching him. Then when his backup came in, we went after him even harder. We wound up winning that game, and I know that I had a big part in that. You can't quantify what I did on paper, but believe me, I know that my tactics helped us win that game—and a bunch of others over the years, too."

Randle definitely got into the heads of his opponents, although some more than others.

"I remember one time when I was with Kansas City and we were playing Minnesota," recalled quarterback Rich Gannon. "Randle was one of those guys who would never shut up. He would start yapping on the first play and wouldn't quit until the end of the game. That was part of his M.O., to trash talk out there. It fired him up and really got him going. He wanted to

E.J. Henderson, Linebacker, on Trash Talking

"People talk trash all the time out there, but people's families are off limits to me. The wife or the girlfriend and the kids, that is off limits. That is highly disrespectful to talk about that, in my opinion, and it is a big violation of the code in my eyes."

intimidate guys and get in their heads, and he was pretty good at it. Well, our offensive line was really strong, and we were beating them up that day pretty good. Our offensive guard, Dave Szott, was a really religious guy and never swore or anything like that. To hear him and Randle go at it all day was absolutely hilarious. During those long TV timeouts, I was almost pissing my pants I would be laughing so hard. It was a riot. We were beating them pretty good that day and Szott just kept asking him questions like, 'Gee John, what happened on that play?' or, 'What are you doing on the ground, John?' or, 'Where were you and your big mouth on that play, Johnny?' It was so funny. Randle didn't have a lot to say back to him because not only was he getting bulldozed, but his team was losing, so his strategy of trying to psych [Szott] out actually backfired on him on that afternoon.

"Trash talking is a funny thing. You don't hear anything from the good teams, because they are professionals and they go about their business as such, playing hard and physical. They don't need to talk. But there are a handful of guys who are either young and inexperienced or insecure, or maybe just feel like that is part of who they are, like [Miami linebacker] Joey Porter. They do that stuff because they feel like it gives them an edge. I can remember when I was a young quarterback, guys would try to trash talk me to intimidate me. I used to say to them early in the games that they were wasting their breath because that crap didn't work on me. They would still say it though because it would make them feel good about themselves. Then later in your career, when you start to establish yourself and go to some Pro Bowls, guys don't want to talk to you out there because the last thing they want to do is piss you off. The veteran defensive guys know better than to get a seasoned quarterback mad because it would just make the guy want to try even harder. John Elway was classic for that. Nobody wanted to talk to that guy out there because it only made him better."

Most players tried to ignore the trash talkers and just play their own game. They had enough to worry about, let alone try to match wits with a world-class trash talker like Randle.

"I never talked to guys out there unless I was talked to," said eight-year running back Vince Workman. "Each guy had his own take on it though and would react accordingly. Take a guy like John Randle, a notorious trash talker. He wasn't mean or vindictive out there or anything like that.

He was more funny and entertaining. He was the kind of guy who might try to get you to laugh out there, to take you off your game that way— not necessarily by trying to be degrading or anything like that. He was relentless though, too, and would just wear you down. His motor was non-stop. He would just never shut up out there, which could be frustrating. Other guys were mean and nasty and would try to either intimidate you or embarrass you by bringing up some dirt or something personal. Stuff like that was just stupid in my eyes. But to each their own. For me it was more about, 'I am going to come right at you,' or, 'Is that all you got?' Stuff like that. It wasn't really anything personal for me."

"I tried to play as clean as possible when I was out there," added former Broncos offensive tackle Jon Melander. "If somebody cheap-shotted you and you got them back, then it would just perpetuate. So I tried to just say something to a guy to let them know I didn't appreciate it, and usually things would get cleaned up from there. Guys who retaliated to stuff like that had to keep their heads on a swivel the entire game because they knew that they were going to get it back at some point, as well. I didn't want to play like that, so I just let stuff go and focused on doing my job to the best of my abilities. It was the same with trash talkers, too. I remember playing against John Randle, who loved to talk. As soon as you engaged him and said something back to him, he would go even harder. That just fueled him. Well for me, hell, I was too damn tired to try to get into a trash-talking contest with a guy like him. I was too worried about catching my breath, let alone try to keep up with that guy. So I just ignored him, and eventually he would quiet down."

"As a long-snapper, I had players constantly trying to get under my skin by talking smack to me," explained 12-year veteran Mike Morris. "I took the reverse-psychology approach to trash talking. Instead of ignoring those guys, like most players, I would completely engage them and have lengthy conversations with them. I would tell them to go ahead and tell me everything they knew about me and my mother, and then I would ask them personal questions. I would just talk to them while I was snapping the ball, telling them what I was going to do and how I was going to do it. I would tell them that I could snap the ball in my sleep and what they were trying to do was just pointless because I wasn't going to be intimidated by them. I knew when the ball was going to be released, so I felt like I had an advantage over my opponent. My ultimate goal was to get them to laugh

Bill Romanowski, 16-Year Linebacker, on Trash Talking

"I would say all sorts of stuff out there. That was fun. Any time I could sense weakness in somebody, I would go for the jugular. I would say stuff like, 'I am going to tear your heart out and feed it to my dog.' I just wanted to get inside guys' heads and get them thinking about me, rather than about them doing their jobs. Whether it was trash talking or taking little shots at guys, like getting your hands up around their neck, the goal was to get them off their game. If you could piss somebody off to where they were going to try to come after you, that was what it was all about. You won at that point because they are not going to be focused on doing what they need to do in order to help their team win."

and diffuse them. I wanted them to know that shit like that didn't work on me, and eventually they would just shut up."

For some players, it was all about having fun with it, sometimes as a way to defuse the tension.

"I used to be a big talker out there. I kind of liked doing that stuff—it fired me up," confessed 12-year quarterback Bernie Kosar. "If guys would get into it with me, I would go right at them. I remember one guy who was a big trash talker, Steelers linebacker Greg Lloyd. He was really mouthy. Stuff like that made me even more competitive. I remember getting into it with him out on the field, just screaming how bad I thought he was and how much I thought he sucked. He was a young guy and didn't show me any respect, so I went right back at him as hard as I could. I would literally yell the plays to him across the line of scrimmage, taunting him, challenging him to stop us. I would tell him that we were going to run right at him and just run him over to shut him up. It was hilarious. My linemen were so pissed at me, but I didn't care. He made it personal, and I wanted to get him any way I could.

"I remember getting into it one time with Raiders linebacker Matt Millen. He was older than I was, so I didn't want to be disrespectful towards him. But we got into it out there. He would scream at me, 'Kosar, I'm gonna get you! You can't run, you're too damn slow!' I would just yell right back to him as I was calling out a play, 'Tell me something I don't know!' Joking around out there kept guys loose, and it made the game fun for me. I enjoyed that stuff. Hell, I thought it was pretty cool that a Pro Bowler like Matt Millen would even want to talk to me, to tell you the truth."

"The most effective trash talking that ever worked on me was when I was going up against Eagles tackle Bob Brown one time," added defensive end Bob Lurtsema. "A lot of offensive linemen are passive-aggressive. They will ask you about your wife and kids, being very nice, while holding you. They want to sort of calm you down and get you to relax a little bit. I tried to tune it out and never get personal with guys out there because it was my job as a pass rusher to beat his ass to the quarterback. Well, Bob was holding me, and I finally just went off on him and screamed, 'You son of a bitch, stop holding me, dammit!' He then just calmly says to me 'Bob, I am so sorry, but you are just too good. This is the only way I can stop you.' Me, being a young player, I totally felt bad about it and kind of calmed down for a few plays. Then, when I realized that I had been duped, I went right back at him even harder. I learned my lesson on that one—never trust an old fat offensive lineman who pretends to be nice."

There was definitely a line that could be crossed when it came to breaking the code with regards to trash talking though, and that was when race was brought into the conversation. You could talk about somebody's horrible athletic ability, somebody's fat butt, and even somebody's mother. But as soon as you made it a black-versus-white issue, all bets were off. You had crossed the line. For white offensive linemen, however, there was oftentimes a double standard when it came to this, which was often a difficult issue to deal with. For Ravens center Matt Birk, it was all about keeping things in perspective and going with the flow.

Stu Voigt, 11-Year Tight End, on Trash Talking

"Bears linebacker Dick Butkus never shut up. Man, he was a talker. He would spit on guys, too—especially the center, who he would always line up against in that 3-4 defense. All of the Bears were talkers. That was part of their game, to try to intimidate guys. They would test you. You would hear them huddle up before a play and see them point at you and say, 'All right boys, let's kill that cocksucker!' Those guys could be pretty intimidating. I mean, when you play in college, everybody is pretty much the same. But then when you get to the pros, there are guys with beards, are missing teeth, are ugly, have bad breath. And a lot of them are dumber than fence posts. You are like, 'Shit, these guys are f---in' crazy!' But after a while, you figure out who's who and what's what."

"I am not a big trash talker, but I have been known to dabble in it from time to time," Birk said. "I don't get into it unless I see something that has to be addressed, or if I am going against a guy who is a little bit of a punk. It can be fun to get into it with the guy across from you. Some guys have fun with it and will try to make you laugh, while others are downright mean and nasty. There is a code even with trash talking, too. You never bring race into the conversation. Having said that, I have been called white boy many times out there, but I don't take it personal. They usually razz me about being a dumb Harvard guy, which isn't too bad in the grand scheme of things. Guys will say stuff in the heat of the moment, and that is just football. Overall, I think that verbal taunting makes the game more competitive, more intense, and more fun. It is just another way to get into a guy's head and mess with him. The bottom line with this stuff though is that whatever you say, you are going to have to back it up. You will dish hits out, and you will take hits. That is the nature of the beast."

Some players simply didn't want to get into a battle of wits with the guy across from him. For Cardinals guard Conrad Dobler, however, trash talking was something he would get sucked into from time to time. It usually didn't take long for things to escalate from there with old Conrad, either. If they were going to verbally assault him, he was going to come right after them and make them pay in any way he could.

"I was not a trash talker. That was bush-league stuff in my eyes," Dobler said. "Plus, I didn't want to waste my breath yapping at some idiot. I was too damn tired to begin with. So when guys started flapping their gums at me, I would just smile and wink at them. I would just say, 'Hey man, if you want to play it that way, we can play it that way.' I was a firm believer that if you were going to talk the talk, then you had better be able to walk the walk. I used to call it victim-precipitated violence, meaning I would play guys straight up until they started getting dirty on me. The first time I got poked in the eye or punched in the nuts, that was it, the gloves came off. If guys wanted to play dirty, then that was fine with me. I could leg-whip, head-slap, or chop-block. I might come at a guy with a hard forearm to his chin or to his esophagus to soften him up. If a guy tried to hurt me, then I was going to try to hurt him. That was my livelihood, and I wasn't about to just sit there and get disrespected. No way. It was my job to make sure the defensive linemen across from me wound up on the ground. Period. So I would do whatever I could to put them there. I was very good at my job, and my teammates appreciated that."

Trash talking, like so many other forms of intimidation and retaliation, still boils down to respect. For nine-year cornerback Irv Cross, it was anything but respectful.

"I never believed in any of that sort of stuff," Cross said. "I think players who do it have no class. Every time I see it, I think it is embarrassing. I respected my opponents too much to do that. I played hard and I hit hard, but I never wanted to disrespect myself by doing or saying something foolish. Even when guys dance around nowadays when they score a touchdown—that is so embarrassing. I mean, you get into the end zone with a total team effort, so to have some clown go in there and start dancing around and showing guys up is completely tasteless. To me it says, 'Look at me, look what I've done,' and that is not what this game is all about, in my opinion. This is a team sport. I always liked it when guys like Tim Brown would score a touchdown and then just hand the ball to the referee. It is a respect thing with me, absolutely."

Excessive Celebration

Another form of intimidation is excessive celebration, which many players view as a violation of the code. There is a fine line between celebrating and taunting when it comes to excessive celebration, and each player's line is different. For most, if a player scores a touchdown or gets a sack or whatever, he can celebrate and high-five his teammates without showing anybody up. However, as soon as choreographic skits are put into place, a la touchdown dances, then feelings start to get hurt, and folks start to feel disrespected. The bottom line with excessive celebration is that if a player does it as a sort of mean-spirited "f--- you" and throws in some trash talking or personal insults to boot, then that has probably gone too far. Again, this is a respect thing, and nobody wants to be shown up out there. Each player and coach has his own personal take on the subject, and the opinions vary from one extreme to the other.

"I wouldn't tolerate any of that kind of stuff for a minute," said longtime coach Bud Grant. "To show up your opponent like that was very disrespectful. I wanted our guys to hand the ball off to the official when they scored touchdowns and act like they had done it before. If the team wanted to celebrate a touchdown or a big play, that was all right, but I

Vince Workman, Former Buccaneers Running Back, on Forgiving and Forgetting

"I was playing with Tampa Bay one time and wound up chop-blocking Bears defensive end Richard Dent. Well, he was pissed. Later in the game, I was sort of walking up the sideline on a play that was on the other side of the field and *wham*! I get blindsided from behind. Sure enough, it is Richard, reminding me what happens to young players who chop-block veteran Pro Bowlers. He just nailed me, and I went down hard. Anyway, we wound up becoming teammates together a few years later in Indianapolis. I remember being in training camp and sitting in an ice bath alone after practice one day. Then, out of the blue, Richard walks over and gets in the tub with me. It was just the two of us. I wasn't sure if he remembered me or knew who I was, but I hoped like hell he didn't all of a sudden have a flashback about my chop block on him four years earlier—because if so, I was going to drown in an ice bath with nobody to hear my screams. Luckily for me, he just blew it off and laughed about it. We actually became good friends."

never wanted to cross that line where we offended anybody. Having said that, this is a different era. The fans seem to like it when the guys dance around on TV and so forth when they score or make a tackle. All I can say is that guys wouldn't last very long in the league if they did that in my day. Things have certainly changed, and I wouldn't necessarily say for the better, either."

"I think that all of the dancing and whatnot is ridiculous," added longtime coach Jerry Burns. "I especially think it is ridiculous when a guy celebrates a sack or a deflected pass or something like that when his team is down 28–0. What the hell is that all about? I can see getting excited with your teammates if you score a game-winning touchdown, but not all of the other stuff. That to me is just basically doing your job. I have always felt that if a guy wants to dance around after doing something like catching a big pass or getting a tackle, then he should also put his hand up and recognize when he drops a ball or gets called offside. You can't have it both ways."

Excessive celebration can also serve as a motivating factor for the opposition, as well.

"Guys hate that stuff, especially the sack dances and stuff by the defensive players," said former Green Bay running back Darrell Thompson. "I remember being in a meeting watching film with my offensive linemen and hearing them talk about Bears tackle Dan Hampton, who used to do a lot of taunting and dancing out there after he would get a big play. Well, they spent the entire time watching his every move just to make sure that they shut him down that next game. So his celebrating actually was the motivation our guys were using to prepare for the game. They did not want that guy dancing on their watch, so they went out of their way to prepare for him. Our linemen just hated that guy and were praying for an opportunity to somehow get him when he least expected it. All I can say is I sure am glad that I was never the subject of a meeting like that!"

It is interesting to note that while excessive celebration is somewhat frowned upon here in the NFL, it is quite different in the CFL.

"This is an issue that is totally different up here in Canada than with the NFL," explained 15-year CFL quarterback Anthony Calvillo. "In the CFL, we are here to please the fans. It is a fan-based league, and we need them to be in the stands supporting us. It is not like the NFL, where we get billions of dollars from TV revenue. So without a doubt, we need to entertain our fans and keep them coming back for more. If that means end zone celebrations and dances, so be it. Our players up here, the receivers and running backs, will choreograph and come up with all sorts of crazy celebration routines. Of course, when a team does it to you, it is no fun. But we all understand that it is for the fans and not intended to be disrespectful toward the opposing team. The fans enjoy it, and to be honest, the players enjoy it. For me, personally, I am pretty low-key and don't do anything too creative. I have seem some pretty wild stuff, though. I know that in the NFL the players can get fined if they do certain end zone dances or certain things, but up here it is actually encouraged."

4

Sign Stealing and Espionage

Sign stealing and the paranoia of sign stealing have been part of football since day one. Just like baseball, the science of espionage has long been part of the gridiron game. There is a constant competition of spy vs. spy going on in every game that most fans are oblivious to. In a typical MLB game, there could be as many as 1,000 signs flashed, including signs from the pitcher to the catcher, from the manager to the third-base coach, from the short stop to the second baseman, from the left fielder to the right fielder, from the home-plate umpire to the first-base umpire, and from the runner on second base to the batter. Usually 95 percent of all those signs are bogus dummies with only 5 percent being hot or live. Sound confusing?

To make sense of it all, the game has sign-stealers. Take a guy like Paul Molitor, a Hall of Famer with a CIA-like ability to decode all of the misinformation and make sense of it. He can study the player's tells and pick up on things that most people never see. From the dugout, Molitor can watch a pitcher flex a vein in his wrist or neck and immediately know that pitcher is about to throw a curve ball. Molitor will then relay that information in real time via coded message to the batter in the batter's box. The message might be a clap, a whistle, or a certain word. Just like that, the power of information has changed hands. Or maybe Molitor will watch the catcher and decipher his indicator for what he wants the pitcher to throw. Maybe he will touch his ankle or adjust his mask. Now he knows when he is going to throw a pitch out to try to gun down the runner on first, so he can yell out to warn him. Or maybe yet, Molitor is in the field and he sees the opposing manager blowing his nose, then touching his elbow, but only after removing his cap. Was that the steal sign? Or maybe the hit and run? Welcome to the world of baseball sign stealing.

In football, sign stealing isn't quite as intense. In baseball, division rivals will face each other nearly 20 times per season, including stretches that include four-game series. If a team can pick up the opposition's steal sign, or perhaps the closer's change-up signal with his catcher, that information can be used almost instantaneously. In football, teams only play 16 games per season, and divisional rivals only face each other twice—once at home and once on the road. So it is a much different animal altogether. To break down the genesis of sign language in football, one can look at it as it pertains to certain eras.

During the early years of the league's inception in the 1920s through the 1960s, sign stealing was almost non-existent. Quarterbacks called their own plays, and if a coach wanted to call in a play, he would send it in via a messenger player who would rotate in and out of the lineup. In those days, it was more about sneaking into practices to see what new plays and formations the opposition was running. Now that is not to say that there wasn't a whole bunch of espionage going on. On the contrary, those were the golden years of paranoia. There are countless stories of coaches trying to spy on opponents' practices in search of their deepest, darkest secrets. That old adage of "cheating versus gamesmanship" comes up a lot in this gray area of the code, as we dissect just what was kosher and what

Steve Young, 15-Year Quarterback, on Signs

"I didn't spend a lot of time worrying about stealing signs. I had other more important things to deal with. Some guys did it, though—some better than others. I think what the Patriots did—which was actually quite nefarious in its own right, to hire guys to do videotaping—crossed the line. A lot of backup quarterbacks studied signs, but there was a lot of pressure to make sure you got it right. I mean, if you were wrong, that could be really bad for your team. For me, personally, I liked the game to go really fast, because I didn't think that defenses could catch up. So the faster I went, the less I had to worry about what they were doing. If they wanted to study what I was doing, I didn't care. I just went out and executed our game plan, which was hopefully too fast for them to keep up with all of the other stuff. That was my philosophy, and over the years, it worked out for me."

wasn't when it came to teams trying to do their due diligence on their arch rivals.

When you talk to the old-timers, they will tell you that things have definitely changed during the past half century. Nobody knows that better than longtime coach Howard Schnellenberger, who began coaching back in the 1950s with Kentucky and is still going strong today as the head coach of Florida Atlantic University.

"The art of espionage sure has come a long way," said Schnellenberger, who has been part of seven NFL playoff teams and two Super Bowl staffs. "I remember starting out as a college coach back in the '50s and '60s, we would go to games and try to take as many notes as we could. We would even subscribe to all of our rival's newspapers to read whatever was being written about them, too. Things were a lot different in those days as far as scouting went. There was no film or anything—just handwritten notes to go back and do your homework."

As technology has grown and become more widespread, the concept of doing your homework has taken on a new meaning. Coaches have long searched for shortcuts and honest advantages. Legendary Cleveland Browns coach Paul Brown used to send fake reporters to other team's games to try to infiltrate the enemy. One of the true pioneers of modern day espionage in the NFL is former coach George Allen, the godfather of deception. Everybody who played for Allen or who coached with him has a story to tell about his extreme passion and paranoia when it came to spying.

"We used to call George '007' because he was always in hot pursuit of what he felt were enemy spies out to get him," Schnellenberger quipped. "We always thought he was just chasing shadows, but he caught his fair share of fellows trying to sneak up on him."

Allen worked so hard to make sure he wasn't being spied on that he would often sleep in his office after working 18- to 20-hour days. He was even known to eat ice cream or peanut butter for many meals because it was easy to eat and saved time, which allowed him to get back to preparing for the next game. The biggest reason why Allen was so worried about being spied upon was because he was notorious for being such a sneaky spy himself.

Schellenberger recalled, "One time he sent his assistant, Joe Sullivan, to Wrigley Field to spy on the Bears before they came out to play his Rams in L.A. So he got Joe a telephone repairman uniform, complete with pole-climbing spurs. Sure enough, Joe climbed up a telephone pole outside of the stadium one day during practice and spied on the Bears as they went through their plays. He stayed up there all afternoon taking notes and then reported his findings back to George the next day."

Everybody was on the lookout for Allen. Former Cowboys executive Gil Brandt recalled the time he got a call from a local airport car-rental agency when Allen coached the Rams. The rental agent said a guy who worked for the Rams had just rented a car and had asked for directions to the Cowboys' practice fields. Sure enough, Allen's undercover agent was captured red-handed.

Allen routinely had his offices checked for bugging devices and even went as far as being the first coach in the NFL to employ a full-time security man to keep potential spies away by patrolling the woods outside Redskin Park. Allen was so worried that he and his practices were being watched that he would often send his trainers into the woods to check for spies, too. They were instructed to remove anyone who looked suspicious, including autograph-seeking fans, who might actually be undercover agents working for opposing teams.

"We had a guy called Double-O," recalled Bubba Tyler, a former Redskins' trainer. "His name was Ed Boynton, a retired cop from Long Beach, and the whole time the team was on the field, he would walk the woods around old Redskin Park. There was a warehouse across the street from us, and we'd see him out there on the hood of a tractor-trailer trying to get a guy's license plate to see if he was from Philadelphia or New York. He was everywhere."

"I remember when I was with the Cardinals just how much our coach, Don Coryell, hated to play the Redskins," guard Conrad Dobler recalled. "Their coach, George Allen, was an espionage freak, which made our lives a living hell the week that we would play them. Don had us taking buses to different practice fields every day, just in case George had spies camped out somewhere. One time there was someone in this big building across the street from Bush Stadium, and there was a guy in a window watching us practice. Don thought it was George up there filming us, so he sent some guys up there to interrogate the guy. Of course it wasn't him, but those guys were so paranoid of each other it was almost insane. Trust me, had they been able to afford it, they would have had satellites up there watching each other."

Rich Baldinger, 12-Year Offensive Tackle, on Signs

"When I was playing right tackle for the Chiefs, our offensive line coach was Howard Mudd. He was the best in the business and was a master at picking off signs. I remember when he would call in the defensive personnel coverage via sign language to our right guard, Dave Lutz, who would in turn tell our quarterback, Steve DeBerg. They had this real elaborate method of hand signaling out there. For instance, if he shook his hand it was a hot call, meaning somebody was coming off the edge in a cover-two formation. If it was three fingers, it was a cover-three, or an open hand with five fingers for a nickel package. This gave Steve an extra 20 seconds to think about what he wanted to do and about what matchups he was going to try to exploit. It was a huge advantage.

"You know, the defenses at this level are so complex. They transpire so quickly and disguise themselves so well. That is the biggest reason in my opinion as to why the vast majority of college players can't make that transition to the pros. They just can't elevate themselves mentally to that next level. So guys who did their homework and really became students of the game, they were the ones who lasted a long time and had a lot of success. I think about our quarterback, Steve DeBerg, who was one of the smartest guys I ever knew. He had like six huge notebooks, one for each system of coverage. He would have detailed notes about every guy we would go up against and about their tendencies. He had a diagram of what every play would look like under every possible scenario imaginable. He would study those books meticulously to prepare himself. He would memorize all of this stuff before games, and I really appreciated that. As his teammate, I wanted to elevate my game to do the same. Knowledge is power, and luckily for me, we had the power."

Allen certainly wasn't the only football aficionado to garner a reputation as a sleuth. Another was the late Sid Gillman when he was coaching the San Diego Chargers.

"When we were quartered at Sunset Park in La Mesa and a plane would fly over, Sid would want to get the number on the plane's wings and call the FAA," said Tom Bass, former defensive coordinator for the Chargers. "I felt that the thing we should have done was to send our playbook to an opponent. They would have gone nuts in a week trying to figure that out."

When Gillman was on the road, he was notorious for leaving dummy playbooks around as a form of counter-intelligence, figuring that whoever cleaned up would find it and give it to the home team's coach. Gillman's penchant for spying started long before he made it into the NFL. In fact,

Dean Dalton, Former Assistant Coach, on Signs

"Protecting your signs and signals is really important. You will hear of players getting fined for losing their playbooks or for leaving a scouting report at a hotel while traveling. That is because if those things fall into enemy hands, your team's entire game plan could be compromised. NFL coaches are a naturally paranoid group of individuals. They are always concerned about being spied upon. If there is anybody that we don't know who is hanging around our facilities or during our practices while we are on the road, it is like a CIA sting. 'Who the hell is that guy up in the stands or on that hilltop or in that window with the dark sunglasses and video camera?!' It is like the Zapruder film on the grassy knoll. It can get crazy. But they wouldn't be paranoid if they didn't have to be, which means that there are a lot of folks out there whose job is to perform espionage on opposing teams."

"When Daniel Snyder opened up the Washington Redskins training camp to the fans a few years ago in an attempt to make a few extra bucks, that made it legal for other teams to send guys over to watch your practice. It used to be unethical to send over a scout with a Brett Favre jersey and a cheese-head hat to watch the Packers practice, but now, thanks to Mr. Snyder, things have changed. The spies can be everywhere. There are plenty of stories of teams being in hotels on the road and finding out that some waiters had been bribed to steal a couple of playbooks from conference rooms. What was fun for us as assistants was all of the counter-espionage that would also go on. We would make up dummy game plans and leave them around the hotel or practice facilities on purpose, just to throw them off. Or we would draw up elaborate plays on the marker boards in the meeting rooms at the hotels or in the meeting rooms in the opposing stadiums and leave them there without erasing them with bogus information. We may even just slightly erase some of it, so they would think that they had discovered some hidden treasure when they found it. It was a big mind game.

"Teams will stop at nothing to get a competitive advantage, even if that means pushing the envelope. Take Spygate, for instance. They got caught videotaping, with the word 'caught' being the operative word in the sentence. One time we were playing the Seahawks out in Seattle, and during the course of a long drive we were on, boom, all of our headsets went out. We had to literally use telephones to call in plays from the press box. It was insane. We even had a backup running back racing messages back and forth from the sidelines up to the coaches for extra security. Mysteriously, the electronics on Seattle's sidelines as well as with their people up in the box were all working fine. Go figure. There is a rule that says if one side goes down, then the other team has to put theirs down, too. But try enforcing that one in the heat of battle. Good luck. Then if you dare call the other team on it and insinuate anything out of the ordinary, they will go ballistic and accuse you of being a whiner and poor loser. Another time during a game against the Steelers, boom, all of a sudden my headset went dead, and all I could hear was country music playing instead. Maybe Elvis was in the building—who knows?

"Videotaping signs is a big no-no. Videotaping anything in the coaches booth up top is illegal, too, but teams get around it by having a guy sit as close to the press box as possible so he can watch the network TV version of the game that is shown for the members of the media. The network feed is different than the live feed, and a lot of times opposing teams won't show controversial calls on the live feeds because that would allow us to see a call that we may want to challenge to overturn with the officials. So we had to literally have a guy on our staff who would run over to watch the TVs in the press box and call us on a cell phone to tell us whether or not to throw our red challenge flag. Fans see it all the time when the guy who runs the giant Jumbotron shows the controversial calls for the home team but never for the visiting team. The crowd goes crazy for that stuff. Every team has their own home-cookin', and that is something you just have to deal with.

"Technology is a blessing and a curse. It really is. Case in point: a lot of rumors swirled around the 2000 NFC Championship Game where the Giants beat us 41–0. It was alleged that the Giants somehow were able to listen in on our radio frequencies. It made for a good story, but personally, I don't buy it. We got spanked that day, and we can't make any excuses. They were up 14–0 before our offense even got on the field, and I am pretty confident that there weren't any jamming signals that caused our returner to fumble the opening kickoff. That was a horrendous loss, but the only people we can blame for that is ourselves. We stunk that day. They got the momentum going on their side and never looked back. You just have to tip your hat to them. We got out-played that day.

"There is so much stuff that goes on behind the scenes in preparation for an NFL game. For starters, the defensive line coaches will get the network TV version of the games and then have all their players sit in a room to watch and listen to the quarterback's cadence. They want to be able to see his mannerisms and pick up on his rhythm, because if they get it down it might mean an extra half-second jump off the line. Another thing they will watch is where the quarterback's hands and feet are on every play. Some guys will offset their feet on a pass play so that they can get out a little quicker or maybe crouch down a little bit on a running play. They study the poker tells. They look at tendencies, like if an offensive lineman's heels were up off the ground, which meant it was a run play. Or they were flat, which was usually a pass play. That is not cheating; that is doing your homework.

"Historically, every team will send an advance scout to watch the following week's opponent. They will be on the field for the pregame and then sit in the press box with binoculars while it is going on. He will size up players, see who is hurt, and study snap counts, stances, and cadences. They will even try to break down which pass-rushing move is the most effective for each defensive lineman, and things of that nature. He will then create a detailed report and meet with each unit of his team the following week to debrief them on what he has learned. They will study the signals, too, and try to figure out as much as they can. Obviously, things have changed now that the defense can use a microphones, too, usually with the middle linebacker. That has helped with all of the sign stealing, but it hasn't ended it. Even with the radios in the [linebacker's] helmet, teams will still have several guys giving signals to that middle linebacker, but only one of them [is] hot. The others are decoys and are on the line just to mess with whoever may be watching or listening in. Nobody trusts anybody, and that is the way it has always been.

"Here is the bottom line with all of this stuff, though. It all comes down to the old Vince Lombardi theory: 'We are gonna run the Packer sweep. We are gonna run it right here. This is how we block it. You guys can watch it because we are still going to execute it.... Try to stop us.' This is a player's game, and it has always been a player's game. It doesn't come down to the brilliance of the coach's masterful game plan, because that only works at the summer coaching clinics and on the chalkboard. I have always been a proponent of the 'simplify and execute' philosophy, and I didn't worry about all of the other crazy stuff that was employed to gain a competitive advantage. It was and still is all about execution. The tricks and espionage may come in handy every now and then, but those times will be few and far between."

as a young college coach at Miami, Ohio, Gillman apparently even sent a graduate assistant to walk-on to the team of the season's first opponent, the University of Nevada. Turns out the assistant practiced for about a week and then mysteriously disappeared just before the first game, only to show up on the Miami sideline next to Sid.

Longtime Raiders owner Al Davis has also been known to dabble in the science of surveillance over the years. Davis, to his credit, has never been caught doing anything underhanded, but there are those who will always wonder. Years ago during halftime of a Chargers-Raiders game at the Oakland Coliseum, San Diego coach Harland Svare apparently began swearing up at a light fixture on the ceiling of his locker room. "Damn you, Al Davis!" he said. "I know you're in there!" "I'll tell you this," Davis said later. "The thing wasn't in the light fixture."

Davis, who lives by the motto, "Just win, baby," understood that unleashing an opponent's paranoia was itself a form of subterfuge. The fact that coaches had to worry about being spied on was a distraction, and that in itself was a tactic that forced them to waste time on non-football matters. When the Tennessee Oilers were waiting for a permanent home, they were using a temporary practice field next to a mall. The week before their season opener against Oakland, one of the coaches noticed a cherry-picker truck driving around in the parking lot, supposedly changing light bulbs. It didn't take long for the Tennessee coaching staff to get suspicious, especially since it was Al Davis' team that was coming to town. So a couple of team employees were told to monitor the supposed bulb changers through binoculars to make sure they weren't up to anything tricky.

"One of the most paranoid coaches I ever knew was Weeb Ewbank," said longtime general manager Ernie Accorsi. "Weeb had learned to coach as an assistant with the Cleveland Browns under legendary coach Paul Brown, who was notorious for his espionage tactics. Well in 1954, Weeb took over as the head coach of the Baltimore Colts. In Baltimore, they played in old Memorial Stadium, which was a half-bowl-shaped venue. One end of was wide open, and there were houses just on the other side of the end zone. It was really unique. Well, the first time Cleveland played Baltimore, Weeb sent the equipment manager across the street to knock on every single door. He would then ask them if anybody had stopped over recently and asked if they could rent a room or anything like that. He than politely asked if he could check their upstairs and roof to make sure there were no spies. The homeowners were all die-hard Colts fans, so they didn't care. But it was pretty amazing. You see, Weeb knew Paul and knew that he would leave no stone unturned in trying to gain an edge. That was how it was in those days. Hell, even today teams are worried about being spied on. There is a very high-rise hotel, the Sheraton Meadowlands, right next to Giants Stadium. From the 20th floor and above, you can look right into our practice field. There have been suspicions about people spying on us from up there ever since it was built. We had hunches that opposing teams would rent out rooms to spy on us with telescopes, but we could never prove it. I wouldn't bet against it, that is for sure."

Another significant saboteur of the early era of football was George Halas, owner of the Chicago Bears. Halas, like Allen and Gillman, was terrified that his opponents were either one step ahead of him or just out to get him. Either way, he was going to be prepared, come hell or high water. Steve Sabol, president of NFL Films, shared some insight into the murky world of the legendary Papa Bear.

"Years ago, after George Halas had died, there had been a fire in the Bears' offices," Sabol said. "They were cleaning out the offices and Ed McCaskey, Halas' son-in-law, came across a box of old film reels. So he called me and asked me if we at NFL Films wanted them. I said sure, so about a month later this big box of old films shows up. I cleaned up a few of them, and we put them on a projector. They were old game films, but they were all out of focus. So I put more of them on there, and it was the same thing—nearly every single one of them was out of focus. I didn't think anything of it the time and just figured that it was a box of bad films that Halas must have been hanging on to for some reason.

"Well, about six years later, Abe Gibron, one of Halas' old players and assistants, came to town on a business trip, and we had dinner together. We started telling Halas stories about how he used to do all sorts of shady things, like loosen the bricks on the first step of the visitor's club house at Wrigley Field, so maybe when a guy ran out he would fall and sprain his ankle. Or how he would never have hot water in the visitor's dressing room, stuff like that. Anyway, we were talking and I brought up this box

Rich Gannon, 17-Year Quarterback, on Signs

"I remember one time when I was with Kansas City and we were playing San Diego. I was a backup at the time and remember watching their quarterbacks' coach pretty closely for the entire first quarter as he signaled in plays in to Stan Humphries. I knew their offense pretty well and understood most of their verbiage, so eventually I was able to figure out some of their key plays. One of them was a hand signal for the slant-and-go route, or 'Sluggo,' which is a double-move route by the receiver that is usually a home-run type of a play. If your defenders bite on it, you are going to get burned for six points every time. Well, I saw their coach give Stan the slugo sign and immediately told our defensive backs coach what was coming. Sure enough, they ran it and we covered it perfectly, nearly picking it off as a result. So that was a case of being rewarded for doing your homework. Hey, if you could figure out the other team's personnel, whether it was three-wide or regular or two tight ends or whatever, that was a huge advantage. As a quarterback, if I knew what the defense was going to do, or if they were going to blitz, that was extremely valuable information."

of old films that was all out of focus. Gibron immediately started laughing. He said, 'You've got the visitors films. That's what those are.' I said, 'What do you mean?' He then proceeded to tell me how back in the '50s, teams were required to send copies of their coaches' practice films to opponents in the days leading up to the game. It was how the teams scouted each other. They all agreed to do it, and it was a sort of gentleman's agreement they all had with one another.

"What Halas did in order to gain an advantage, however, was to hire two cameramen to record his practice—one who shot in perfect focus for the Bears, and one who purposely shot the players out of focus. The Bears would then send the blurry film to their prospective opponents. Then, and this is the great part, when the coaches would get the blurry film, they would invariably call Halas and say 'Jesus Christ George, what the hell is the matter with this film? It is all out of focus.' Old man Halas would then say all disgusted, 'Oh, yeah, that goddamn camera man, he screwed up again. I am going to fire that son of a bitch!' It was hilarious. Halas got away with that for three years before the other coaches finally picked up on it. That was what Halas was known for, always looking for that edge. It is what we at NFL Films now call skullduggery, which by definition means underhanded or unscrupulous behavior, or a devious trick. What a beauty he was. I really miss that guy."

Sign Stealing in the Modern Era

The modern era of sign stealing took place between the early '70s through 2008. This was the period when teams would study the signals being sent in from the sidelines on both offense and defense. As offenses became more sophisticated, more assistant coaches were hired to not only develop more advanced plays, but also to be able to relay that information in to either the quarterback on offense or the middle linebacker on defense. On defense, if a team knows when an offense is going to pass on a certain down, or to which side of the field they are going to run, then they will win the game every time. Conversely, if an offense knows when a defense is going to blitz or to which side of the field they will allow man-to-man coverage, then they too have the advantage.

However, there has always been a right way and a wrong way to steal signs, which makes for a fine line between cheating and gamesmanship. Like in baseball, if a batter peeks back at the catcher to see a sign or to see where he is lining up, that is a no-no and he can expect to get drilled in the ribs. Conversely, if that same guy sees the shadow of the catcher or hears him clumsily move around behind the plate on a hot day, without turning or squinting to peek back, then that is okay. The same is true in football. If you can decipher the hand signals of your opponent by doing your homework, then that is all right. However, if you cheat by using video to tape signs or maybe even bribe a mole, then that is crossing the line. Regardless, even if a team does get the signs, they still have to know what calls are coming in certain situations in order to make sense of them and actually benefit from them.

"Sure, you have guys looking across the sideline trying to figure out what the signal is going to be," said former Cleveland Browns coach Romeo Crennel. "Everybody looks across the field to see if they can determine what the signals are. But that doesn't necessarily help you. Your guys still have to go play, and they still have to make the plays themselves."

Until the early 1990s, coaches would send in plays via hand signals. Then in 1994, the league passed a new rule allowing for one-way radios

Paul Wiggin, Longtime Coach, on Signs

"Sign stealing is a huge part of the game. Teams have always done it, and they are not even subtle about it. Teams want to be able to steal any sign that they can in order to gain a competitive advantage. You can gain insight with regard to matchups, personnel, down and distance, zone or man-to-man, or whatever is going on out there. There are signs for everything, and the more you can decipher, the better your odds are. I mean, if you can predetermine whether or not a team is going to pass, run, or blitz, that is extremely valuable information. To be able to call a play where you know that your primary receiver is going to be open because he has man-to-man coverage, then that is a big advantage. Information and knowledge is power. There are right ways and wrong ways to get signs, though, and you can't cross that line. That is the key. Filming is cheating, but doing your homework is gamesmanship in my book. Hey, if you can read lips and figure out whether a team is going to call a run or a pass, then that information is fair game. I will say this though—as a head coach, it was tough to change up your signs all the time because some of the players just couldn't handle too much information. You had to keep your signs relatively easy but hard enough so that the other team couldn't figure them out. You had to be clever how you displayed them, when you displayed them, where you displayed them, and to whom you displayed them."

to be placed inside the quarterback's helmet. This was revolutionary. Offensive coordinators could now have direct contact with their signal-caller without having to worry about relaying hand signals, which could be stolen by enemy spies from across the field. The defenses would have to wait another 14 years before they would be allowed to use the same technology. During that 14-year window, teams put a lot of time and resources into not only protecting and disguising their own defensive hand signals, but also into stealing those of their competitors.

It is interesting to note that while the league first officially put radios in helmets in '94, unofficially, they first showed up some 40 years prior. According to longtime general manager Ernie Accorsi, "Back in the early '50s, legendary Cleveland coach Paul Brown actually installed a radio into his quarterback's helmet. Paul was an innovator and really pushed the envelope. There was no rule about radios in helmets at the time, so it wasn't illegal. I mean, nobody had ever even thought of it, that was how far ahead of the game Paul Brown was. So one day they are playing a game, and he is calling in plays to his quarterback, Otto Graham. At one point, Graham can't hear anything, and so he calls his own play, which results in an interception. Paul is upset and calls him over to talk to him. He says, 'What's the matter, didn't you hear my call?' Otto apparently just looked at him and said, 'The only thing I am getting on your radio is the dispatcher calling in routes for his cab drivers!'"

As for protecting their signs, teams would usually have at least two or three signal-callers on the sidelines. Two of them would be dummies, with one being "hot" or "live." Coaches would instruct the players as to which coach would be hot at various times throughout the game, always trying to stay one step ahead of the bad guys. Some of the coaches might wear different colored wristbands as well, so that the quarterback or middle linebacker could pick them up easier on the sidelines. Some teams would often have a coach on the sidelines wearing a headset that wasn't plugged in and giving bogus signals to throw off the scouts as well as the opposing team.

As for stealing signs, this practice is much more involved. Teams go to great lengths to get this information, which makes for a steady flow of information and disinformation between the two warring factions. Teams have long employed advance scouts, who are assistant coaches trained in the art of deception. Some scouts will travel to games of future opponents and do nothing but monitor plays. These scouts use binoculars to focus on a different signal-caller from the press box, and they write down every move. Every single play is documented on paper, followed by the down and distance. He also writes down every movement of the coach. For instance, the scout may write down, "Third-and-4 from the 22 yard line; the coach pumped his fist, rolled his fists, waved to his left, then saluted with his right hand. He then touched his nose, then his elbow, then his ear." After recording every play, the advance scout returns home to try to make sense of it all by matching it up to the video feed that the network shot. From that information, he may be able to pick up a blitz package or maybe when it will be a running or passing play. It is a tedious, boring, and often frustrating job. After all, there is a 66 percent chance that the guy he watched all afternoon was one of the dummies.

Sometimes the advance scouts go to team practices, especially when those teams are on the road and doing their walk-throughs, to watch what plays the teams are running. If they are closed practices, then they may try to sneak in disguised as a fan, a random electrician, or whatever. Visiting teams know that they are being watched, however, and put counter-measures into place, such as either not running their best gadget plays, or they may just run a bunch of bogus plays that they will never use during the actual game. This is known as "clogging" or "cluttering." Certain coaches, the real anal-retentive ones such as Jon Gruden, are obsessed with cataloging opponents' plays. So teams will try to overload opposing coaching staffs with extra dummy plays just to clutter their game plans. They want them to have to do more work than necessary and prepare for way more than they need to. They want to tire them out and get them chasing ghosts. Again, it is spy vs. spy, 24/7, 365. They all know each other, and they know which guys don't sleep.

"It is a lot of charting, down and distance, time on the clock, that sort of thing," revealed one advance scout who insisted upon remaining anonymous. "It is monotonous and tedious. It is like chess. We sit up in the box with binoculars and chart every play, looking for patterns or tendencies. Then you go back and try to match it all up back at the office. There are about 60 plays on defense in a typical game, and you chart each one of them. Here are a few examples of some sample plays: 'Okay, it's first-and-10 with the ball on the 23-yard line. The signal-caller, coach X, grabbed his right wrist, touched his head, clapped his hands.' Or, 'It is

Anthony Calvillo, 15-Year CFL Quarterback, on Signs

"Up until very recently, there used to be no written rules whatsoever regarding stealing signals up in Canada. So it came down to your own morals and ethics as far as just what you were comfortable doing. It is an interesting issue that varies from team to team. Some teams don't care if you videotaped them. They figured that you still had to go out there and stop them. Other teams were completely paranoid and had all sorts of counter-measures to prevent people from stealing their signs. One of the big things, especially on defense, was the advent of wristbands. Now instead of signaling in plays that could be stolen, a defensive coordinator can just signal in a number. There might be 20 plays on a guy's wristband though, so maybe No. 4 is the same as No. 10 and No. 13. Or they may call in an even number or an odd number or whatever. They want to try to confuse the sign stealers and keep them guessing—that is the ultimate goal."

second-and-8 with the ball on the 28. The signal-caller grabbed his right wrist, touched his right knee, then touched his right ear.' Eventually you see patterns developing. Every time they ran cover-two, for instance, the signal-caller touched his face. Pretty soon you are on to something. But teams will fake signs if they think they are being stolen. So you have to really be careful of that stuff. I remember one time a team knew that the other guys were stealing their signals, so they faked a blitz and then dropped back into coverage, which led to an interception and a touchdown. So it can really backfire on you if you are not careful. The big thing now is stealing personnel signals, which can by deciphered pretty easily. By someone stealing those signals, they can get their defensive calls made quicker. That is all it will do, speed it up. But that is an advantage, and we will take it."

Teams with the best advance scouts had a real advantage. The guys who could break down statistics, crunch numbers into spreadsheets, study probability analytics, then match it all up to video were coveted. Teams paid big bucks for guys who could do this stuff and still be able to fly under the radar. Eventually, teams started having entire video departments full of scouts and analysts who made a science of breaking down film. To gain an edge in the ever-escalating never-ending war, teams eventually started to videotape the opposing signal-callers. This is when things started to go from above-board to down-right cheating.

Jerry Glanville, Longtime Coach, on Signs

"This stuff has been going on since day one. This is nothing new. Filming them, however, is new, and it's something that won't be tolerated—as the Patriots found out with Spygate. Everywhere I have ever coached, teams have always tried to steal our signs, and we have always tried to steal theirs. That is how it is. They have been stealing signs ever since they started sending them. You just can't get caught; that is the key. For us, we always had three different people sending them in, which made it very difficult for the opposition to figure out which one was live and which ones were decoys. We always figured out which guy of the three would be hot before every series. It would change that frequently. Why do I always have three people signaling in signs? Because I know that there is always somebody out there trying to steal them. If you can get the other team's signals, that is a huge advantage. For instance, the minute you call a man-to-man coverage package on defense, which means you are going to blitz and leave the corners with single man to man coverage, and the offense stops and calls an audible on the line, they have picked you. So if that happens, then as a coach I have to react and change our defense in a split second to react to that. Then you have to factor in a guy like Peyton Manning, who will call an audible to try to get you to check out of what you were doing, even though he doesn't really know what you are doing. That type of cat-and-mouse game goes on all day out there. It is a big chess game."

While most teams have done it from time to time, off the record and out of sight, it is still illegal. Enter Spygate.

Spygate

Like Watergate and every other scandal that is now given the "gate" suffix for dramatic effect, Spygate was actually a pretty big deal. Spygate refers to an incident in the 2007 season when the New England Patriots were disciplined by NFL Commissioner Roger Goodell for illegally videotaping New York Jets' defensive coaches' signals during the September 9, 2007, game from a sideline location. After a lengthy investigation, the NFL fined Patriots head coach Bill Belichick $500,000 for his role in the incident—the largest fine ever imposed on a coach in NFL history. Goodell also fined the organization $250,000 and stripped the team of its first-round pick in the 2008 Draft. Belichick admitted to taping signals dating back to 2000, but he said he believed he was operating within the rules as long as the tape was not used during the same game.

As part of its probe into the allegations, the league demanded that the Patriots turn over all of the tapes they had made of their opponents' defensive signals. The Deep Throat in this "gate" turned out to be Matt Walsh, a Patriots video assistant from 2001–02, who told the media that he had information regarding the team's videotaping practices but demanded an indemnity agreement before speaking with the league's top brass. They agreed, and Walsh sent eight videotapes containing opponents' coaches' signals from the 2000–02 seasons, including regular-season games against the Dolphins, Bills, Browns, and Chargers—and against the Steelers in the 2002 AFC title game. In that game, the tape was edited together to show Steelers coaches signaling plays, followed by two different camera angles of the actual plays that were called on the field. It was the proverbial "smoking gun."

Later that September, Belichick was accused by the Jets of authorizing his staff to film the team's defensive signals from an on-field location during a game, a violation of league rules. NFL security then confiscated the video camera used by Patriots video assistant Matt Estrella to film the signals. Two days later, Belichick apologized "to everyone who has been affected." The league's position was clear. Page 105 of the 2007 NFL Game Operations Manual states, "No video recording devices of any kind are permitted to be in use in the coaches' booth, on the field, or in the locker room during the game.… All video shooting locations must be enclosed on all sides with a roof overhead." Belichick stated that he believed that if footage collected was not used during the game, its collection was legal, as the NFL Constitution and Bylaws stipulate that "Any communications or information-gathering equipment, other than Polaroid-type cameras or field telephones, shall be prohibited…including without limitation…any other form of electronic devices that might aid a team during the playing of a game." In a September 2006 memorandum sent out by NFL Vice President of Football Operations Ray Anderson, though, all teams were told that "videotaping of any type, including but not limited to taping of an opponent's offensive or defensive signals, is prohibited on the sidelines, in the coaches' booth, in the locker room, or at any other locations accessible to club staff members during the game."

The reaction was swift, as all of the media pundits jumped on the bandwagon to talk about what was now being hailed as Spygate. You see, New England was the powerhouse team in the NFL at this time, having won a trio of Super Bowls in 2002, 2004, and 2005, and they were poised to win a fourth in 2008 at the time of the scandal. Many opposing teams had venom to spew and were now convinced that their teams had somehow been duped by the Patriots, who were now known cheaters. Shortly after everything went down, footage from the actual tapes that had been made was shown on FOX NFL Sunday.

Former Cowboys head coach Jimmy Johnson, a commentator on the show, saw the tape. "This is exactly how I was told to do it 18 years ago by a Kansas City Chiefs scout. I tried it, but I didn't think it helped us." He went on to add, "Bill Belichick was wrong because he videotaped signals after a memo was sent out to all of the teams saying not to do it. But what irritates me is hearing some reactions from players and coaches. These players don't know what their coaches are doing. And some of the coaches have selective amnesia because I know for a fact there were various teams doing this. That's why the memo was sent to everybody. That doesn't make [Belichick] right, but a lot of teams are doing this."

"The Spygate thing has diminished what they've accomplished," added former Dolphins head coach Don Shula. "You would hate to have that attached to your accomplishments. They've got it. I guess you got the same thing as putting an asterisk by Barry Bonds' home-run record. I guess it will be noted that the Patriots were fined and a No. 1 draft choice was taken away during that year of accomplishment. The sad thing is Tom Brady looks so good, it doesn't look like he needs any help."

Pittsburgh wide receiver Hines Ward also chimed in, believing firmly that there was more than just good scouting to New England's 24–17 upset win over his Steelers in the 2002 AFC Championship Game. "Oh, they knew," Ward said. "They were calling our stuff [audibles] out. They knew a lot of our calls. There's no question some of their players were calling out some of our stuff."

As for the fall-out, even Pennsylvania Senator Arlen Specter got involved, calling for independent investigation as to why the league destroyed the tapes before any further questioning could be conducted. Specter also spoke of his own meeting with Walsh, who "told Specter of a former Patriots offensive player who told Walsh about being called into a meeting with Belichick, Adams, and then-offensive coordinator Charlie Weis before a September 3, 2000, game against the Tampa Bay Buccaneers, at which point the player was instructed to memorize previously recorded defensive signals on tape, watch for the signals from the sidelines during the game, and relay them to Weis. This, according to the player, allowed the Patriots to anticipate 75 percent of the defense's plays being called."

As for Matt Walsh, he said that he was surprised when he heard of Belichick's comments that Belichick "couldn't pick Walsh out of a lineup" because Belichick had spoken with Walsh on more than one occasion and that Belichick's former wife even gave Walsh a sweater for Christmas in 2001. Is it a case of he said, she said? Who knows? Meanwhile, the entire saga was finally put to bed in May 2008 when Senator Ted Kennedy, who along with Specter sits on the U.S. Senate Judiciary Committee, spoke of Specter's initiative by saying, "With the war in Iraq raging on, gasoline prices closing in on $4 a gallon, and Americans losing their homes at record rates to foreclosure, the United States Senate should be focusing on the real problems that Americans are struggling with."

In a bit of espionage karma, the Patriots, who had won their first 18 games in the 2007–08 season (an NFL record), lost in the Super Bowl to the Giants, 17–14. Part of the reason, some will speculate, was because

Bernie Kosar, 12-Year Quarterback, on Signs

"I have no problem with stealing signals. That is just a part of the game. Look, if you are playing the Steelers and everybody is wearing black, but one knucklehead is wearing something totally out of the ordinary and really sticking out like a sore thumb, standing five yards away from the sideline, it doesn't take a rocket scientist to figure out what that guy is doing. So if I am stupid enough to flash signals in those types of situations, then that is my own fault. Conversely, if I can look over to the other bench and see what they are doing, then that is their fault. They need to come up with tougher signals or hide them better, plain and simple. Watch and learn—that is such a simple concept, yet so many players were clueless when it came to that stuff. Signs and signals are a huge part of the game. I studied that stuff as much as I could. I would watch guys on the sideline, and sometimes you would see or even hear what they were doing. Or when I was playing, I would listen to how they were calling their defensive signals when they were making adjustments to our motions and formations coming out of the huddle. It amazed me how much you could learn if you just listened once in a while. Some guys would just blurt stuff out and maybe yell, 'Cover three!' or, 'I got this guy or that guy!' It amazed me, it really did."

in the week leading up to the game, Spygate was rekindled when Walsh claimed to have information about taping the Ram's walk-through prior to Super Bowl XXXVI in 2001—a game the Patriots won. As one writer put it, "The lighter fluid had been sprayed, and the story burst into flames all over again." Perhaps the distraction proved to be too great. Nobody will know for sure. One thing they did know, however, was that Bill "Belicheat" wasn't going to get much sympathy from the league. For better or worse, Spygate will forever be linked to Belichick's legacy.

The last word on Spygate goes to Steve Sabol, the longtime president of NFL Films, who has seen his fair share of espionage on the gridiron over the years. "I think in the NFL, knowledge is power," Sabol said. "And you try to get the knowledge by whatever means. The difference between Belichick and the long list of coaches before him who tried to win with trickery and deceit is that Belichick crossed the line and actually broke a league rule. He had been warned and continued to do it. The others? They just smudged the line between right and wrong. The media is everywhere now. In the '60s and '70s, a network had three cameras at a game, and now it has 20. The game is under CAT-scan scrutiny. There is no way you can get away with anything."

Ernie Accorsi, Longtime General Manager, on Signs

"There was a great sign stealer in the league about 20 years ago working for Seattle, and he was so good that we stole him and hired him in Cleveland. Do you know they have card counters in Vegas? Well, he was just like that. He was amazing. We would get him tickets to our road games the week before we played, and he would sit in the stands and figure everything out. The guy was brilliant. He would then come back and report to us what he learned, and it was a huge advantage for us. Our players told me that he was phenomenal. For our offense, it was immeasurable because, thanks to him, he would have the opposing team's defense completely figured out. It wasn't cheating because it wasn't illegal. I remember back in 1977 we won a divisional championship with the Colts in a game against New England. It was late in the game, and we were rallying. One of our guys up in the booth was really good at picking off signals. He had been doing his homework, and with a few minutes to go, he read a double-safety delayed blitz. We immediately radioed the information down to our quarterback, Bert Jones, who was able to capitalize on it for the game-winning 78-yard touchdown. It was huge. That guy was the unsung hero, but nobody knew it."

Green Dots, Lip Readers, Film Stars, and Double Agents...

In 2008, the NFL finally allowed for one defensive player per team to have a radio in his helmet. To identify the designated offensive and defensive players, they are also given green stickers, or dots, that are placed on the backs of their helmets. Only one live helmet can be on the field at a time. Coaches have 25 seconds to make their calls, starting when the play clock begins to tick down from 40 seconds. While offensive coaches tell the quarterback what play to call, defensive coaches call in formations, stunts, and blitz packages. The radio transmitters, which are only one-way communication devices—meaning only the coach can talk—automatically shut off at the 15-second mark. To make sure nobody cheats the system, a designated backup player will also have a live helmet in case of injury to the primary player, which is stored in a secure, 3' x 4' trunk that is off limits to players, coaches, and team personnel. A league-appointed monitor even stands sentinel on each sideline over the dual backup helmets, just in case. The defense must designate a primary and a backup player authorized for receivers in their helmets 90 minutes before each game. With more than 268 million different military-grade encryption codes protecting the frequencies, the helmet transmissions are virtually impossible to tamper with. "Each team has it own code, indecipherable by any other team or person attempting to listen in," said league spokesman Greg Aiello, "and there has never been evidence of a team tampering with the current frequency system."

One would assume that with radios in place on both sides of the ball that sign stealing and counter-intelligence is gone. Wrong. It has just evolved to the next level. Teams still use video in questionable manners, especially home teams, which place cameras on the sidelines under the guise that they provide extra game tape for the home team's coaches to study. It has been alleged, however, that occasionally cameras will get "bumped" from time to time and wind up "accidentally" recording the opposing team's signals. Meanwhile, when road teams attempt to get credentials for their sideline cameramen, their applications are usually denied. Go figure. Teams have also been chastised for having a second camera in the press-box area—one camera shooting the game, and the other for sneaking a peek at the opposing team's signal-callers.

One of the more recent phenomenon finds coaches holding their play-calling charts in front of their mouths when they're sending in the play to the quarterback via the radio headset system. Why? Teams now have scouts who are adept at reading lips. Heck, that has been going on in baseball for years, with both English- and Spanish-speaking lip readers. The pitchers hold their gloves over their mouths when they talk to their catchers so that they can change up their signs, especially when there is a base runner on second base who can see in and communicate what the pitch will be to the batter. Football isn't quite the same, but lip reading has definitely become a new trick of the trade. Scouts know that if a coach speaks for a long time that he is usually calling a pass play because those calls take longer to say. A running play, meanwhile, is much shorter, so coaches shield their mouths and will even try to throw off the spies by moving their gums to pretend to be speaking on a running play, just to keep them honest. Sign stealing is all about studying habits and tendencies, so the coaches have had to learn how to be a bit more abnormal and unpredictable.

Veteran players know how important things like lip reading are and try very hard to take advantage of those things.

"Because the terminology is so similar form system to system, it is not very hard to figure things out if you know what to look for," confessed 13-year offensive tackle John Alt. "Even now when I am home watching TV, I can read the coaches lips at least 80 percent of the time and know exactly what play they are going to run. Trust me, lip reading is something that has been around for a very long time, and it will continue to be. Teams understand how important it is and have people who practice this stuff. Look, the league is so competitive now that any little advantage they can get they will take."

"I try to hide behind my big offensive linemen in the huddle when I am calling plays because I know that there are defensive linemen just a few feet away trying to read my lips," added 15-year CFL quarterback Anthony Calvillo. "If they can see me or even hear me if I talk too loud, that puts us at a serious disadvantage. You have to be very cognizant of that stuff out there, especially in the heat of battle or when you are on the road and it is really loud."

Lip reading isn't just for the scouts, either. Good defensive lineman can watch the quarterback's lips and often figure out the play from how quickly he blurts out the call in the huddle. Such was the case early in 2008 when the Steelers stopped 264-pound Giants running back Brandon Jacobs on a key goal-line play late in the game. Steelers defensive end Brett Keisel

Sean Payton, Longtime Coach, on Signs

"There are many teams in our league, us [New Orleans] included, who have guys in the press box with binoculars focused on the defensive coordinator or the signaler, trying to get his signals. He would then relay that information to me on the sidelines. Maybe he could identify a pressure or a cover-one or cover-two formation. I would in turn relay that information on to the quarterback through the radio in his helmet. That all happens very, very quickly. You always had to be aware of sign stealers, though. Everybody had them, and everybody tried to prevent them from having any success. We always assumed that we were being watched, so we went with multiple signalers to try to stay a step ahead of them. I would never have thought that anybody would be videotaping us from inside the stadium, however, and that is where New England got into trouble with Spygate. There you had actual filming, which was obviously against the rules and crossed the line. We certainly didn't do that. Stealing signals in my eyes is gamesmanship, versus cheating, which was what happened in Spygate. I would be surprised if more than a couple of teams got into the actual physical videotaping of that coordinator or signaler. It wasn't a widespread thing, I don't think. Now that the defensive helmets are wired for radios, all of that stuff is kind of out the window anyway."

saw Giants quarterback Eli Manning mouth the play call and lined up his defense accordingly, stopping Jacobs inches short of the goal line.

"I was watching Eli's lips the whole time, and I saw him say '32,' so I went over and tried to tell everyone, 'It's right here,' and we stopped it," Keisel said. "That was a big play in the game. I'm guessing it's the two-hole, which is right off center guard. And that's the play they ran, and we stopped them."

"I always tried to watch the quarterback very closely in the huddle," said former Raiders defensive tackle Otis Sistrunk. "I got pretty good at reading lips over the years. You could tell by his eyes as to whether or not he was going to pass or hand it off on a run. On a run he would just look anywhere, but on a pass it was totally different. When he was going to pass, he would always look over to see who was going to be coming after him and try to knock him into next week. I tried to pick up on that stuff. Every quarterback was different, but they all did little things that would give stuff away—especially the younger players."

"I got to be pretty good at listening in to the offensive huddle and was able to pick up a lot of snap counts," added eight-year defensive tackle

Keith Millard. "I would watch their lips, too, especially the younger quarterbacks. In the heat of the battle, they don't realize just how loud they are talking. And when they do talk loud, they really use their lips to enunciate what they are saying, which made it easier to pick up what they were saying. That was a huge deal for me. I didn't share the info with my teammates though, because if it was wrong, then I didn't want them to get penalized for it."

Even now, with both teams having radio communications, the offensive and defensive coordinators try to wait until the last second to call in their plays to prevent the other guys from being able to adjust. On defense that might mean calling formations and blitzes with only 10 or 15 seconds before the play-clock expires. They will not want to show blitz until the last second so that the offense won't have time to call an audible and change the play at the line of scrimmage. There is s a lot of jockeying going on in those final few seconds before the ball is snapped.

One of the best ways for coaches to communicate today is via wristbands. The coach will touch his wrist to indicate to the quarterback or linebacker that he wants him to look at his wristband. He will then signal him a

Bud Grant, Longtime Coach, on Signs

"I never bothered with any of that stuff. Look, I played baseball and occasionally when you were up to bat, you would get a sign from your teammate who was on second base about what pitch was coming. Well, maybe he would tell you it was a curve ball, but in reality it was a fastball that wound up right under your chin. It only took one time to get fooled like that before you became leery of all the disinformation that goes on out there. It is the same in football, too. My philosophy on all of that was that there were a lot more important things to worry about out on the field. You could never know for sure what signs were coming, so why bother? As often as they flash them, they change them. Then what? It was unreliable information. I wasn't a gambler like that, so I just ignored all of it and did my own thing. Look, even if I had all of the film, like New England supposedly got, I wouldn't know what to do with that information. Or if a guy was spying on our practice, I didn't care. It is very difficult for a coach to interpret what another team is doing during one of their practices, let alone an untrained observer. Even today when the coaches cover their mouths with their play sheets, that is crazy to me. I never worried about people reading my lips. So I never put too much stock in all of that stuff, I had more important things to worry about, like winning football games."

number that corresponds to a number on the wristband. This is pretty effective. They will change up their wristbands every quarter, just to keep the other guys honest, or they will make it all even numbers or all odd numbers. Or maybe they will call out a number, then the quarterback or linebacker will add a number to it, such as what quarter it is. Advance scouts watch this information very closely from their perches high above the field in the coaches box and try like hell to decipher the code. And once they have it, they can do some damage.

Beyond spying, another way teams get information is through interrogation. With the advent of free agency, the movement of players and coaches from team to team is more prevalent than ever. As such, there is a venerable treasure trove of information about player inclinations and play-calling tendencies that is readily available and just waiting to be mined. So when players are signed as free agents or come to teams via trade, one of the first things the coaches will do is to sit that guy down and interrogate him—especially if he is a former enemy coming from a division rival they will play that season. In essence, the coaches want to debrief him for inside information. They want him to go Benedict Arnold and spill his guts. They will want to know his quarterback's audibles at the line of scrimmage, his defense's blitz tendencies, and any other insights that can be helpful in preparing a game plan. On the other hand, teams know if one of their former players is on the sideline of an opponent, they will change their line calls. They all know the drill.

"One of the hardest things for coaches was when we had to cut a player just before the season would begin at the end of training camp," revealed longtime coach Tom Olivadotti. "Those guys were very desirable to conference rivals and would often get signed for a week or two. Opposing teams knew that the player would know the signals and have in-depth knowledge of the playbook, and that was pretty valuable information. So they would sign the guy, give him a few bucks, and basically interrogate him. There is no loyalty in this game. That guy would be upset about being cut, so he would spill his guts. The same was true for signing guys who had been with teams for several years. Those guys were always a wealth of information, especially for getting hand signals. If you could get a team's blitz signal, for instance, that was a huge advantage. The first thing you would try to do with those guys would be to find out what his former team's automatics were. We would want to know what the codes were for the automatics, or audibles. What was the live color? How did they run their automatics? What did they do when they executed their automatics? Most teams nowadays will change their automatics from week to week, but years ago teams would stick with certain things and not change it up. So if you knew what that was, that could be a huge advantage for your defense. Espionage is a big part of the game, and there are some teams who would go to extreme measures to get that kind of information. I never did it, but I know of a lot of other guys who did."

According to eight-year linebacker Carl Brettschneider, "When I was a rookie, I signed with the 49ers as an undrafted free agent. I wound up playing during the preseason but then got cut after our final game with the Chicago Cardinals. I then wound up signing with the Cardinals that next week, and we later played the 49ers next season. Well, they hadn't changed any of their signals, so I knew every play when it was coming. As a result, I had one of the best games of my career. *The Chicago Tribune* even wrote a big article about me and about how I had made all of these unbelievable tackles out there that day."

"The players who get released late in training camp or who are traded during the season are interrogated big time by the coaches and scouts," said Packers running back Darrell Thompson. "First and foremost, they will interrogate the guy to figure out what his former team's check-offs or audibles are. Maybe they are 'hot' or 'red' or whatever. Teams rarely change up that terminology during the course of a season, so it is extremely valuable information. I remember when Darren Sharper signed with Minnesota in 2005 after spending eight seasons in rival Green Bay. You don't think we changed up all of our terminology after that? We knew he

Conrad Dobler, 10-Year Guard, on Signs

"Do you think all of the millionaires on Wall Street come across any inside information from time to time? Of course. Everybody is looking for an edge. I don't care if it is in business or in football or in raising your kids or even in romance—everybody wants to get ahead. Those who are able to find that edge are usually the ones who are the most successful. Now whenever you cross the line and go too far to gain that edge, that is when it all comes tumbling down. That was the case for all the Wall Street brokers who got busted, and it was the case for Bill Belichick in New England. They took it to an excess, and they got burned."

Peter Najarian, Three-Year Linebacker, on Signs

"I needed every little edge I could get, so certainly studying signs and becoming a student of the game was in my best interests. I would do everything I possibly could to understand every scenario under various down and distances or formations. It was like chess. I would always stare at the offensive linemen's hands to see which way they were leaning. Then I would look at the quarterback and running back's eyes to see what they could tell me, too. Any sort of tip that you could get to tell you it was going to be a run versus a pass was huge. You could tell nine times out of ten what was going to happen, and that was a big advantage. I watched ungodly hours of film, though, because you had to really study this stuff to get comfortable with it. I needed every advantage I could get out there, and this was certainly one of them."

would spill his guts and tell them everything, so we redid all of our calls. Even so, I am sure he was able to tell them a wealth of information that was extremely helpful in them playing us. He knew blocking schemes, formations, even Brett Favre's tendencies on snap counts and stuff like that. What are you going to do? That is just the way it is in this league—it is just business. It is not a violation of the code either, because you gotta pay the bills. Your loyalty ends the minute you are cut or traded.

"What guys learn in training camp is pretty basic," he added. "The meat and potatoes don't really come in until the final roster has been set for the first game of the season. That way if guys get cut they won't be able to reveal too much to whomever they next sign with. Football isn't very different from team to team. Teams will have wrinkles, but the offenses are all pretty much the same systems. Everybody runs slants, everybody runs go [patterns], everybody pulls, everybody zone blocks, and so on. It is mostly the same stuff from team to team, but it is the order that the coaches call stuff in that makes the big differences. Teams even employ offensive and defensive quality-control specialists whose job it is to study tendencies. They will point out when the offense and defense do certain things, what their wrinkles are, and when they like to employ them. It is their job to watch film 24/7 and make sure the play calling is not predictable and has no pattern. They break stuff down in spreadsheets, and it gets pretty technical with a lot of statistics and probability."

Bob Lurtsema, 11-Year Defensive End, on Signs

There were no signs back in my day. Hell no. We had pictures, though. I remember playing with New York back in old Yankee Stadium. They would have a wire that ran down to the field from the press box on which the coaches would send Polaroid pictures. They would use this clothes-line clip and just let gravity take it all the way down to the field for the coaches and players to look at. We would look at those things and marvel at how technology had changed the game. Boy, how times have changed."

One way teams still try to gain an advantage is by studying the opposing quarterback's cadence. They know that if their defensive linemen can get off the ball a split second faster, then that might be the difference between a sack and a hurry. To help in analyzing the quarterback's verbal tendencies, teams will watch the network TV feed of the game (the one the fans watch on Fox or NBC on Sunday). They will then have the players all sit in a room to just listen and learn. The coaches want the players to listen for the voice inflections and try to identify them. It is an audio visualization, so to speak, and it's actually quite effective. Teams have learned that quarterbacks, especially the younger and more inexperienced ones, tend to do the same things over and over. They will not only call the same snap counts over and over ("On one!" or "On three!"), but they will also use the same pauses and inflections to call them, too. Teams have even been known to place hidden microphones on their defensive linemen to tape the opposing team's audibles.

"We used to get the video of the actual TV broadcasts of our games and then all sit in a room with the volume blasted as loud as it could possibly go to listen to the quarterback's snap cadences," said Mike Morris, a 12-year veteran long snapper. "We would sit in a dark room and watch it with and without volume, over and over, trying to pick up any subtle hints they might give away. We would also study check-downs and the lingo of the quarterback. This was especially useful when you played divisional rivals, who you would face twice a year. Those rematch games were huge because both teams knew a lot more about each other that second go-around. Quarterbacks will use certain terminology, such as colors or numbers, when calling audibles. So if you could pick up on that stuff, it was a huge advantage."

Beyond that, teams will also get together to watch the film of every other camera angle that they can get their hands on, including shots from the press box, end zones, and sidelines. They will even watch the Sunday night television shows of opposing coaches for tips. Then they hunker down and watch the footage with the same scrutiny as FBI agents on an undercover sting. "We want to hear what's being said in case you hear an audible or a [defensive] check," said Chiefs coach Herm Edwards. "Coaches have a saying: 'Anything you say can and will be used against you.'"

Film study has always been an integral part of the game. Players who put in the time by studying their opponents are usually rewarded come game day.

"Film study is so important," Thompson said. "You can figure out pretty quickly what guys' favorite moves are. Everybody has one, from Michael Jordan to Lawrence Taylor. They will usually do it early in the game too, right when they start out the game. They will adjust from there and get creative, but they usually always go with their signature move right away. Good players will adjust many times over and become incredibly unpredictable. So if you can identify their favorite move, that is a huge advantage. I remember playing Buffalo one time and studying up on their big-time safety, Leonard Smith, ahead of time. I knew that as soon as he blitzed, he was going to dip his outside shoulder in and try to rip and come underneath. That was his move. He had gotten sacks in every single game that year doing that. It was an amazing move. Sure enough, he blitzed on the very first play of the game, and I recognized it immediately. He came around the outside, faked, and put that shoulder down. I picked him up

Joe Theismann, 15-Year Quarterback, on Signs

"To me it wasn't stealing—it was interpreting. I was trying to gain a competitive edge. The league is very unique in this regard, too. It doesn't say you can't do it. It just says you can't do it electronically with video, which is what Spygate was all about. Stealing signs has been a part of the game for a long time, and it will continue to be. Why do you think coaches put their play-sheet over their mouths when they call signals? To check their breath? Hell no. This is valuable information. Take baseball, for instance. If you can study and figure out what pitches the pitcher is throwing, then that is a tremendous advantage. Let's say a guy is on first base and is looking to steal second. If he knows that the next pitch is going to be a curve ball coming in at 70 mph versus a fast ball coming in at 95 mph, that is the difference of about one step in real time. That one step is usually the difference between being called safe or called out. That could be the winning run. So I am a big believer that if players or coaches in any sport want to do their homework, then they should be rewarded accordingly."

out of the backfield and put my helmet right on his shoulder pad, driving him straight into the ground. He even said to me, 'Damn, good block kid!' That is how you earn respect in the league, by doing your homework and executing what you learned. Afterward my coach even came up to me and was super proud of me for what I had done."

"Every week we would watch film of our opposing team that we were going to play," said 14-year defensive tackle John Randle. "We would see two angles of the plays that they were running, a sideline view and a front or game view. We watched a ton of film, a ton. Watching film is almost like being a stalker. You watch it over and over and try to find things that are out of the ordinary. You look at the space between the linemen, their splits, on certain plays. You look at whether a lineman will line up on a two- or three-point stance. You look to see if a lineman is leaning a certain way, indicating whether or not he will pull, or if it is a pass or run or maybe where the play is going. You watch it over and over until you can pick up the tendencies or poker tells. I remember playing against Cincinnati one time. We studied their quarterback, Boomer Esiason, so much that we were almost obsessed with him. Well, sure enough, we finally picked up one of his tells: he would button both of his chin straps if it was a run but only one of them if it was a pass. We figured that out, and we burned him on it the entire game. That was awesome. That wasn't cheating—that was doing our homework. Another guy who gave stuff away was Cleveland quarterback Bernie Kosar. He had a bad leg and would tend to favor it when he was going to drop back for a pass. We would just watch him and key off of it. Again, that was just gamesmanship. Beyond that, we had coaches breaking down our opponents every week. They would work with you to help you figure out

Fran Tarkenton, 18-Year Quarterback, on Signs

"None of that stuff was prevalent in my era. None. I used to call my own plays and never had to worry about sign stealing. Even if the coach called in a play, he would send it in with a messenger guard or some other player from the sideline. So we didn't have people stealing signs because we didn't have any signs to steal. As for all of the other stuff, hell, I never once in 18 years of playing in the NFL saw another person's playbook, game plan, or scouting report. What was I going to do with it? After studying film all week, we knew what people were going to do. There was no mystery there."

their tendencies. Together, you would analyze players and see what he did well and where he was weak. Then there were magazines that would do the same thing, and the Internet, so there was a lot of information out there if you were willing to do your homework. But even with the film and all the other stuff, you still had to line up and play the game. That was the bottom line."

"As a lineman, I studied a lot of film," added former Chiefs offensive tackle Richard Baldinger. "Good players recognize tendencies on certain downs and distance scenarios. I looked for irregularities in a guy's stance, where he was leaning, where his weight was shifted, where his eyes were focused, and any other mannerisms that he was displaying. Film don't lie. If you did your homework, you would have an edge. It was definitely a cat-and-mouse game between the offensive and defensive linemen. In my world, you could flat-back a guy sixty straight plays, but on the sixty-first, if you give up a big sack, people think you played a terrible game."

One of the byproducts of free agency today is the fact that more and more players become friends, whereas in the old days, everybody hated everybody. Your opponent back then was your mortal enemy, and you wouldn't dare speak to him. Now with so many players sharing agents and getting together in the off-season for celebrity charity golf events and whatnot, they become pals. As such, they talk, and they share secrets. According to *Washington Post* writer Les Carpenter, Redskins cornerback Shawn Springs revealed that he regularly calls friends on other teams after they played teams he will face soon. They compare notes on that team's cadences and terminology, all of which might give him a hint of what they might try in a game. What he's come to learn is most quarterbacks don't have a firm grasp of the team's offense to throw out fake calls while on the field. What they shout at their teammates before the snap is often what they are going to do. According to Springs, that little bit of understanding is the difference between an interception and perhaps a touchdown.

Yes, despite the green dots, paranoia is still alive and well in the new millennium. Coaches still fear moles and worry about counter-intelligence. In fact, many coaches now have their garbage segregated and shredded independent of everyone else's at the team offices. Coaches are control freaks who want to manage the flow of information down to the smallest minutia. They watch everything from who has access to team files on encrypted computers to who's driving the team bus to who's cleaning

Pete Bercich, Six-Year Linebacker and Coach, on Signs

"Studying and stealing signs was huge for me. I was a middle linebacker and was the signal-caller on defense, and I later did some coaching where I became very involved in signage. We used common-sense signs. For instance, we had a blitz for one of our linebackers, Keith Newman, who went to North Carolina, so we called it the 'Tar Heel' and would call it in by tapping the side of your head, like a ram. Another was called 'Nike,' to which you would call it in by tapping the side of your sneaker. We tried to keep them simple, because there were so many of them and they could get confusing. You can't give guys too much information or they won't be able to process all of it. It was either myself or [defensive coordinator] Ted Cottrell who would signal them in to the defense. One of us was live, and the other was a decoy. We were constantly changing it up. We knew that the other team had guys watching us, trying to steal our signs, so we would mix things up in a constant game of cat and mouse. It was a lot of fun.

"When you look at what New England did with Spygate, the reality is that almost every team does that stuff. The difference is that they don't videotape it. Instead they will send some pre-scouts there with binoculars to try to steal their signals. He will sit there and watch the other team, meticulously writing down each signal that is called on every play and how it coincides with down and distance. He will then come back and put together a scouting report that details what each signal represents as it pertains to a certain personnel group on the offense or defense. Then that same scout or pro personnel guy will sit up in the booth with the coaches at games, looking through his binoculars and trying to identify certain matchups or situations out on the field. He may see a signal and then tell the coaches, 'Okay, we have a cover-two here,' or something like that. We would even wait until the microphone to the quarterback would cut off before signaling in the defensive play, just to make sure the quarterback couldn't all of a sudden change the call in the huddle.

"Or sometimes when it was really noisy in the Metrodome, we would wait until the quarterback would take his hands off of his ears to send in our signals. When it was really loud in there, the quarterback would have to hold his hands over his ear holes to be able to hear the coach talk to him on the headset in his helmet. We knew that the microphone had cut off at that point, so we would hurry our defensive calls in. Those little games are going on constantly out there, and the fans are completely oblivious to it.

"Here is another thing: teams that travel will always go through a walk-through practice the day before the game at the stadium. Well, there is always a guy from the home team at the stadium behind some darkened glass somewhere watching everything that is going on. Are they videotaping? Who knows? They are definitely watching and listening, trying to pick up any little thing that they think might help their team win. The point-counterpoint gets so crazy that teams will actually type up dummy play sheets and crumple them up and put them in the trash. They know that the other team will go dumpster-diving as soon as they go back to the hotel. Or they will type up entire dummy play books and leave them in hotel rooms, in hopes of some local fan finding it and hoping it somehow finds its way to the home team.

"Lip reading is big, too, especially for West Coast offenses, which are very verbose. When a coach calls out a typical play in the West Coast offense, he will give the formation, the motion, the protection, and then the route of every single wide receiver. An example would be something like, 'Dot right, shift to slot right, C-motion, X-post, Y-dodge, Z-comeback.' Conversely, when they call a run, it would be something much smaller in length, such as, 'Dot right, 53 power.' So if you saw a coach calling in the play over his headset and it didn't take him very long to say it, you would know that it was a run versus a pass. That is a big deal. You could then set your defense to counter that and have a distinct advantage. You just had to hope that you weren't getting decoyed, which would really suck. And that happened, too. It was a big game out there, a game within a game. Anyway, that is why you see the coaches covering up their mouths with their play sheets.

"It is the same thing with the hand signals, too, where you are calling in fronts, stunts, and coverages. People could decode those just as easy, so teams all went to wristbands. Now all they have to do is signal in a number or a color or whatever, and the quarterback or linebacker can just look it up on his wristband. Football players are not rocket scientists, though, so you had to change up those things pretty regularly. Now they have the radios in the defensive helmets, so a lot of this stuff is a moot point. Back when I played, though, it was a big deal. Football is a thinking man's game. There is a ton of shit going on at all times, and you can't overwhelm your players with too much information or they will just overload. The simpler it is mentally, the harder it is physically. So if you are a cornerback or defensive end, there is not a whole hell of a lot to think about. But if you are a quarterback or a linebacker, then you have a hell of a lot to think about.

"There is a fine line between spying and cheating, though, and the Patriots got caught because there was evidence. Another thing that goes on, but is nearly impossible to prove, is when teams listen in on opposing teams' radio signals. I played in the 2000 NFC Championship Game where the Giants beat the Vikings 41–0, and it was alleged that the Giants had somehow tapped into our radio signals and could hear our play calls. There is no way to prove it, but there are a lot of people who believed it to be true. I don't know. We will never know. We got beat pretty good and I don't want to take anything away from the Giants, but you can't help but wonder about stuff like that. I just hope it wasn't true."

the offices at night. They have small inner circles that are reserved for only the most loyal and trustworthy. Jobs are on the line, and there is a lot of money at stake in this multi-billion-dollar industry. Everything and everybody is scrutinized.

Even the little things, like players losing their playbooks, is a big deal today. Since day one, coaches have reminded their players to guard their playbooks with their lives. Even so, they still occasionally fall into enemy hands, either through ignorance or grand larceny. Either way, they can often yield a treasure trove of information that can be used for nefarious purposes. Stories along these lines have run rampant over the years, from teams hiring kids seeking autographs at training camp to pull the old bait-and-switch to literally breaking-and-entering to heist what many coaches believe to be the holy grail. Teams are cognizant of just how much information they will give to a free agent or a rookie who may get cut, so they limit how many plays that guy will get for his book. Once that guy signs a contract and is officially a part of the team, then he will get more information on a need-to-know basis.

Marc Trestman, Five-Time NFL Offensive Coordinator, on Lip Reading

Sign stealing has always been a part of the game. It is not cheating if you know that the other team is going to blitz and you counter that to your advantage. What is cheating or unethical is if you break the rules in order to get that information. Videotaping is against the rules, so that is something that I would never do. If I could see a coach hold up two fingers, however, to indicate a cover-two defense, then I was going to use that information to my advantage. It could go both ways though, because maybe that coach was trying to psych you out and throw you some dummy signs. You never know. Now, with the defensive headsets, sign stealing is a thing of the past. Lip reading is still out there though, and teams have seen that as a path to gathering intelligence. You know, I was one of the first coaches ever to cover my mouth with my play-sheet. I knew that there were people, advance scouts, up in the box trying to ready my lips so I did what I had to do in order to protect my plays. I ran a lot of plays from the West Coast offense, which uses words and terminology, versus numbers, so they are easier to detect and decipher. I certainly did everything within the rules to gain an advantage, but I never tried to do anything that was cheating or unethical. I just never wanted to disrespect the game or the league.

5

If You Ain't Cheatin', Then You Ain't Tryin'

There is a fine line between cheating and gamesmanship in sports, and athletes have always tried to push the envelope in order to gain an honest, or dishonest, advantage. Just like there is a right way and a wrong way to steal signs, there are also right and wrong ways to beat your opponent down in the trenches at the line of scrimmage.

Stickum

Arguably no team in NFL history is more associated with toughness and grit than the Oakland Raiders. In the late '70s, the heyday for the silver and black, the Raiders would seemingly try any tactic if it helped them to fulfill team owner Al Davis' notorious phrase: "Just win, baby." The faces of the franchise in those days included defensive back Lester Hayes and wide receiver Fred Biletnikoff. One of the little intangibles that gave those guys that edge was a sticky, gooey, brownish-yellow substance that they would rub on their hands, otherwise known as Stickum. Oakland's players learned about the glue-like substance when their former equipment manager Dick Romanski introduced them to it in the mid-1970s.

Biletnikoff loved to use it because it helped him catch the ball. Hayes, who rubbed it on his hands, wrists, and forearms, liked it because it helped him keep his hands on opposing receivers and disrupt their pass routes in the bump-and-run coverage that he became known for. It also helped him to pick off balls, too. In fact, he swiped a total of 18 of them in 1980, which garnered him NFL Defensive Player of the year honors.

"The sole focus of our team was to win consistently," said Hayes, who helped guide the Raiders to a pair of Super Bowl wins over Washington and Philadelphia. "Whether it was a mental or a physical advantage, we were going to do whatever was necessary to win. Our attitude was that if we could get away with something, we were going to do it."

The downside to using it was that it stuck to everything and everybody it would touch. "You practically had to pry the ball loose from him whenever he got his hands on it," said Raiders linebacker Ted Hendricks.

And it made for one hell of a mess. "That stuff would get all over everything. It was awful," said Raiders safety Jack Tatum. "I remember always telling Lester, 'Don't touch me, man! Don't touch me!'"

"That stuff was the stickiest, greasiest, slimiest, grossest stuff," said Vikings linebacker Matt Blair. "I was friends with Lester [Hayes], and he would harass guys with it. It was pretty funny. I remember one time at the Pro Bowl he came over to say hi to me right before the game and hugged me and shook my hand. I was totally covered in that crap. It was awful. Here I was at the Pro Bowl and I wanted to look good, and then I got covered in that stuff. He just laughed and walked away."

Visions of Biletnikoff's and Hayes' Stickum-coated jerseys are now synonymous with the team's bad-ass, rebel image. The stuff was legal at first, but it was declared illegal by the league in 1980. That didn't stop the Raiders from using it, though—they just hid it in their socks or under their shoulder pads until they needed a quick fix for a big play. After the league outlawed the axle-grease-like substance, Hayes' interception numbers plummeted. His security blanket was gone, and with it went its placebo-like benefits. He later said that without it, he became a "mere mortal."

Oakland wasn't the only team to use it, either.

"I used it occasionally," confessed nine-year cornerback Irv Cross. "I would put some on the inside of my socks and grab a little bit every time I would return a punt or kick. It would give you that little extra grip, especially if it was wet out."

The guys who hated it the most were the referees, who had to police the players from using it after it was outlawed.

"In the '70s, Stickum was all the rage," said 23-year NFL referee Jerry Markbreit. "In those days, players would smear that stuff all over themselves to help them catch passes. They used to put it under their arms so they could reach under there and reapply it whenever they felt like they needed to. It got so bad that guys could darn near catch passes without even closing their hands. Eventually, when it became illegal, we had to police it, which was a real pain. If we detected it, we had to send the player out of the game to either change his jersey or get cleaned up. I remember working a Raiders game one time. Now the Raiders were notorious for using that stuff, and they would try to hide it everywhere. I stepped into the Raider huddle of this particular game and could smell it like crazy. So I stopped the game and said, 'Okay guys, lift up your arms.' It was like an old cops and robbers holdup, with all the guys being under arrest. Sure enough, one of their guys had a big blob of it hidden under his arm, so we had to send him out of the game. You would have to search guys, and it would get all over you and make a real mess. If they got caught the first time, nothing happened. If they got caught a second time, it was a five-yard penalty. And it was 15 yards for the third offense. It was a joke. As officials, we were thrilled when that junk finally went away for good. What a mess!"

"I was glad when they eventually outlawed it because it made for such a mess," added 25-year NFL referee Dick Hantak. "The balls would come back so sticky from the receivers that the quarterbacks couldn't grip the ball after that, so they finally banned the stuff. I remember the old Raiders, guys like Jack Tatum and Lester Hayes, they would goop that stuff on their jerseys so much so that the ball would almost stick to them like Velcro."

Silicone

The exact opposite of sticky Stickum was slippery silicone, and it too became the substance of choice for offensive linemen who were looking for a sneaky edge. You see, defensive linemen have always tried to grab onto the offensive linemen's jerseys to gain leverage and to move them the way they wanted them to go. With silicone, the linemen's hands would just slip off. And the silicone would stay on there, so they couldn't just wipe it off. The defensive linemen would complain, to which the offensive linemen would just say, "Hey, what are doing grabbing me anyway? That is a 10-yard holding penalty!" While it was never legal, the substance was outlawed by the league in the late '80s. The referees were thrilled to see it go, but like Stickum, they hated trying to police it.

"Offensive linemen used to spray it on their shirts, and the defensive players would holler like hell about it," said 23-year NFL referee Jerry

Markbreit. "Nowadays the officials regularly conduct what are called 'shirt inspections' during every game, where certain position players are checked before games and then again at halftime. Players would use Vaseline, too, especially when it was cold—because they would say it was to keep them warm. Well, sure enough, they would smear a dab on their face to stay warm, along with another handful all over their arms or jerseys to prevent anybody from grabbing onto them. I remember one time working a Denver vs. Kansas City playoff game. Denver had the ball, and on the first series, the Chiefs players were hollering to us officials about how the Broncos players were all covered with grease.

"So my umpire and I went over to check it out and sure enough, all five Bronco offensive linemen were covered in Vaseline. It was zero degrees out, and they didn't have any shirtsleeves on or anything, just their bare skin exposed—so they could be as slippery as possible, I suppose. These guys each had about an inch of Vaseline on their arms. It was the darndest thing I had ever seen. Well, as per the rules, we had to send all five of them out of the game to get cleaned up, and they had to stay out for at least one play. Meanwhile, I am thinking to myself, 'Do I really want to send out the entire Denver offensive line and risk having their superstar quarterback John Elway get killed on my watch?' If that happened they would blame me, and I wouldn't make it out of there alive. So I stopped the game and sent the entire line to the sideline to get cleaned up. I then let them back in to play without taking a play off. The supervisor of officials later came down hard on me for not penalizing the players. I told him that I could not, in good conscience, take them all out at once for fear of what may happen out there, and he understood. He respected my good judgment in that particular situation, and it all worked out."

"We would get a list of names before every game of who the league wanted us to check," added 22-year NFL referee Bernie Kukar. "It was random. So we would then stop and check those players as they were coming out of the locker rooms. We will check guys out on the field, too, if we have reason to believe that they have used it. We will then tell them that they have to leave the field and change their jerseys. There is no penalty for it, but we do write them up, and they will usually then be fined by the league."

The offensive linemen loved to use it, feeling that it gave them an edge over their constant nemeses across the line of scrimmage.

"Hell yeah, we used that stuff all the time," confessed former 49ers offensive tackle Keith Fahnhorst. "It came in an aerosol can, and it stunk. The trick was to not get any on yourself, otherwise you would have problems. In San Francisco, the entire line would get their shoulders sprayed down. That was just part of the game in those days. We eventually got busted doing it, which only meant that we had to be more sneaky about it."

Eventually, after it was outlawed, the linemen had to move on to other slippery substances.

"I remember during a game one time versus the Raiders when their center kept grabbing our nose guard, Greg Kragen, right between where his shoulder pads hooked together," recalled Broncos linebacker Karl Mecklenburg. "He would do this and yank him down and then jump on. Finally, Greg went to the sideline and put a huge glob of Vaseline right between his pads where he had been grabbing him. Well, sure enough, the next play he grabbed onto him and got his hands all up in there really good. The next play the guy tried to snap the ball and he couldn't even get a grip. It was hilarious. His hands were just covered in Vaseline and were slippery as hell. It was pretty funny."

The next great thing in the evolution of anti-holding counter-measures was double-sided carpet tape, which they would use to tape the insides of their jerseys to their shoulder pads. From there, they evolved to custom fitted jerseys.

"As an offensive lineman, you wanted to get as much of an advantage as you could out there," said former Broncos tackle Jon Melander. "In addition to putting silicone on our jerseys, we also had a tailor come in who would custom-fit our jerseys so that you could barely get the thing on. We needed them to be that tight so the defensive linemen couldn't grab on to us. They were so uncomfortable, but you had to do it, otherwise those guys would throw you around out there."

The Spoken Word

Good quarterbacks can use deception, both legally as well as illegally, when making play calls. When a quarterback steps up to the line and sees something he doesn't like, he will call an audible, which will change the play to something that will either capitalize on a weakness he sees in the defense or defend against a weakness he sees in his offense. Either way, he will bark out his call to his receivers and linemen alike to warn them of the impending change. The defense, meanwhile, will also adjust accordingly. If they were going to blitz, maybe now they won't. It oftentimes depends on the reputation of the quarterback. Perhaps the most feared and respected player in this regard is Indianapolis quarterback Peyton Manning, who is known for doing his homework. He is also known as a master of deception.

The NFL has a rule in place that mandates that a quarterback must snap the ball if he places his hands under center. Manning, who regularly walks up to the line after breaking the huddle, will often get right up next to his center, reach out to extend his hands, but then will quickly back away to call an audible. Many times his audibles are meaningless dummies, but Manning, widely regarded as one of the smartest players in the game, uses this trick to see how the defense will shift their formations. Defensive coordinators argue that Manning comes close to violating the new rule, but he gets away with it time and again. Is that cheating, or is that gamesmanship? The consensus is that if they don't call a penalty, it's the latter.

Another trick quarterbacks will use to draw offside penalties deals with voice inflections. It is illegal for the quarterback to change his voice inflection while he is barking out the cadence on the line, and it results in a 10-yard unsportsmanlike conduct penalty. But a veteran quarterback can change it up a little bit and throw in a good head bob to get an overly aggressive defensive lineman to jump.

One of the best in the business when it came to deception was quarterback Earl Morrall, who learned plenty of tricks during his 21 years under center in the NFL. "I used to use the head bob quite effectively in my day, which was a great trick to get guys to jump offside," Morrall said. "They outlawed it, of course, but you could still get away with getting guys to jump with your voice inflection."

"Sometimes teams would sucker you into to believing a count was on two, when in reality it was on three," added eight-year defensive tackle Keith Millard. "So you had to be careful. The veteran quarterbacks like John Elway were great at drawing you offside with their snap counts. Those guys could really change things up on you and keep you guessing. Elway got me three different times in a game one year, he was just that good. He would just look over at me and laugh, too, which just sucked. You had to really do your homework and try to find the little things that would give you an advantage. Sometimes you could just get lucky, too. I remember playing a wild-card playoff game against New Orleans when I was with Minnesota. I was able to pick up Bobby Hebert's snap count almost every time; it was either on two or four. You knew that if it wasn't on two, then it was on four, and he kept doing it the entire game. I have no idea why he never changed the count, or even his rhythm for that matter, but I certainly didn't mind. I was flying that game and just tore it up. We killed them."

Conversely, the defensive lineman can't yell out a fake 'hut' call either because that will result in a penalty, as well. Chicago Bears Hall of Fame linebacker Dick Butkus was so adept at learning his opponent's snap counts that he would yell it out as soon as the quarterback started his cadence. Guys will get away with things down there from time to time in the heat of battle, especially when the crowd is loud. As a result, both the offensive and defensive linemen would be in a constant state of trying to get each other to jump offside.

"The Raiders were notorious for trying to steal snap counts," said former Chiefs offensive tackle Richard Baldinger. "So we would try to sucker those guys into jumping offside every now and then. One time during a game, we set the snap count at two, but as I was walking up to the line of scrimmage I asked my right guard, Dave Lutz, what the snap count was. He then sort of angrily said 'one,' out of the corner of his mouth, to act like he was pissed at me for forgetting the count. We of course planned this, but we were trying to mess with Raiders lineman Howie Long, who was trying to sneak a peek into our huddle. Anyway, it was a tight third-and-4 situation, and sure enough, DeBerg barked out, 'Hut one!' At that point, Howie jumped offside. Mission accomplished. The only problem was that I jumped right along with him and offset the penalty. I just had to chuckle and kick myself in the ass—I never could remember the damn count. I caught hell for that one."

The offensive line could also steal the signals of the defensive players. Often during a game when a linebacker is going to stunt, he will signal to the tackle which hole or gap he is going to run through. In so doing, he will either tap his right or left butt cheek, which can be seen, or he will use a verbal code word.

"One thing you would listen for on the line of scrimmage as an offensive lineman was when the guys across from you spoke in code," said Howard Mudd, seven-year offensive guard and 36-year NFL coach. "If a linebacker said to a defensive tackle a word that started with the letter 'L,' then that usually meant he was going to go to the left, and visa versa if he said a word that started with the letter 'R.' So if he said something to him and used the word 'Louie,' then you knew which way he was going. The defensive guys weren't too bright, trust me on that one."

Sometimes during an audible, things need to be said without tipping off the defense as to what it is. As such, the players have to be creative. One of football's most colorful characters was Packers Hall of Fame receiver Johnny "Blood" McNally. Blood was lightning quick and even scored 13 touchdowns in 1931, a single-season record at the time. In Green Bay, it was said he broke as many rules as he did tackles and ignored team curfews just as he did Prohibition. Once during a play at the line of scrimmage, Blood saw a weakness in the defense that he knew he could exploit, so he turned to quarterback Arnie Herber and shouted, 'Arnie, throw it in the direction of Mother Pierre's whorehouse!' Herber, like Blood, was no stranger to the Green Bay nightlife and knew he was going to be headed for the goal post at the northeast corner of the stadium. Needless to say, the pass was there, and so was Blood for the touchdown.

Tricks of the Trade

Players at every position have little tricks, techniques, or secrets to their success that they try to exploit to gain an edge. Let's start with cornerbacks. When Pro Bowl defensive back Eric Allen covered a speedy wide receiver on a deep route, he would lock his arm with the receiver's arm to slow him down and keep him close. It was illegal, but he knew how to position his body away from the referee so he wouldn't get caught. "If the receiver tried to push me away, it would either disrupt his route or make it look like he was pushing off, resulting in a penalty," Allen said. "I also knew when the ball was coming without even having to turn and look because I could feel the receiver's arm coming up to make the catch."

For former Raiders defensive back Lester Hayes, it was all about intimidation. Hayes used to get on opposing receivers right on the line of scrimmage and then strike them in their throats when they tried to get past him. It even had a term—to get Adam's appled. It wasn't a legal move by any means, but it was highly distracting and very effective, so much so in fact that Hayes swears one opponent actually changed to a longer face mask whenever he played the Raiders.

"When I played back in the '60s, we could bounce receivers around all over the field," explained nine-year cornerback Irv Cross. "We had what we called an axe routine, where you would roll up and actually chop the guy down at the line of scrimmage. You don't see that stuff today, with all of the rule changes. Stuff like that was legal back then, so we did it. I never wanted to hurt anybody or anything like that. I just wanted to play hard and do my job, which was to prevent that wide receiver from doing his job."

For one veteran cornerback, the secret to his success was all in the hands.

"I used to size up my opponents by looking at their hands," revealed former Minnesota cornerback John Turner. "If they had pretty hands, I knew that they weren't very tough. You see my hands, they are all beat up with a whole bunch of busted fingers and knuckles. Anybody who wants to be taken seriously at this position in this league has to have at least one finger that sticks out to the side and is all crazy. I've got one, and I am proud of it. I was a cornerback in this league for 10 years, and I have the scars to prove it."

Receivers had their tricks, too, such as setting illegal picks. Just like in basketball where players are routinely blown up, football receivers will also position their bodies in the defensive backfield to create a venerable minefield for the opposing cornerbacks. If one came running across the middle in coverage and smashed into a receiver who was set in stone, it was like hitting a brick wall. The veteran wide-outs with proper technique can make it look accidental or at least unavoidable, thus avoiding a penalty. The really good ones can even make it look like the defender actually ran into him and do the pretend flop to show how he was run over. So who is cheating? The player for doing it or the coach for teaching it?

And just like cornerbacks can hold receivers to dictate plays, good receivers can do all sorts of tricks to draw pass-interference penalties. It is a real art. They are big plays, too, which result in big yardage and automatic first downs, usually coming on key third-down conversions. Those are momentum-changers.

"Players will try to get away with whatever they can. It has always been that way," said former Vikings coach Bud Grant. "For instance, tripping and holding are both illegal, yet guys continue to do it and continue to get away with it. Is that cheating? Not if you can get away with it. Take pass interference, which has always been a battle between the receiver and the defensive back. Officials see things very differently, and sometimes a player can sell a call to make it go his way. Today, however, a lot of the wide receivers are prima donnas, if you ask me. Every time they run a route and get bumped, they throw up their arms to signal to the official and everybody else that there should have been a penalty called. That is just ridiculous. Back in my day, we used to get hit the whole way down the field, way before the ball was in the air. Now they only have five yards to be hit, and believe me, there isn't a hell of a lot a defensive back can do to slow you down in five yards. So I don't know what these guys are always complaining about, to tell you the truth. Hell, we lost a chance to go to the Super Bowl back in 1975 when we lost to Dallas in the playoffs when Drew Pearson pushed off on Nate Wright. He not only pushed off, he pushed him down. We didn't get a penalty on it, and that cost us our season. Should there have been a penalty called? Absolutely. But the official didn't see it that way, and that was that. Some officials are good, and some are bad. What are you going to do? Those things happen, and that is just football."

Defenses key in on tendencies, and good players will make sure that they don't become creatures of habit, otherwise they will become predictable—and predictable players don't last very long in the NFL. One of the league's most dynamic players is wide receiver Randy Moss. Moss is anything but predictable now, but early on in his career, he had garnered a reputation for getting lazy after running deep routes. Many receivers do, but defenses knew this about Moss in particular because the media really played it up. However, in 2004 during a game between the Vikings and Eagles, Moss' predictability was used in the form of an amazing trick play that didn't quite work out in the end. Former assistant coach Dean Dalton explained why.

"Randy had a tendency that when things didn't go well, he would kind of mope his way off the field with his head down, sort of pouting," Dalton explained. "So we practiced this play where we capitalized on Randy's reputation. The situation finally presented itself during this game against the Eagles and just like we had drawn up, we had Randy slowly jog off the field on a missed third-down conversion while the field goal unit sprinted out there to kick a field goal. Well, just as Randy was about one foot from the sideline, he stopped, and then turned just a second before the ball was snapped to get set and was now lined up as a receiver. No one was there to cover him because they all just assumed he was moping off the field. Well, everything worked, except for the fact that one of our guys got confused and went into the game when he wasn't supposed to. As a result, we were penalized for 12 men on the field. It was a bummer too, because Randy was so open it was sick. Had the play worked, he could've caught the ball and walked into the end zone. It was perfect. We practiced it all week and timed it out perfectly, but one guy who wasn't paying attention killed the entire thing. It was a one-time deal, too, because every team watched for that for the rest of the season. The element of surprise was gone. Hey, sometimes that is just football."

For defensive linemen, it is all about being able to execute a variety of stunts by using tactical rush maneuvers and techniques. Some could "swim," others could "spin," and for the big boys, it was the "bull rush." For Hall of Fame defensive end Reggie White, it was the "Hump" move, where he would lure his opponent into rushing at such a torrid pace that he eventually would lose his leverage and tip over. Good linemen could get holding calls, and that was a big deal. Holding penalties were 10-yard momentum killers and could destroy team morale.

"Defensive guys hold too, absolutely," explained former assistant coach Dean Dalton. "They will grab an offensive lineman's hands and pull them in tight and then fall back, like being pancaked, in a certain way that looks like he is being held. Talk about jumping on the grenade and sacrificing your body for your teammates for 10 yards. I mean to fall backwards with a 330-pound lineman on top of you says to your teammates that you are all about the team. Drawing a penalty like that could be a huge momentum-swinger. In a case where there is a defensive lineman who gets out on the edge and is not going to be able to make the play, the smart ones will roll their shoulders and flop to make it look like he had been hooked or held. Knowing how to fall and how to garner the attention of the not just any official but the right official out on the field is an art form all to itself. Odds are if that guy can sell it and be able to convince the official that he had been held, he will get his team a 10-yard penalty. That is a big deal. For guys who play that way, it is a lot of live by the sword and die by the sword because for every great play you pull off, you will also be getting burned a fair share, too. He will either get an ass-chewing or an 'Atta boy!' from the coach, depending on how things go out there for him. It is all about calculated risks at this level, and you can't afford to get burned too much or you won't have a job for very long."

Conversely, the offensive linemen had all sorts of tricks that they would use to deter their rivals across the line from penetrating past them. One of the best deception moves that they could make was to pretend like they were going to chop-block the guy and pretend to go after his knees. Defensive linemen are so worried about this that it will cause them to hesitate even if only for a second. That extra second, however, is an eternity in the NFL.

For 12-year offensive tackle Rich Baldinger, it was all about having strong hands.

"I did 1,000 hand exercises and 500 wrist curls a day during the off-season," Baldinger said. "That was the secret to my success as an offensive tackle. I was a really good pass blocker and had a few tricks up my sleeve, but they all started with a killer grip. It got to a point where I could have popped Godzilla's head in half with my bare hands, they were so strong. Out on the field if I could grab a jersey, it wasn't coming loose. I was going to hold on for dear life, either until the seams came out or I could see blood come out of my fingernails. Those defensive ends were so big and so fast that you had to do whatever you could to slow them down."

For 13-year offensive tackle John Alt, it was the split.

"Everybody has a few tricks up their sleeve, you have to," Alt said. "For me, I would really vary my splits, or the distance between me and the offensive guard. Sometimes I would go way wide and try to get the defensive tackle to move out there, too, to decoy him or force him to go outside versus inside. Being so tall, I felt like I could cover a lot of ground as a tackle. It eventually got to the point where my guard next to me, Dave Szott, would kiddingly tell the coaches that he wanted a bigger contract because he was having to play two positions, guard and inside-left tackle, because I would get so far away from him and leave such a gap between us. Defensive tackles weren't the brightest bulbs on the tree and they were always taught to line up across from the tackle, so I would just steer them over a little bit to either create a hole for my running back or else just force him to have to take an extra two steps to get to the quarterback. It was a good trick."

Holding has always been the biggest issue with offensive linemen. They will try to get away with whatever they can because it is only what gets called by the refs that matters. So offensive linemen will do whatever they can to get away with holding their defensive counterparts.

"I was pretty good at holding guys," admitted 14-year NFL offensive tackle Keith Fahnhorst. "I could get in tight and grab hold of them inside their frame. I got my share of penalties but was pretty successful in getting away with it, especially against the big guys like Too Tall Jones, whose first move off the line was to open up his chest. I would then latch on and take him for a ride. There was a science to it, believe it or not, and it was something I worked very hard at."

"Certain linemen can hold guys all day without getting caught," said 12-year long snapper Mike Morris. "It is an art form almost to itself. The savvy veterans have all sorts of tricks that they use and have the mangled fingers to prove it. It all comes down to how they sell it to the officials. There is a lot of acting that goes on out there, believe me."

Centers are the quarterbacks of the offensive line and have their own unique tricks that they can do. Longtime Vikings center Matt Birk explained some of the secrets to his success. "As a center, I can try to draw guys offside by doing little things on the line of scrimmage. It could be as subtle as wiggling a finger or squeezing the ball, anything to get that guy to jump offside. If I can get him to jump across the line into the neutral zone, I will just snap the ball and we will get a free play. I have even had quarterbacks do stuff like that as a decoy, where they open their hands up wide on a certain count as if they are preparing to get the snap. The defensive guys key in on all sorts of different things, and if you can get them thinking just a little bit about stuff like that, you will get lucky from time to time.

"Holding is something you can get away with from time to time, too. You know, you always hear about how they could call holding on every play with the offensive linemen. Well, I've got news for you. They could call it on every play with the defensive linemen, too. They are taught to hold just as much as we are. Let's get real. Sure, there is a certain amount of holding that is allowed, and you just have to deal with it. That is just a part of the game. If you are getting held by a guy and it becomes excessive, though, then you might have to sort of 'over-accentuate' it, or sell it, to make your case to the umpire. That is where a veteran with a few tricks up his sleeve can get away with certain things."

"As a snapper, you could glitch it or play little games with your hands to try to trick the defensive linemen to jump offside," added 12-year long snapper Mike Morris. "They are always looking at your fingertips to see when they turn white, so you could squeeze it prematurely and do things like that. You could tip your rear end down or flinch with your head a little bit or flex some muscles in your arm. All of those things have worked from time to time in getting guys to jump. And hey, if it's fourth-and-4 and you can get your team a first down by doing that, that is gamesmanship in my book. There are all sorts of things going on with the linemen down there that most fans are oblivious to."

Kickers

Last, but certainly not least, are the kickers. Kickers deserve a category of their own when it comes to cheating and skullduggery. Like a bad case of the hiccups, every kicker had his own remedy for what would make the ball go farther, and the stories of kickers tampering with balls are endless.

"I have seen kickers putting balls in clothes dryers, microwave ovens, you name it," revealed longtime NFL equipment manager Bob Monica. "They will try to manipulate it based on the weather conditions. They usually want to over inflate it, or make it fatter. Kickers love to kick fat balls, no pun intended. Ray Guy, the old Raiders punter, used to supposedly put helium in there, although I can't confirm it. That one is sort of an urban myth, but I wouldn't put it past him—he was a classic."

"My biggest trick was to go through the bag and find all of the old balls," said 15-year kicker Fred Cox. "You see, the old balls would fly much better than the new ones because they would get rounder. You can kick a soccer ball a lot farther than you can kick a football. Aerodynamically, round goes further because there is less wind drag. Other than that, I didn't do too much, other than battle my equipment manager who always wanted to take all of the balls out to the field a couple of hours before our games. He was real punctual and wanted to get his job done. Well I would argue with him all the time, telling him that by the time I got out there, the balls would be frozen rocks. Hey, it's cold up here in Minnesota!

"Beyond that, I was a pretty good actor out there, too, if I do say so myself. If a guy came rolling into me, I was going to do a pirouette, no question. Sure, I tried to draw penalties if I could. That was a tactic. A roughing penalty would result in a first down, and that was a big momentum-changer. The officials knew who the best actors were, though, and they took pride in

Greg Coleman, 12-Year Punter, on the Punter Code

"There was a code for punters, absolutely. We are in a vulnerable spot with our heads down and can get really hurt if we are cheap-shotted. When I was back there punting and the defenders were coming at me, the veterans would holler your name to let you know that they were coming, whereas a rookie who was trying to make the team, he would try to take your head off. Rookies are young, dumb, and excited. They didn't know the code so you cut them some slack, but only for a while. The veteran guys understand that this is a business, and they don't want to injure you. I had a great deal of respect for guys like [Bears linebacker] Mike Singletary, who pulled up on me many, many times over the years. He could have laid me out, too, but he didn't."

not being duped, so you had to sort of choose your battles out there. You couldn't go to the well very often with that stuff."

For the referees, it was all about trying to stay one step ahead of those oh-so-sneaky kickers. The rules eventually got changed because of all the tampering, which makes the officials now part-referee and part-security guard.

"Those guys would do all sorts of tricks with the balls, everything from microwaving them before games to even filling them with helium with the hopes that it would fly farther," said 25-year NFL referee Dick Hantak. "We used to get all kinds of complaints from opposing teams, and it eventually got so bad that we eventually decided to keep all of the balls quarantined until the games started. It got crazy. We would have the balls securely delivered to our hotels the day before the game so we could rub them down and prepare them. We would then take them to the games with us in bags, making sure no one on either team could get a hold of them and tamper with them."

According to 23-year NFL referee Jerry Markbreit, "The kickers used to try all sorts of little tricks to doctor those balls. They would put them in ovens to bake them; they would over-inflate them when it was warm out and under-inflate them when it was cold out; and there were even rumors of guys putting helium in them to get them to fly farther. They would do whatever they could to give themselves an advantage. It eventually got out of hand. So a few years ago, to prevent anybody from tampering with the balls, the league designated kicking balls or K-Balls that are just used for kicking. Believe it or not, the balls are inspected and then sent express to

Greg Coleman on Acting

"Sure, I would try to get roughing calls for my team. Look, the rule clearly states that you cannot touch the punter. So I did whatever I could to make contact—without getting caught, of course. I went down a lot in those days and still have the neck and back pains as a reminder. I got pretty good at hanging my foot out there though and having it 'accidentally' get trapped into opposing defender's body parts. I just called it follow-through. I remember getting hit 13 times in 1984, and out of those 13 times, we scored either a field goal or touchdown 11 times. That was significant. As a result, Bears coach Mike Ditka, who was on the league's competition committee, lobbied to get the rules changed to prevent punters or kickers from diving. Under the new rule, if the punter or kicker got called for diving, he would be called for a penalty. Proudly, that is what they call the 'Greg Coleman Rule.'

"In order to get the roughing call, you would have to sell it by lying there in agony a little bit, too. That did two things. First, it let the officials know that you had indeed been hit; and second, it let your team catch their breath. I knew that my quarterback was already upset about not converting the third down on the play before, so I would lay on the ground for a few minutes to let the offense catch their breath and regroup. You would sort of peek to see if you got the flag and then wait for the trainers to come out and check you out. The coaches loved little things like that, and your teammates did, too. And it would get you some quality TV time, too, for all the boys back home."

Greg Coleman on Teams Trying to Take Out the Punter

"Teams only carried only one punter or kicker, so if you could take him out, then that could be an effective tactic. Chicago and Tampa Bay were notorious for trying to take out punters. I tell you what, when you see 10 guys all screaming and yelling at you, and you know that they are all about to come at you full speed, wanting to kill you, that can be intimidating. They wanted to get your attention to throw off your rhythm and timing. The whole process would start during the pregame, too, when you were out on the field for warm-up. Guys would come by and start in on you, reminding you about what they were going to do to you later in the game. They would talk about your momma, too, which if you are a brother, you know is a no-no. They would just do anything to get in your head."

Greg Coleman on the Perils of Punt Coverage

"I always kept my head on a swivel, and I always knew where the last guy was. Every now and then you would get caught up in traffic, and that is when guys would find you and go after you. Generally though, you would hang back and use the sideline as your friend. Your job was to stay back as a safety and make sure nobody beat you. And unlike a lot of punters of my day, I was pretty athletic and wasn't afraid to get in there and make some tackles. I only had four runbacks for touchdowns in my entire 12-year career, which I was very proud of. Two of those were by Billy 'White Shoes' Johnson, and on one of them, when I was a rookie with Cleveland, he reached out of bounds to catch the ball and then brought it back in before taking it 87 yards to the house."

Greg Coleman on the Myth that Punters Weren't Tough

"Hey, we were tough…sometimes. I remember one time playing the Giants, I was the holder on a PAT and we had a botched snap. I looked up and saw a guy coming at me out of the corner of my eye. I thought he was going to go for my knees, so I grabbed his helmet and slammed it into the turf. Then when the guy stood up, I realized that it was none other than No. 56, Lawrence Taylor. I turned around for backup and realized that everybody had cleared out and were on their way back to the bench. I had two choices at that point: turn around and run, or try to talk my way out of it. I saw my life flash before my eyes at that point as I quickly thought about what I was possibly going to say to this beast to prevent him from killing me. I then remembered that we had played in a celebrity golf tournament together one time, so I frantically said 'L.T., if you hit my knees man, then we can't play golf!' Just then I immediately saw the death look leave his eyes and shift to a more agitated gaze. I literally saw him then unball his fists as he calmly backed off. Luckily for me, I had somehow escaped a serious butt-whooping. I learned my lesson, though—you just didn't do that kind of stuff to Hall of Famers like him."

the hotels of the officials, so that they can personally bring them to the stadiums under security. They are then washed and put into special bags by league-approved ball boys. Those guys then carry those things around like precious jewels, never letting them out of their sight."

"The kickers were always looking for an edge, so we had to put a stop to that a few years ago," added 22-year NFL referee Bernie Kukar. "They would harass the ball boys and try to finagle the best balls for field goals and so forth. They would put them in microwave ovens and cook them and do all sorts of crazy things to them. So now we have kicking balls that are labeled as K-Balls, which come to the officials in sealed boxes before the games. We won't accept any balls that don't come in sealed boxes from the league. We open them right there and check them. We then wash off the residue, check the air pressure, and we then carry them with us right on to the field. We check the game balls the same way, too. Even when the balls are out on the field, we leave them in a protected area with a guard next to them to make sure nobody will tamper with them. That is a big time fine if they get caught doing any of that crap, let me tell you. We also check the tees the kickers use to make sure they are not too high. We even check the kicker's shoes to make sure they don't have a steel toe in there or anything. These guys will try everything, so we have to try to stay one step ahead of them. The league doesn't want them affecting the integrity of the game. That is the bottom line."

Foreign Objects

Some players have been known to push the boundaries of cheating to the point where they actually employ using foreign objects as weapons against their opponents. For instance, they might overload the pads on their forearms by shoving pieces of wood underneath them, or they might reinforce plaster casts to make them into club-like battering rams. Guys will try almost anything if they think they can get away with it. Will Wolford, a 13-year offensive lineman, once bragged on a radio show that he used to line the padded gloves he wore in games with Kevlar that was given to him by a police officer.

Hall of Fame offensive tackle Bob Brown apparently persuaded the NFL to let him wear braces on his wrists. The braces, unbeknownst to the league, however, were made out of hard leather and could be slipped over his entire hand and knuckles. Brown would slip that thing into position once the ball was snapped and use it like a frying pan on opposing defensive tackles. His signature move was to take two steps back before driving his fists into the oncoming pass-rusher's chest. Dan Dierdorf used to refer to it as the heart shot, because it would nearly knock guys dead right on the spot. "Eventually, the league made Bob put rubber padding over those things," said former Raiders defensive end Ben Davidson. "But they still turned out to be pretty good weapons for him."

Raymond Chester, a former tight end with the Colts and Raiders, reminisced, "I can remember when defensive linemen taped hockey pucks and ashtrays to their hands to use in a head slap."

"I will never forget the time Conrad Dobler hurt his hand and got a cast put on it," recalled 11-year NFL defensive end Bob Lurtsema. "He doctored that damn thing up with about an 8-inch extension on it, and he would use it like a weapon. I remember going up against him one time during a game. He rammed that cast under my armpits until I was finally able to throw him off of me and knock him down. Then as I ran past him, he leg-whipped me, which was also illegal. Then to make matters worse, the announcer, Howard Cosell, says, 'What a great second effort by Conrad Dobler!' When I watched the film on that one, I just had to shake my head and laugh. Unbelievable."

Sometimes guys will just snap and lose it. Such was the case back in the early '70s when Steelers defensive end Mean Joe Greene allegedly tried to bring a foreign object into the game. According to *Sports Illustrated*, during a game with Minnesota, Greene was upset about being cheap-shotted. So between series he opened up the equipment manager's tool chest and pulled out a screwdriver. Whatever he intended to do with it remains a mystery because he had second thoughts and threw it down before re-entering the game.

Coaches Can Push the Envelope, Too

One of the ways coaches cheat is for them to manipulate injury reports in order to hide a star player's health status. Such was the case back in 1998 when the league fined Broncos coach Mike Shanahan $15,000 for failing to list quarterback John Elway on the injury report, despite the fact that Elway had ribs so sore they eventually prevented him from starting that week's game. A disgusted Shanahan responded by listing 22 players on the next week's report, 20 of whom were labeled "probable."

Another odd violation occurred in 2005 when the league levied a $25,000 fine against Atlanta Falcons coach Jim Mora for using his cell phone during a game against Tampa Bay. Mora had apparently used the phone to find out how a tie would affect Atlanta's playoff chances. Evidently he didn't get through to the right person because his team lost to the Bucs in overtime.

Other rule violations—that some construe as forms of cheating—are more overt. For instance, on January 2, 1996, during the Citrus Bowl game between the University of Tennessee and Ohio State, Buckeye coach John Cooper accused Tennessee of using "illegal cleats" in its 20–14 victory on a very muddy field. NCAA rules limited the length of the cleats to a half inch, but Cooper claimed that the Vols used illegal three-quarter-inch cleats. Just to prove his point, he even had an assistant run over to the opposing locker room and confiscate one of the player's shoes. Sure enough, they were three-quarter-inch cleats. Cooper demanded an explanation, to which the Vols said that the shoe company incorrectly shipped them the wrong cleats. The ones they got were supposed to go to a soccer team somewhere else but miraculously wound up in Knoxville instead. (One can only assume that the "phantom" soccer team in need of 20 pairs of size 16 cleats probably wasn't winning a whole lot of games.) Needless to say, the next year the NCAA instituted the Tennessee Rule, which states that any player wearing illegal cleats will serve a one-game suspension. Case closed.

While there are some gray areas when it comes to cheating, other areas are pretty black and white.

"I once knew of an assistant coach at the collegiate level who would go through the other team's locker room in search of playbooks," revealed longtime coach Tom Olivadotti. "He would then run off copies of whatever he could find and return it before anyone knew it was gone. Amazing. That is beyond cheating and just plain stealing in my eyes."

The Home-Field Advantage

Teams have long used the "home field" moniker to their advantage over the years. One of the most common forms of home cooking are deals with groundskeepers.

"I remember whenever we would play the Raiders, they were notorious for doing all sorts of shady stuff to get an advantage," said former Chiefs linebacker Bobby Bell. "We had a really fast team that year with a lot of quick players. One time we went out there to play and it hadn't rained in like six months, yet the field was soaking wet. I mean there was standing water out there. It was crazy. And they hadn't cut the grass in weeks, either. They wanted to slow us down and were going to do whatever little tricks that they could to do so."

One time in 2004 when the Patriots played host to the Colts and their high-octane offense in the AFC playoffs, the field at Gillette Stadium was left uncovered the week before the game, exposing it to the sleet and rain. The wet and icy field was perfect for New England's ground-attack game plan that day, and the Patriots beat the Colts, 20–3. When asked about why the stadium was left open to the elements after the game, Patriots coach Bill Belichick simply said, "My job is not to pull weeds."

Perhaps the most infamous story involving a member of the grounds crew took place on December 12, 1982, when Patriots coach Ron Meyer sent out Mark Henderson, an inmate on furlough, to start up a plow and clean off a spot in the middle of a snowy field so that their kicker, John Smith, could kick a game-winning field goal. Smith made the kick for a 3–0 Pats win, infuriating Miami coach Don Shula. "That guy [Henderson] was out on the field and finished before I knew what had happened," Shula said. "I talked with the official on our side of the field, and he said the same thing happened to him. The guy was on the field before they knew what he was doing. The Patriots will have to live with doing something like that."

Teams have used the weather to their advantage for years. For instance, the Raiders swore that the Steelers cut the edges off the Three Rivers Stadium tarp to leave the outside part of the field exposed to the rain in order to make the turf more slippery for the Raider receivers.

"George Allen had a system in RFK Stadium in Washington, D.C., where whenever the visiting team was about to try a field goal, he would have the doors open at the far end of the stadium, which would in turn let in a huge draft," recalled Steve Sabol, President of NFL Films. "We got that one when we had Marv Levy miked up for a game one time when he was coaching the Bills and they were playing the Redskins at RFK. He was reminiscing about being an assistant under Allen and laughing about how they would open those doors to get the wind stirring up in there. It was pretty hilarious."

Even today, teams in domed stadiums have been suspected of opening doors to let in sudden gusts of air that have affected kicks. Not to mention the fact that they pipe in artificial fan noise to make it harder for the visiting team to hear the play calls. To counter that, it was alleged that the 49ers used to have microphones in their offensive linemen's helmets for road games in domed stadiums so that they could hear the quarterback's snap count. It is an urban myth, of course.

Any time the home team can make the visitors uncomfortable, they will do so. Former Cleveland Browns owner Art Modell and Oakland Raiders owner Al Davis didn't much care for each other. When their teams met in a 1980 AFC divisional playoff game, Modell "forgot" to provide heated benches on the sidelines for the Raiders in frigid Municipal Stadium. Once Davis heard what was going on, he called his buddy Wellington Mara, the owner of the New York Giants, who loaned him some of his extras. Incidentally, Davis' Raiders won the game, 14–12.

Another owner who loved to rub it in was the Bears Papa Bear Halas, who once sold tickets to the visitor's benches at Wrigley Field. When the Vikings showed up for their game with the Bears, they found fans sitting on their team bench. Unwilling to move because they had paid good money to sit there, the Vikings players had to sit on the grass or on their helmets. The Bears were fined by the league, but Halas figured it was money well spent.

The Seahawks used to put the visitor's benches at Qwest Field on the east side of the stadium, right in the path of the wind and rain that often came off of Elliott Bay. Meanwhile the Seahawks players stayed warm and dry under a giant roof on the west side of the stadium.

Other teams were notorious for shutting off the hot water in the visitor's locker room showers. "I remember whenever we would play in Cleveland in that old raggedy Municipal Stadium, they would get back at us by turning off all the hot water," recalled wide receiver Ahmad Rashad. "It was brutal. We would play there, and immediately after the game guys would sprint to the locker room to get in the showers and get whatever hot water that was left in the pipes. It was nuts."

"If we were playing somewhere cold, like in Cincinnati, I would shut the heat off in our locker room and open all of the windows," admitted longtime coach Jerry Glanville. "That way, at halftime, the locker room would be nice and cold. You see, if the players came in at halftime and it was nice and warm, then there was no way in hell that they would want to go back out for the second half. As a result, they couldn't wait to get back out on the field where they could run around and warm up."

Maybe the best home-field advantage story of them all comes from legendary Colts defensive tackle Art Donovan. "We played the Giants in an exhibition game in Louisville one time back in 1954," Donovan recalled. "They had just built a brand-new stadium, and the first thing they had in there was a circus. Well, every time you took a step out there, you would wind up in a big pile of elephant crap. Even when you had to go down into your stance, it was everywhere. So we had some fun with it. As soon as the Giants offensive linemen got set and couldn't move, we'd throw globs of that stuff at them. It was hilarious."

6

The Referee Code

There is also a code between the officials and the players, as well as the coaches. The zebras have a tough job trying to officiate the action on the field while dealing with the politics and the drama that occur on the sidelines. While most officials are like Switzerland—completely neutral—players and coaches have found that they get further when they treat the officials with respect. Some players and coaches have even alleged that they actually studied the officials to the extent that they knew which ones would call certain penalties. In baseball, managers will come out of the dugout to scream at the umpires to swing the momentum of a game. In football, the coaches will also try to get after the referees. Sometimes they think it will work, and they will either get calls or non-calls. Who knows? One thing is certain—the fans love to see their coaches go off on the guys in the stripes.

"The key to having success with the officials was to always include yourself in the conversation," explained longtime coach Jerry Glanville. "For instance, if I would let them know what I thought about a questionable call they had made, I would start if off this way: 'The good news is you are not the worst guy in the stadium; there is one guy doing a worse job than you, and that is me.' You see, that keeps you from getting a penalty. You can then continue the conversation by letting him know why you think he is the worst guy that you've seen. I never went after a guy without including myself as a part of the problem. I would say, 'I thought you stunk today, but I think I am worse than you are.' That was a big part of the referee code with me. Believe it or not, I never got a penalty or thrown out or anything like that while I was coaching, and I was pretty damn vocal out there, trust me. And it's funny because NFL Films has things on tape of me that I can't show the public!

"Although I was never penalized, I came pretty close on several occasions. I was coaching during a game in San Francisco one time and was getting after an official over what I felt was a blown call. He finally just looked at me and said, 'If you speak one more word to me in this ear, you are getting 15 yards.' I just smiled and casually walked around to his other side and said calmly, 'Okay, well now I am over at this ear, and I still think you're horseshit.' He just walked away. It was beautiful.

"Another time I came out during a pregame warm-up and one of the officials who I had known came over. I said to him, 'Holy cow, you got a new pair of glasses. They look nice.' He smiled and said, 'I have been married 33 years, and my own wife doesn't even know that I have new glasses.' I said, 'The reason I know and your wife doesn't is because you screw me more than your wife!' He never dreamed about giving me a penalty for the rest of his life after that.

"You could antagonize the younger officials from time to time. Another time when I nearly got penalized came after I asked a rookie official, who I felt had just blown a call, 'Hey, do you know what the NFL stands for? It stands for Not For Long when you keep making those stupid calls!'

"One of the biggest compliments I ever got came one time after I was out of coaching in the NFL and a group of officials told me what they were always told by the league: 'He knows the rules better than anybody in the league, so he doesn't complain just to complain. He knows that there was an error or injustice that occurred.' In fact, the head of officials himself once told me that he would tell the younger guys in their training that if I was ever complaining to them about something, I was probably right. So I had a good reputation with them, and I took that as quite a compliment.

"You know the greatest line ever was by someone I greatly admired, legendary Bears coach Papa Bear Halas, who was asked one time why he would retire when he was still winning games. Old Papa Bear said, 'Last Sunday I was chasing an official down the sideline, only I wasn't gaining on him. I knew it was time to go right then and there.'"

For longtime coach Paul Wiggin, it was about knowing when to say when.

"I remember one time when I was coaching with the 49ers and we were playing the Rams at the Coliseum in L.A.," Wiggin said. "The Rams running back had this one particular play where he got knocked over but got up and went on to score a touchdown. Well, I saw the play and was sure that his knee had hit the ground, which should have ruled the play dead right then and there. I was irate about it because it was a big play. So at halftime I went over to give the ref an earful as we were walking off the field. I was screaming at him as we entered the tunnel and eventually he had had enough. He told me to shut up or he was going to throw a flag. I said a few more choice words and sure enough, he threw his flag up in the air. He then told me to inform the rest of the coaching staff in the locker room that we had been assessed a 15-yard penalty and were now going to be kicking off in the second half from the 25-yard line. After halftime we headed back out onto the field and gave the officials hell for what they were doing. They eventually gave in and overruled the call, which was good for me because I really had my tail between my legs on that one. Afterward, the league made a ruling that the officials could, in fact, call penalties anytime and anywhere during the game. It was even referred to as the Wiggin Rule from that point on, in my honor. What a legacy!"

Hall of Fame coach Bud Grant's approach was completely and totally unique.

"My philosophy on dealing with the officials was simple," Grant said. "I never talked to an official during a game. Ever. I didn't talk to them before the game, during the game, or after the game. I never acknowledged them. I had a lot more important things to do than to scream and holler at those guys. So I ignored them. I just didn't want to spend any time talking to them. It was a complete waste of time."

Maybe longtime coach Jerry Burns had it right all along.

"I have been guilty of raising hell with an official before, sure, even when I knew I was wrong," Burns confessed. "You do it to let them know that you are paying attention and that you care. You also do it with the hope that the next time around, that official will think twice about making a questionable call against your player. Maybe he doesn't want to deal with an angry coach or doesn't want to look bad on TV being yelled at. Or maybe if the ref thinks that you got a horseshit call, he may even it up the next time. You never know, you might just catch a break down the road. As a coach, we would like to believe that our actions on the sidelines—

what we say and what we do—have an influence on the game. You never know, but either way sometimes if just felt good to scream and holler at somebody."

Some players are skeptical of the officials and have their own conspiracy theories about what really goes on out there.

"I am completely convinced that officials know how they are going to officiate certain players going into every game," said six-year linebacker and assistant coach Pete Bercich. "For instance, take a guy like wide receiver Cris Carter. If he catches a ball and pushes off a guy in the process, they sort of let him slide a little bit because he is a well-respected Hall of Fame–type player. Same thing with a guy like Jerry Rice. But if you get a guy like Randy Moss, who squirts water on officials, they are never going to give him a call."

Yes, during a playoff game between the Vikings and Rams in 2000, Moss—despite catching nine passes for 188 yards and a pair of touchdowns—got upset at an official about what he felt was a blown pass-interference call late in the game. So he went over to the sidelines, grabbed a water bottle, and proceeded to soak the official. The commissioner's office responded sternly by fining him a whopping $40,000.

"Because the game is so fast, I mean lightning fast, I really believe that officials have a preconceived notion of who guys are and what they do," Bercich continued. "If they think they see what they see, then they will call it. That's why the coaches will meet with them ahead of time to let them know who they think is dirty, or who has been holding on the offensive line, or whatever. Randy shot himself in the foot when he disrespected the officials like that because they will now never give him a break. He won't get the same sort of respect calls that Carter and Rice did, no way. Those guys earned that respect though hard work and by not talking smack to the officials. There is a human element to the game that just can't be taken away."

As for the officials, they just try to take it all in stride. It is just another day's work for these guys, who also have actual day jobs on the side.

"There is a code between the officials and the players and coaches, absolutely," explained 23-year NFL referee Jerry Markbreit. "The secret to success in professional football is to establish a line of respect and trust from the coaches and players that you are officiating for. That stems from the way you treat them under the extreme pressure of the game. Coaches holler and scream at you all the time, but you can't take it personally. You have to treat them with respect, even though they are not treating you with respect. I just listened to them and tried to be fair. I didn't treat Don Shula any differently than I treated Tom Landry or Bill Cowher. Sometimes we had to tell them that we missed a call and that we are sorry, but we are human. They may not like that, but they can respect it.

"Occasionally you would get coaches who would try to intimidate you out there. I remember one time back in 1968 when I was officiating college football. I was working a Miami of Ohio game, and their coach at the time was Bo Schembechler. We had a rough day out there, with a lot of controversial calls. Anyway, after the game he ran out onto the field and let me have it. He said, 'What's your name?' So I told him, and he said, 'Jerry Markbreit, you're the worst goddamned referee I have ever seen. You will never work another game for me as long as you live!' Then off he went, just like that. Well, the following year he took over as the head coach at Michigan, and I was officiating their opening game of the season versus Vanderbilt. He came running out onto the field before the start of the game and he saw me. He looked at me and then came over toward me. He got to me and he said, 'I'm Bo Schembechler. Do I know you?' I said 'Of course you know me. I am Jerry Markbreit, the guy you said would never work for you again!' He just looked at me and said, 'Well, I guess I don't have very much influence around here then, do I?' We both just laughed like hell after that. It was the beginning of a long friendship.

"I remember officiating a college game one time between Michigan and Michigan State. Michigan State head coach Duffy Daugherty was very upset about something and signaled me to come over to talk to him during a timeout. He then proceeded to read me the riot act and just really went off on me. I just stood there and didn't say a word. He finally stopped and said, 'Aren't you going to say anything?' I said, 'Coach, you are upset, and I understand. I am not going to argue back with you. I have too much respect for you.' He just looked at me with a smile and said get the hell out of here. Every time I worked with him after that, he always tipped his hat to me. If coaches or players feel that you have lost control of the game, then the trust that they have in you to run that game properly goes out the window.

"Look, we try to get it right, and sometimes there are going to be some controversies. The most controversial call I have ever been involved with was the Holy Roller, which took place in the final moments of a game between Oakland and San Diego back in 1978."

For those who don't know about this one, here's the gist. With 10 seconds left in the game, the Raiders had the ball at the Chargers 14-yard line, trailing 20–14. Raiders quarterback Ken Stabler muffed the ball, and it rolled forward toward the San Diego goal line. Several players then fumbled and bumbled the ball into the end zone, where Raiders tight end Dave Casper eventually fell on it for the game-tying touchdown as time ran out. Oakland then went on to kick the extra point and won the game, 21–20.

"I ruled that Stabler had fumbled the ball," Markbreit said. "That was how I saw it. I know that there are fans out there who believe that it should have been called an incomplete pass, but I called it the way I saw it, and the league supported me. I have seen the thing a thousand times, and even to this day it is extremely difficult to tell. You try to get things right, and you just do your best. What can I say, we are human."

"Sure, there is a code between the players and the officials, without question," said 22-year NFL referee Bernie Kukar. "The players know that if they push things too far that they will get a 15-yard unsportsmanlike conduct penalty, which could kill a potentially game-winning drive. So they know just how far they can go without overstepping the boundaries. Sometimes if the younger guys don't know the boundaries, then we will remind them and tell them when enough is enough. If they push it too far, then they will learn a tough lesson. The vast majority of players are respectful toward the officials and understand that we have a job to do out there just like they do. I have been injured from players running me over, but it was never intentional. It is a tough job to be out there with all of those massive bodies running around and colliding, but it was a lot of fun, too."

One of the biggest fears the league has about its officials is that they will be tampered with by someone associated with illegal gambling. Various players were involved with gambling probes over the years, including Alex Karras and Paul Hornung, who were suspended for a year for gambling on NFL games, though it was never suggested that they shaved points. However, the refs have stayed clean through the years—a true testament to the league's commitment to play it straight.

"You would hear stories of the mob trying to get to guys and all of that other stuff from the old days, but that is all from a long, long time ago," Kukar added. "Today the league has a security department that is made up of ex-FBI agents. They don't mess around with any of that stuff. Each club has a security representative. The NFL even has people in Las Vegas and Atlantic City to monitor and watch out for suspicious activities. That is the thing that the league is the most careful with, the gambling aspect. We even have to pass security checks continuously. In order to get into the league, your background is checked out thoroughly. Periodically throughout the course of your career, they will do additional background work on you, just to make sure. If we as officials have any inclination that somebody is trying to approach us or is suspicious, we immediately call the league office. [For example,] I might go out for lunch with a buddy during the off-season, and maybe he will bring another buddy I don't know. Well, if I wanted to, I could call the league office and tell them who he was. They will do an immediate check on him and let me know if I need to stay away from that guy or not. So it was serious. They don't mess around. As a crew chief, I was responsible for six officials. If I had any inkling of anything going on, I was on the phone immediately. To my knowledge, in my 22 years in the league, no officials have ever been tampered with or anything like that. Unfortunately, it just happened in the NBA with Tim Donaghy, and that was a really big deal. The NFL is always extremely concerned about that sort of thing and goes to extreme measures to make sure it never happens."

"One of the things that NFL officials can be most proud of is that there has never been a hint of suspicion that any of us have been involved in anything like that," said 25-year referee Dick Hantak. "We are held to an extremely high standard and pride ourselves in having a lot of integrity."

"One of our perks as NFL officials was that we got to fly first class," explained longtime NFL field judge Dick Dolack. "I remember one time being on a flight to Chicago along with seven other officials. We were all up in first class, and unbeknownst to us, there was an NFL security agent sitting up there with us. I don't know if he was there to protect us or to keep an eye on us. Either way, he was there. You see, the league was always concerned about us traveling in large numbers and about the possibility of a shady character who might try to sit with us to listen in on our conversations. Or worse yet, I am sure they were always concerned about the possibility of someone who might try to bribe one of us, maybe a bookie or somebody like that. Thank goodness none of that stuff ever happened when I was around, but the league wanted to make sure that we got to where we were going without any problems."

7

The Training Camp Code

Each summer, veteran players and undrafted rookie free agents descend upon small towns throughout the Midwest and East Coast to gather for the annual rite of passage otherwise known as training camp. Once there, teams will prepare for the ensuing season by whipping their boys into shape. Long, hot, two-a-day practices are punctuated with autograph sessions, team meals, film study, and then lights out. The players usually stay in college dormitories and live a no-frills existence for the roughly one month of hardcore learning and team bonding. The older players know the drill, but the newbies often get into trouble. They don't know the ropes and want to make a name for themselves, so they will try to get noticed by the coaches by doing anything they can. For them, it is fight or flight in the truest sense. They will say and do just about anything to make that team. As a result, tensions will escalate in camp between the youngsters and the grizzled vets, which usually leads to some skirmishes or even some good old-fashioned brawls. Bad blood is also exposed in camp between the older players who are battling for positions on the depth chart. Or maybe so-and-so used to date so-and-so's girl. Things like that tend to make for good fodder, too. Eventually the long, hot, monotonous days in camp start to pile up, and tempers inevitably flare.

"You're hot and tired and somebody just pushed a little bit extra on the pile, and now you want to get a little get-back, so you push back," said Eagles linebacker Omar Gaither. "At that point, it's blah-blah-blah in somebody's face, and then everybody starts pushing. Later on, you laugh about it in the locker room."

"I love fights, personally," said Browns receiver Braylon Edwards. "I think they serve a purpose. When fights happen, it shows you that the guys there aren't just going through the motions. When you've got guys going after it, when they're intense, when guys are trying to get better on every play, you get fights. I like those fights."

Training camp fights are usually more pushing and shoving than anything else, but that stuff also contributes to team-building and camaraderie.

"You want guys to be aggressive," said former Browns head coach Romeo Crennel. "You want them to be physical. And when it's hot outside like that, sometimes tempers flare. As long as it doesn't get out of hand, sure, it can be useful. It changes the monotony of practice. It picks everybody up, gets everybody excited, and they're talking and it generates some energy. You can tell when guys are fighting or just pushing and shoving. When they're fighting, then you need to try and get in there because that's when someone swings and breaks a bone in a hand or something like that."

"We had some good fights at the Giants because you had big egos and competitive guys," Crennel added. "But there are all different ways they can start. I think sometimes early in camp there might be a bit player starting a fight with a veteran because he's trying to get noticed by the coaches. But then as things go along in camp, it can be one good player against the next good player. I've even seen two best friends go at it."

"I've seen a couple punches here or there," said Browns receiver Donte' Stallworth. "But it's usually nothing personal. It's the competitiveness in everyone. It usually happens around now, when you're in that sixth, seventh, or eighth day of camp, after that first week. You're just tired of seeing each other, and you're not able to beat up on another team yet. That's when tempers flare. The only negative that can come out of those is if someone gets hurt. But otherwise they're definitely good because at the end of the day we're all teammates and we're all going to be in the locker room laughing and joking about the fight right after that. It's just a little spark, and sometimes you need that to keep everybody's attention."

Sometimes tensions can mount and guys will snap, causing serious injury. Such was the case in 2003 when Raiders linebacker Bill Romanowski punched teammate Marcus Williams in the face during training camp, shattering his eye socket. Williams' playing career ended shortly thereafter, and Romanowski agreed to pay a $415,000 settlement two years later.

Another thing that the older players don't like is when the hotshot rookies don't report to camp on time. In fact, they have their own sort of vigilante justice for just that sort of thing.

"If a guy was holding out in training camp for all the wrong reasons, we as veterans would do little things to remind him that the game was bigger than he was," said 14-year defensive tackle John Randle. "Then maybe when he finally reported, to punish him a little bit we might tell him the wrong plays when he came into a preseason game. He would be lost as hell out there and then get screamed at by the coaches. It's pretty funny. Little things like that could be used to send powerful messages."

One of the hallmarks of training camp is rookie hazing, where the older players will initiate the rookies by having them do all sorts of silly and ridiculous things. The goal was to embarrass or humiliate them, but it was all in good fun. Most guys got off pretty easy.

"I have heard a lot of horror stories, but when I was a rookie with Green Bay, we didn't get it too bad," said eight-year running back Vince Workman. "They used to make the rookies sing during training camp, but not their college fight songs. It had to be some other song. Well, I must not have been too bad because they kept asking me to get up and sing. There was other little hazing stuff they would do though, like having to carry a veteran's shoulder pads and helmet to practice—stuff like that. Or maybe each rookie would have to buy his position teammates dinner. We also had to ride little kids' bikes to practices during training camp, which was fun. It was a tradition and we had fun with it, it wasn't mean-spirited or anything like that. There were a couple of butt-holes on our team who enjoyed terrorizing the rookies, but once Mike Holmgren came in as the head coach in 1992, all that stuff was outlawed."

For others, it might have been a little tougher.

"We used to make our rookies play 'Cardinal Puff,' which was a drinking game that we would play in training camp," said 10-year guard Conrad Dobler. "We would go out to a local bar and line up tequila shots. The rookies would then have to repeat things, sort of like the game Simon Says. If they screwed up, they would have to take a shot. Well, we had the bartender in on the fix, so us veterans were actually drinking water instead of tequila. Sure enough, we would get these guys good and liquored up, and then the next morning at practice they would be puking all over the place. It was pretty hilarious."

"I remember when I was a rookie, guys would get ambushed in the middle of the night and get their heads shaved," recalled 12-year center Matt Birk. "Too many guys looked good bald though, so then they started shaving just clumps of hair out. The rule was that you had to go to at least one practice like that before you could shave it all off and make it look normal. That eventually evolved to them getting their eyebrows shaved, which really started freaking guys out."

"Beyond taping them to goalposts and dumping water under their doors at training camp, my favorite was to take their clothes during a practice late in the season and soak them in water and then letting them freeze all day outside in the snow," said 14-year defensive tackle John Randle. "That was awesome. They would get back after practice and have to thaw everything out. It was pretty funny."

"We used to love getting guys with paintball guns during training camp," added 10-year defensive tackle Keith Millard. "We would have all-out wars. It was crazy. We would give the rookies a pistol with one clip, then give them two minutes to go hide in the dorm. We would then go after them with these machine guns and just blast them. Guys would wear their hunting camouflage and really get into it. I remember one rookie who really got it bad. He got ambushed and just got pelted. We saw him the next day in the showers, and it looked like he had chicken pox from all the bruises and welts. I felt really bad for him. It had to have been painful. I think it all sort of ended after that. We kind of got out of hand. It was fun though and nothing malicious or anything."

The fun with training camp was that you never knew how those rookies would ultimately turn out.

"I remember back in training camp we had a guy, Jim Lindsey, who showed up as a rookie, and then every year after, with what he called an 'Arkansas suitcase,'" explained Vikings tight end Stu Voigt. "It consisted of a couple pairs of underwear, a pair of shorts, a pair of jeans, and a couple tee shirts, all wrapped up in a towel. That was it. He would just show up with that towel under his arm, all ready to go. It was hilarious. We didn't know what to think of him. Well, wouldn't you know it? Nowadays he is a really successful businessman and even has his own jet. So you never know. It's like they say, you can't always judge a book by its cover."

8

The Locker Room Code

There is a sign that hangs on most NFL locker rooms, and it goes something like this: "What you see in here; what you say in here; what you hear in here...stays in here!" It's like Vegas, baby—you don't kiss and tell when it comes to matters discussed in this most sacred of football shrines. If a player hears something and mentions it during pillow talk with his wife or girlfriend and it gets out as a juicy rumor, he could get seriously reprimanded and worse yet, even banished. Players are not very forgiving when it comes to guys throwing them under the bus and will blackball or alienate players who do so in a heartbeat. With the scrutiny that the media has on the players these days, the locker room is the last bastion of free speech that the players enjoy. Even the media understands this strict off-the-record code about things that they see and hear in the locker room. The same goes for reporters, too. If they break that code, then they too will be disciplined. Worse yet, the reporter will be ostracized by the players, who will unite to make sure nobody gives that guy or gal an interview ever again.

An extension of the locker room code deals with players talking badly about other players to the media. Occasionally coaches will do that, but it is usually a calculated move in order to call someone out or stir up a premeditated controversy. The players know that if they call out an opposing player in the media for some reason, the story will invariably become bulletin-board material in that player's locker room. It will then serve as a motivating factor in that team wanting to get revenge on the guy who called him out. The same is true for players calling out teammates in the media, as well. When stuff like that happens, it usually only fuels the impending media firestorm, which can turn into a viral soap opera.

A recent example of this occurred in 2009 when Philadelphia quarterback Donovan McNabb hinted on a radio interview that the Eagles' defense was to blame for the NFC championship loss in Arizona. McNabb was asked why his team could not score another touchdown after the Cardinals took a 32–25 lead.

"We were up 25–24," McNabb said. "[The Cardinals] drove down 72 yards by running the ball probably what, eight times? And it reminded me so much of [the NFC Championship Game in] St. Louis where, coming back in that second half, they ran the ball nine times with Marshall Faulk to keep our offense off the field because they were terrified of us going back out and scoring more points."

"Some people will say it's not a big deal, but it is," said former Eagles defensive end Hugh Douglas. "When you break that team code, it hits home. When you call someone your teammate, you're calling him your brother. Be loyal to your teammates. It's easy to point fingers. Brian Dawkins is a team player. He would never do that.

"I know Donovan. I respect Donovan. In his mind, he didn't say anything wrong," Douglas added. "But a leader thinks before he speaks. That would never come out of a leader's mouth. Every year, Donovan says something that's inflammatory, then he doesn't explain himself. Explain yourself. When you alienate people who have your back, I need to understand why. I need to understand how he thinks. Right now, I don't."

Another example occurred in 2007 when former Giants running back Tiki Barber made some disparaging remarks about his former teammate, quarterback Eli Manning, on the *Today Show*.

"I think back to the comments Tiki said, and I didn't think that was too cool," said former Packers running back Darrell Thompson. "You don't want to go back and blast your old teammates and the way they play. That is not cool at all; it really isn't. That is not the way guys want to be known or remembered. Even though Tiki could probably care less, I still think some things are better left alone. There is enough other stuff out there to talk about; it is not necessary to talk about your old teammates that way. I mean, Tiki doesn't need to go after people. He is a good speaker, he is handsome, he is a nice guy, and he is well liked. It is not like he is some up-and-coming journalist who needs to talk about his former quarterback in order to get ratings. He could've said the things he said, but he could've worded it differently so he didn't throw him under the bus. He kind of went at him, and that was really disappointing. Eli played the game and he was your teammate, so you don't need to do that stuff, especially on a huge TV show like that."

Every player has his own take on what the locker-room code means to him.

"You can't talk, no way," said Pete Bercich, six-year NFL linebacker and coach. "What goes on in the locker room stays in the locker room. You don't talk about stuff with wives, either. If you say something about someone or about an incident to your wife, and then they tell the ladies club, it is all over. The wives always talk; that is what they do. Once rumors or innuendos get around and it comes back to you, you are screwed. There is some crazy stuff that goes on in professional sports, and we are talking about stuff that can ruin families. So even if you are out and you see somebody doing something they shouldn't be doing, you just keep your mouth shut. You can talk about it with other guys in the locker room, but you cannot tell your wife or girlfriend or you will be completely ostracized by your teammates. Other teams find out about that stuff, too, and nobody wants those guys around because they are perceived as cancers for your locker room. So it is a bigger deal than people think. It can cost a guy his career. It really can."

Bercich continued, "The locker room is one of the most unique places on the planet. You don't care what religion the guy sitting next to you is, what color he is, or what he does off the field. All you care about is the fact that on game day you can trust him to have your back and to help your team win. That is all we care about. And that is why players look past all of the personal problems that they may have. People wonder how we can support a guy who beats up his wife or does drugs or whatever. Nobody gives a shit in the locker room. That is just how it is. They don't care. All they care about is winning. If the guy is a great teammate and covers your ass, you support him. You don't care what he does when he leaves the locker room. Sure, you want your teammates to be happy and all of that, but winning is what it is all about at this level. And the sad thing is the better the player you are, the more baggage you can have that other people will accept. Case in point is Randy Moss. He is a hell of a player, and nobody can deny that. That may sound cold, but it is the truth."

Things can get even more dicey when one of your teammates is romantically involved with a celebrity. If the tabloid paparazzi eventually come out, it can be a huge distraction to the entire team.

"This code was put to the test the most for our team back in the early '90s when the whole O.J. [Simpson] trial was going on," said 13-year offensive tackle John Alt. "Marcus Allen was with the Chiefs in those days, and he had allegedly been romantically linked to Nicole Brown Simpson. So that was certainly an interesting time for all of us. He couldn't even be on the bus with us at one point because the feds were going to subpoena him for the trial. Well, he obviously wanted no part of that stuff, so he hid out. He would literally come to the game and then take off immediately afterward through a back door. They never got a chance to get him. He would even fly out separately from the whole team to our games. It was crazy. Well with him gone, the media wanted to talk to all of us about it, and we couldn't say a word. Some guys even got pressured to talk, but that is what the code is all about. You just can't throw a teammate under the bus."

Today's locker rooms are vastly different from those a few decades ago, that much is for certain.

"Things change," remarked 11-year tight end Stu Voigt. "In my day, most of the guys smoked and drank coffee right before games. They would take bennies or pep pills, too. There were no health drinks, no supplements,

---

Dan Dierdorf, 13-Year NFL Offensive Tackle, on the Locker Room Code

"We severely adhered to the clubhouse code, absolutely. That sign, 'What you see in here, what you say in here, what you hear in here...stays in here' was a way of life for us. I believed in that very, very strongly. If you broke that code, that was very serious."

no carbohydrate diets, nothing. We would eat two or three donuts for breakfast on practice days, and that was considered healthy. We would wash that down with a couple of Tom Moore soda pops, either orange, cherry, or grape flavor. The pregame meal for game day then was always steak and eggs with dry toast. I remember they told us we couldn't have any butter on our toast—as if that made a difference with all of the other stuff. Who knew? I mean, we were eating a big New York strip steak at about 9:00 AM, just a few hours before a game at noon. Hard to believe, but that was the way it was. It was a totally different era.

"I remember our training facilities, too, back when we used to practice at old Midway Stadium in St. Paul. We had this tiny little locker room. It was a real dump. Bud [Grant] hated smoking and wouldn't allow it in the locker room, so guys would go back and smoke in this little bathroom. It had two urinals, two toilets, and about 10 shower heads for our entire team. You would go back there, and you would see guys in their full uniforms, even with their helmets on, smoking and drinking coffee in there before practices. It was a sight to see, just incredible.

"The veterans ran the locker room in those days, too. It wasn't Bud's locker room, it was the older guys, the team leaders: Jim Marshall, Grady Alderman, and Mick Tingelhoff. They set the tone for what went on in practice and everything else. They enforced the dress code, they would tell you what time to get on the bus, and they might even fine guys if they felt it was necessary. If there was a problem, like if a guy was late to practice or something, then Bud would just tell one of those guys and they would deal with him. Even during games, if a young guy started jawing with a referee, a veteran would drag him away. If somebody got a 15-yard unsportsmanlike conduct penalty, we were all going to catch hell for it. Lastly, we weren't allowed to talk to the guys on the other team after the game or anything like that. There was no visiting before the game during warm-ups or any other fraternizing allowed. Bud had a rule about that stuff and wouldn't tolerate it. There was no team prayer afterward or walking off the field hand in hand like you see today. No way. So that was how it was in those days. That was the code."

Back in the day, coaches would let the players have long leashes. With all of the media scrutiny these days, things are much different.

"The rule was that if a player lied, we all swore to it," said 11-year defensive end Bob Lurtsema. "Everything had to stay in there, that was just the way it was. Today it is a lot different, with all of the media and whatnot. I feel sorry for the guys today. I really do. They have no private life. Between cell-phone cameras and blogs, they can't do anything without being seen or heard. The locker room is a sanctuary for these guys. They need to have a place where they can get away and come down from the emotional highs and lows of the game. It is a place that needs to be protected. It is sacred.

"You know, when I was with the Vikings, Bud Grant was great at dealing with a lot of that stuff. Because he was a former player and understood the pressures from the media, he used to be able to deflect stuff away from the players and onto himself from time to time. I mean, if there was some gossip or juicy story about a player, Bud would distract all of the media and steer them toward him for something totally unexpected. He didn't talk very much, so if he had something to say, it was newsworthy. Maybe he would make up some bullshit story about how the team was going to incorporate some new offensive strategy that meant passing 35 percent of the time, something really bizarre that would focus all of their attention on that versus what was really going on in the locker room. Bud could control the media in his own way without them really even knowing it. That was why the players loved Bud—he was the consummate players' coach, and he treated them like men. Even when we were down in training camp and we would sneak out at night to drink some brewskis, he didn't care. As long as we didn't get into trouble, he was fine with it. In fact, he liked the fact that we were bonding as teammates and building that team chemistry together. He trusted us, and as a result, he earned our respect. He pushed us and he was tough on us, but we loved him."

The older players take great pride in the fact that back in their days, things were run by the players, not the coaches or even the media.

"The locker room belonged to the players," said quarterback Joe Theismann. "Period. I played for coach Joe Gibbs in Washington for six years, and I don't think I ever saw him come to our locker room but maybe four times during that time. Any strong, good football team will be that way. It is controlled by the players."

And just like rookie hazing, the locker room is a safe haven for pranksters and practical jokers.

"It was a safe haven and our home away from home," said 12-year long snapper Mike Morris. "My favorite thing about the locker room was all the pranks we would pull. I loved stealing guys' keys and moving their trucks during practice. We would hide them on people and just mess with them. We would shut off all the lights and have wars with footballs. We would soak guys' clothes in five-gallon buckets of water and let them freeze outside during practice. We would put itching powder in guys' underwear, throw stinkbombs in the reporter's media room, and just raise holy hell in there. Tony Dungy once gave me a master key for every dorm room at our training camp. I assembled a group of henchmen, and we absolutely terrorized the rookies. It was beautiful.

"One time we handcuffed Dave Huffman to a locker. Well, he eventually got the key and got loose while we were out at practice. He then proceeded to take everyone's clothes and put them into one of the cold whirlpool tubs. We came in after practice and there was all of our stuff, floating, soaking wet. He didn't just do clothes either, he threw in watches, rings, wallets, you name it. He got us back pretty good on that one. We had to give it to him.

"My favorite thing to do was to tape guys up and leave them for dead. We had a saying: 'There was no guy too big to be taped.' It didn't matter how big you were, how much money you were making, or anything else. We were going to hunt you down and tape you up, that was the law. Well, David Dixon nearly killed five guys when we tried to tape him. He was so damn big; he was a beast. He was claustrophobic and absolutely terrified of being taped up, which did not bode well for us. We ambushed him one night after practice while he was getting dressed, and it got ugly. It was myself, Todd Steussie, Randall McDaniel, and Jeff Christy—all giant slug linemen. We all piled on him, and he went down like a redwood. He was madder than hell, just pounding on us like a crazed madman. We were all terrified that he was going to kill us. It was like wrestling an alligator in one of those old *Mutual of Omaha* TV shows. It was nuts. He stood up from being flat on the ground with me on his back, that was how pissed he was. We eventually got his ankles taped and then decided that we had

Sean Payton, Longtime NFL Coach, on the Locker Room Code

"When a player talks about another player's contract, that is out of line and really a big part of the code in my opinion."

better quit while we were ahead. We figured that was as much tape as big Dave could handle and crossed him off the list.

"Another time Pete Bercich and I moved Matt Birk's entire locker out to the 50-yard line of our practice field. We reassembled it out there and just sat there on the stools drinking coffee waiting for him to show up. It was like 20 below zero that day, too; just colder than hell. Sure enough, he came lumbering over just pissed as hell. We got the hell out of there before he could kill us both. I miss those days. You could truly digress to being a kid. It was wonderful, just pure fun."

"Locker-room antics are a part of life in the NFL," added former Cardinals guard Conrad Dobler. "We were constantly pulling pranks of one sort or another on each other—things like filling jockstraps with heating salve, nailing shoes to the floor, swapping helmets, throwing ice water at guys in the sauna, changing shower settings when guys had shampoo in their eyes, wrapping a lower-level assistant coach in athletic tape, stuffing guys' equipment into plastic garbage bags so they thought they'd been cut when they came to work in the morning, giving a rookie a false message that the head coach wanted to see him and to bring his playbook. The worst thing that ever happened to me was the time I was going to do a TV interview with the lovely Phyllis George for the CBS *NFL Today* show. I even bought a new pair of Levis for the occasion. Finally, after primping and getting ready after practice one day, I went to put on my new jeans...my new one-legged Levis! Man, I was really pissed. Dan Dierdorf and Jackie Smith were the culprits. I had to hand it to them though—that was pretty good."

Pranking your teammates was one thing, but to go out and get the opposition as well? That took big balls.

"Oilers defensive end Andy Dorris was a great prankster," said seven-year linebacker Bob Stein. "He and his buddy, Steve Baumgartner, went to a pharmacist one time years ago and got some empty capsules. They then went to a butcher and got a bunch of that blue dye that they use to stamp meat and filled the capsules with it. They snuck into the Houston Astrodome at about six in the morning before a game one day against Pittsburgh and unscrewed the shower heads in the visitors' locker room. Sure enough, after the game the players hit the showers, and after a few minutes the capsules would melt from the hot water and start coming out. Well, this dye was like semi-permanent, and these guys started turning blue. It was a classic. They went undetected for a long, long time until finally coming clean years later."

Lastly, racism has always been a part of the clubhouse code, to some extent. The locker room is a mixing bowl of all sorts of ethnicities and characters from all walks of life. If players can't get along in there, then there is little hope for them getting along on the field. Personal problems that players have with one another can be discussed openly in the locker room and are expected to be resolved, one way or another. If a player can't get along and play nice, then he will usually either be shipped off somewhere else or cut. A cancerous player can destroy team chemistry and divide a team, so the bad apples are weeded out pretty quickly.

One guy who dealt with more than his fair share of racism was defensive back Johnny Sample, a self-proclaimed trash-talker and cheap-shotter who played in the '50s and '60s with the Baltimore Colts, Steelers, Redskins, and Jets. Sample literally wrote the book on dirty play in 1970 when he penned his autobiography, *Confessions of a Dirty Ballplayer*. In it, Sample made it clear that the objective of dirty play is "to get a good guy, maybe a player of greater talent than your own, to blow a fuse and retaliate, with the good guy getting the penalty and maybe even removed from the game." Sample also spoke out about the treatment of blacks in the NFL, something for which he believed he was blackballed.

Blacks, whites, Asians, Latinos, and Polynesians all come together in the locker room, as do Christians, Jews, and Muslims. The one minority that has been ostracized, however, are homosexuals. Esera Tuaolo, a Samoan from Hawaii, played defensive tackle for nine years in the NFL with Green Bay, Minnesota, Jacksonville, Atlanta, and Carolina. In 2007, Tuaolo came out in his book *Alone in the Trenches*, in which he revealed many of the struggles he faced in keeping his secret of being gay.

"During my nine years in the NFL, I lived that close to the edge of destruction," Tuaolo wrote. "My success tormented me. The better I did, the more exposure I received. The more exposure, the greater the chance of someone discovering my secret. A secret that a man who plays the most macho of team sports is not supposed to have. The stress nearly killed me.

"The dream to succeed in the NFL and achieve all that football had to offer was at times a nightmare," he continued. "I struggled to survive the combative, macho world dominated by a culture that despised who I really am. Had opponents and teammates known I was gay, they would

Matt Birk, 12-Year Center, on the Locker Room Code

"You just don't talk publicly about one of your teammates and expose them or call them out on something. You just don't do that. This is a respect thing. I have been outspoken on certain matters with the media, but I am very careful about what I will and won't say publicly. Sometimes veterans will call out the entire team when things are down, as a sort of way to rally the troops, but they won't call out individuals unless they are doing things that might somehow affect the entire squad. I mean, even though this is a game, it is also a business. Guys make their livings as football players, and if one guy is doing something detrimental to the team, then that is a different story.

"I remember a few years ago when we had the whole Love Boat scandal here in Minnesota. As a veteran, I was pretty vocal about the entire situation and took some heat from a few of my teammates for commenting publicly to the media about it. The thing that was so frustrating about that whole situation was that it was all the guys who weren't there that night who were having to sit there and face the music. That wasn't fair in my eyes. I felt like the media was coming down on the entire team, when in reality it was just a handful of guys who were involved with it. You know, scandals like that can really have an adverse effect on your entire organization, so you just hope that your teammates will make the right choices in those situations. Look, I don't preach to guys or tell them what to do. That is not my place. We all have our own values and ethics. I just stressed the concept of putting the team first."

have mocked me the way I heard them ridicule others with sexual slurs. More than likely—as several former teammates admitted—they would have tried to injure me so that they would not have been viewed as guilty by association. In other words, they would have taken me out so that their own masculinity would not be questioned for playing alongside a sissy. It's rough down in the trenches, where linemen weighing more than 300 pounds hurl themselves at one another in brutal hand-to-hand combat, but it is nothing compared to the pain I kept buried inside so I could play out my dream."

Only one of three former NFL players to ever come out of the closet, Tuaolo's secret crippled him, leading him to drink excessively and even contemplate suicide. He led a double life that deeply depressed him, but he now looks back upon his time in the NFL with new perspective.

"Being a gay man in the National Football League was tough," Tuaolo revealed. "The code is an important thing. We all lived by it. Even when my book came out, I was careful not to break that code of silence, even though I had long since left the game. I didn't want to name names or throw anybody under the bus. I wanted to be respectful. That was tough. The locker room was a difficult place for me to be. On one hand, it is a sanctuary for the players. There are no repercussions in the locker room. None whatsoever. It is a safe zone where players can do and say whatever they want to. On the other hand, there were many times where I felt terribly uncomfortable in there. There were things that were said and that were done with regard to homosexuality that really upset me and offended me.

"As a minority player, I saw my share of racism during my time in the league. Sure. It was in the locker room, too, but the N-word was only thrown around among the brothers. Nobody else dared go there; that was off limits. If someone had a problem with black people, then it would be discussed and resolved. Being gay though, everybody talked about that in a derogatory way, only I couldn't say a word. You see, teams are all about chemistry, and if you have people who are unaccepting and ignorant, then that can be a real distraction for the team. That was why it was so difficult for me because I could never talk to anybody about my true feelings in there. You just didn't want to ruffle any feathers in there and make waves. You didn't want to get that label. So I laid low and kept my secret hidden. For me, this was my career, my livelihood, so I wasn't about to rock the boat and get blackballed. I had to keep quiet. I just kept up the façade and did whatever I had to do with the guys. I dated girls, went to strip clubs, and talked the talk. It was a big lie. I had to make sure that nobody ever found out my secret.

"I just bit my tongue whenever I heard things being said about gay people. I felt embarrassed and ashamed that I didn't say anything, either. That was tough. I felt that they were talking about me, but I knew that they weren't. They were just talking. I mean that is the one minority you can pick on in the locker room, homosexuals, because they know that nobody in there is gay. Or so they think. Even if they are though, like myself, they are in the closet and don't talk about it. Either way, it was very difficult. It wasn't even 'Don't ask, don't tell,' it was just don't anything. In the NFL, the mentality is that there aren't any gay people. They were very ignorant. There can't be any gay players in the NFL, right? If they only knew."

9

Drugs and Steroids

Perhaps an extension of the locker-room code, the NFL has another code that deals with drugs and steroids. The reason the two codes are linked is because the same veil of privacy and secrecy shrouds both topics. There has always been a don't ask, don't tell policy when it comes to drugs and steroids in football, which has changed in recent years for the better. In looking at the genesis of the problem, we have to go back decades. Long before the days of performance-enhancing steroids, many players in the 1960s and '70s used to take what were known as greenies or bennies, which were euphemisms for amphetamines or speed. Nobody thought that they were bad for you, either. In fact, a lot of team trainers used to have bowls of them sitting out before practices and games for the players to take at their leisure.

"Players have always been on the lookout for an edge," said Bud Grant, six-year wide receiver and longtime coach. "I remember when I played in the NBA with the Minneapolis Lakers back in the late '40s and seeing George Mikan, a future Hall of Famer, guzzle four or five bottles of orange pop during halftime. I couldn't believe my eyes. I thought that was almost sacrilegious when I first saw that, but I later learned that he felt that it gave him an advantage. Not only did he get rehydrated, but the sugar gave him a boost, as well. Other guys smoked cigarettes at halftime. Anyway, a few years later when I jumped over to playing in the NFL, I remember my first game with the Eagles. I came in to the locker room at halftime, and there were team doctors there to meet us, handing out bennies or amphetamines.

I thought, 'What in the world are those?' and my teammates proceeded to tell me that they would give me a boost for the second half. Well, I didn't think that I needed that sort of thing, so I stayed away from them. A lot of guys took them though, and in those days it wasn't a big secret. Nobody really knew a lot about that stuff, drugs, in those days. I mean, as far as I was concerned, Coke came in a red can."

Nobody really knew what the downside of taking speed was at the time. They just knew that the players got a lot of extra pep from taking them. Sometimes, however, if a guy took too many, he could snap. Former Chiefs linebacker Bob Stein, who played back in the 1960s and '70s, recalled one such incident.

"A lot of guys took amphetamines in my era," Stein explained. "Hell, the trainers handed them out to us like candy, and nobody really knew what the hell was in them. Guys would take them and then get so jacked up that they wouldn't be able to sleep for days. It was crazy. One time we were playing Denver, and they had this big nose tackle by the name of Dave. I don't want to mention his last name. Anyway, we all came to the line for the first play of the game and he looked like a madman. He had white shit foaming all over his mouth, his eyes were bugging out, and he looked like he was going to explode. Our center was wondering what this guy was up to and sure enough, before he could even snap the ball, Dave jumped offside and knocked out one of our center's teeth. Our center, stunned, cocked his arm back to punch him in retaliation. Just then, before he could get the punch off, Dave screamed, 'I'm sorry, I didn't mean it! I overmedicated this morning!' It was the craziest thing I had ever seen. We all just had to laugh."

While the topic of steroids has become very prevalent during the new millennium, especially in baseball, steroids have actually been around for quite some time. Stein remembered the first time he ever saw them and about the immediate pressure he felt to take them.

"I first got introduced to steroids when I was in high school in 1965 just before I was about to play college football," Stein said. "A bunch of guys were talking about this new drug, Dianabol, that they said would make you big and strong. Some of my teammates were taking it and I didn't want to fell left out, so I took some pills home with me. Then, in a rare moment of clarity, I decided to call my uncle Jules, who was a physician, to ask him about it. He told me all about steroids and about

Conrad Dobler, 10-Year Guard, on Steroids

"I never took any. Ever. Steroids have been around for a long, long time though. How do we know who did them going back 50 or 100 years? We don't. So instead of calling this the 'steroid era,' I prefer to call this the 'steroid-testing era.' However, my roommate, Bob Young, certainly took massive amounts of them. He was the strongest man in the NFL, no question. A lot of guys took them in my day, but not nearly to the extent that these guys do today. These guys today are massive giants. I am 285 pounds, and I look a midget next to some of these guys. It is ridiculous."

how in World War II the doctors would give soldiers steroids in order to help them generate muscle tissue in their recovery. He told me that it would indeed help me build muscle and get me stronger, but there was just one more thing. He then just stopped talking. I waited and waited and finally I said, 'What's the one thing Uncle Jules?' He said, oh yeah, the steroids substitute your natural hormone production, which will oftentimes make your testicles shrivel up. My jaw just dropped to the floor at that point. Needless to say, Uncle Jules had successfully scared the hell out of me, and I immediately went and flushed the pills down the toilet. Luckily, that was as close as I ever got to taking any steroids."

Steroids would, of course, grow and expand in popularity over the ensuing years. By the late 1970s, the pills had found their way into most professional sports teams' locker rooms. Many professional wrestlers had been taking them at this point, and it didn't take long for the other athletes to see the results. The guys had gotten bigger, faster, and stronger. They were ripped. The league didn't have a firm policy on steroids at this point, nor did it have any sort of testing program in place. As a result, a lot of players, especially linemen, started to take them. Nobody knew for sure, but guys could start to tell something was up.

"I didn't even know what steroids were until I got out of football in 1978," said quarterback Fran Tarkenton. "I knew that they were around in my day though. I remember playing the Pittsburgh Steelers in Super Bowl IX in New Orleans in '75 and standing out on the field before the game. I was there with my center, Mick Tingelhoff, and he looked like a normal 235-pound offensive lineman. We both stood there watching the Steelers linemen, and you could see their bulging biceps popping out of their arms.

I then looked over at Mick and kind of sized him up and said, 'What the hell are they doing that you're not?' I didn't know anything about steroids at that point, but my guess was that the Steelers did."

By the early '80s, the popularity of anabolic steroids exploded. Certain teams around the league started to garner reputations toward their tolerance of these drugs, as well.

"They started to get popular towards the tail end of my career in the early to mid-1980s," recalled 14-year offensive tackle Keith Fahnhorst. "There were certain teams in those years where guys were just expected to do them, like Cincinnati and Pittsburgh. Luckily in San Francisco, where I was, they didn't stress for us to be really big, but rather they wanted us fast. So there wasn't that same pressure on us to do them. I remember going to the Pro Bowl one year with a couple of my linemates, and when we got to the beach, we took our shirts off. Once we started looking around and seeing all of the other guys from the other teams who were clearly enhanced, we humbly put our shirts back on. Those guys were huge, it was scary. Luckily, I never got into all that craziness. It was bad news."

For the linemen especially, the peer pressure to take steroids was intense. The league was onto them, but the testing had become almost laughable.

"When I came into the league in the early '80s, it was just expected that you were going to use them," explained 13-year offensive tackle John Alt. "In so many words, the staff people told you to take them. I came

Pete Najarian, Three-Year Linebacker, on Steroids

"I played in an era when they were very prevalent, so I was around it big time. First and foremost, I never took them. I had a lot of teammates who did take them, however. Because they knew I was so against them, there were even instances where guys would ask me to help them pass tests by giving them my clean urine. I probably understood more about steroids health-wise than the other guys because of my father, who is a very respected doctor. Because of that, I wanted no part of that stuff. Incredibly though, I knew of other players who also had fathers who were doctors, and they still took them. In fact, some of them even got them from their fathers, which blew me away. We all knew of the long-term health risks, but it was an individual decision. Players knew that their jobs were on the line, which represented a lot of money. It was just an unfortunate part of the game. I was clean and had to work twice as hard as everybody else just to keep up, which was unfair in many ways."

into camp and had never really lifted weights before. I was naturally a big guy and just wasn't that into it at the time. Well, I got the message loud and clear that if I wanted to stick around that I had better get on something in a hurry and get my strength up. All that did was piss me off, because I certainly didn't want some idiot telling me that I had to take steroids in order to do my job. So I went out and hired a personal trainer. I then proceeded to work my ass off, ate right, and build up my strength naturally. Proudly, I can say that I have never taken steroids."

"There was a lot of pressure on the guys who weren't taking [steroids] to start taking them," Alt continued. "I remember sitting in the training room getting some treatment on my back when I was a rookie. Two of my teammates came over, both were wide receivers, and they started calling me out. They were saying, 'You were a first-round draft pick, and you aren't even willing to do this for the team? Our arms are bigger than yours!' It was pretty intimidating, but I held to my guns. I got a lot of crap from my coaches and trainers, even the doctors, after that and started hearing the 'first-round bust' label being thrown around as a sort of tactic to pressure me into it. It was sick. Ethically, I just couldn't do it, and I am glad that I didn't because so many of those guys who did them are just a mess now. They are in really poor health, and their bodies have just fallen apart. Hey, I played for 13 years in the NFL. I must have been doing something right.

"The thing that bothered me the most about it was just how much of a joke the testing was. You would see guys getting caught with nine times their normal testosterone and they would somehow get off scot-free. They would just say that was their baseline testosterone, which is B.S. It was so unclean, the whole thing, across the board. Plus, you would definitely see rookies and free agents who were taking them having a distinct advantage over guys who didn't. They would test out really well on a lot of stuff at the combines or whatever, plus the coaches just knew that those guys were going to be stronger. The guys on the juice didn't last as long career-wise though, because your muscles get stronger real quickly and then your tendons and ligaments go to hell. So they became very injury-prone after a while."

For former Broncos offensive tackle Jon Melander, it was all about making tough choices.

"I honestly never took them, but I certainly stared them in the face and asked myself if I should be in order to gain an advantage out there,"

Melander admitted. "Luckily, I said no, but there was a whole lot of pressure to take that stuff. I certainly knew a lot of guys who did take them though, and I even helped a few of them inject themselves in the ass. It wasn't pretty, but some guys wanted to have that edge. To each their own, I suppose. The money that is at stake nowadays is absolutely incredible. It has exploded, so guys will always be looking for that edge because of that. When you have that much money at stake and the celebrity perks that come with it, you will get guys doing things that they wouldn't necessarily do in a normal career. The stakes are just so high now that people will do unethical things that they didn't think they were capable of doing. The younger guys want to make the team and get paid, and the older guys want to keep their jobs and stay in the limelight. So it escalates and escalates. Guys who don't take them suddenly find themselves at a disadvantage, and then they have to make some hard choices. They know that the opposition is taking them too, which only increases the paranoia. I think the league has done a good job of cracking down on it with all of the testing, but I am sure it still goes on behind the scenes somehow, someway. It is sad, it really is."

Into the late 1980s, the heyday for steroid use in the NFL, the players could see the effects it was having on the long-term users.

"All I can say is that I played in the late '80s when [steroids] were at their peak in popularity, and I saw a lot of guys with bruises on their back hips in the shower," said former Redskins offensive guard Ray Hitchcock. "I will just leave it at that. You could tell which guys were on the gas. They were much physically stronger and much more aggressive, both on and off the field. And most of them could do Clearasil commercials, too, because of all the purple acne they would break out with. The testing was such a joke back then. We would report to training camp on a Sunday night, physicals were on Monday, and the urine test for steroids was on Tuesday. That was the only test. That was it. Talk about taking a test that you didn't have to study for! So guys would just stay clean until five minutes after the test and then start a new cycle. What a joke."

Some guys just said no, and for those who did, they count their lucky stars now that they are retired and don't have to deal with the long-term side effects to their health.

"When I first came into the league back in the early '80s, it was everywhere," said 12-year offensive tackle Rich Baldinger. "A lot of guys were taking them, there was no question about it. Personally, I never used it. I had enough weight issues just trying to stay under 300 pounds. I had been lifting weights since I was a kid and was big naturally, thank God. Even in high school and college, I worked heavy construction, which helped a lot, too. The sad part about that stuff now is that those guys who used back then are paying the price for it now. Some of those guys look like they are 100 years old. They are getting new hips, knees, and ankles. It is sad. But hey, that was their choice to use that garbage. Weight lifting was a big deal. You had to lift 24/7, 365 days a year if you wanted to stay in the NFL. It was all about being bigger, faster, and stronger. You needed to condition your body to hold up for 16 games, or you were going to be out of a job. Some guys could do it and see big gains, while others had to take short cuts. To each their own, but the guys who cheated are definitely paying the price today."

For 11-year linebacker Mike Walter, the problem wasn't with the league, it was with the player's union, which enabled many players to keep using.

"While I am proud to say that I never took steroids, there was definitely a disadvantage for those players who didn't," Walter said. "I remember being at training camp and waiting in line to do a drill. I looked down the line and realized that of the four guys in line, I was the only one who was clean. When you are competing for a job with those guys, that was a tough pill to swallow. The code says that you can't say anything though, so it was always this big dirty secret. Looking back, I really think the union was way off base. I mean, every time a guy got busted for steroids, the union would step in and protect him. The union, which was basically against testing, should have been protecting guys like me instead, who chose to stay clean and just work harder. It wasn't fair. A lot of guys got pressured into doing them. It was crazy.

"Guys used to hate getting tested. It was really invasive, where somebody had to basically stand there while you peed into a cup. So to have a little fun one time, we had our food service guy order in a ton of asparagus for one of our training table meals. Asparagus, of course, makes your urine really smell. We knew we were going to be tested the next day, so we told all the guys to eat as much of that stuff as possible. All I can say is I am sure the testers got bombarded with some nasty smelling pee that next morning. Whew!

"There was a time back in the early '90s when they started testing for them. As a result, a lot of guys went off of the old-school anabolics and started to experiment with the designer human-growth hormone stuff that the Bill Romanowkis of the world made famous. What was so interesting about steroids that a lot of people don't realize is that guys become mentally addicted to them too, where they thought that they had to be on them, otherwise they couldn't perform out there. We had a guy on our team who was using them, and he was an awesome player. He didn't need them, but he used them anyway. As soon as they started testing, he went off of them and from that point on, his career just fizzled. Psychologically he couldn't perform, and he crumbled."

Eventually, the testing started to work. Players were getting deterred from using them, knowing that fines and suspensions could cost them their careers.

"Steroids were huge before I got into the league in the late '80s, and the guys were open about talking about it, too," said former Green Bay running back Darrell Thompson. "It was a different time. I would guess at least 50 percent to 70 percent of the linemen were doing it in the early-to-mid-1980s. The juice could make a good athlete into a great athlete; that was the difference. I remember one of my teammates telling me about it one time. He was like, 'Dude, I was the strongest guy in the weight room. You know how you feel on Mondays, strong and refreshed like you can lift the world on your shoulders? Well, I feel like that every day.' He loved it and thought it was the greatest thing. He said he could do reps with 275 pounds and do it all day. He said he had zits and mood swings, but when it came time to lift, he said he felt like a million bucks. One of the guys on our team that had juiced was Tony Mandarich, who was pretty much

Pete Bercich, Six-Year Linebacker and Assistant Coach, on Steroids

"I knew a lot of guys who took them. The guys who got all 'roided up suffered a whole host of funky injuries because their muscles got stronger but their tendons and ligaments stayed the same. So they were tearing calf and bicep muscles and all sorts of odd things. The bottom line with steroids is that they were bullshit—and more importantly, they were cheating."

deflated by the time I got there. As soon as the testing kicked in, he went from like 325 pounds—rock hard on the cover of *Sports Illustrated*—to 285 pounds of mediocrity. It was sad."

Through the 1990s, the league really cracked down on steroids. And during the 2000s, the problem has been cleaned up a great deal. Many players got busted using though, with many more playing undetected and getting away with it. Sure, a lot of big issues still exist, but many of the players from this era feel good about the progress that has been made.

"I think the NFL has done a good job of policing [steroid use] and cracking down on it," said former quarterback Steve Young. "When you think back to the early '80s, those steroids were scary. They were not created for skill players. They made guys huge, which was why the lineman wanted to use them. That has obviously changed nowadays, but they are still scary. I am glad football cracked down on it the way they did. It has no place in the game. They policed it so well that I don't think it is a problem anymore."

"We test so much for it now, so I would hope that we have a handle on it," said Saints head coach Sean Payton. "But I am not so naïve to think that it still doesn't exist to some degree. I think the NFL is a little bit ahead of all the other leagues in that regard in how much we test. Now there was a time in the late '70s that steroids were very prevalent in the game. Players have become much more educated about the dangers of steroids and are thinking about life after football much more so now. There are still probably some players that feel that they need that edge, but overall I think our league is doing a pretty good job of getting rid of this stuff."

"I really don't think that it is an issue in today's game. I really don't," added Ravens center Matt Birk. "I am sure that there are a handful of guys who are staying ahead of the curve and able to cheat the system, but overall I think the league has done a fantastic job of staying on top of things. Our testing program is very thorough, and it is pretty tough to get around. That probably hasn't always been the case, but it certainly is now. I will say this about steroids too—they don't necessarily mean you will be a better football player if you take them. A lot of people think that if you are big and strong then you are automatically good at football, and that is not the case. As an offensive lineman, and I hesitate to put us in the category of 'athletes,' but there are a lot of 'athletic' things you have to be able to do with your body to be successful. I can go to Target right now and find at least a couple of guys walking around who are bigger and stronger than I am, but they can't play professional football. So steroids might get a guy bigger and stronger, but that doesn't necessarily equate to being a better football player. While I have never done [steroids], I can see how guys can get sucked into taking them. Playing football is more than just a job; it controls your life to a great extent. So the guys who do get hooked on them, a lot of them will have serious medical problems later in life. That to me is really sad."

Former Giants wide receiver Stacy Robinson serves as the NFL Players Association Director of Player Development and oversees the policy on anabolic steroids and related substances on behalf of the players. He is on the front line of steroid abuse and feels good about how far the league has come in regard to keeping these drugs out of the game. There are many problems facing the players today, however, and it is his job to help them navigate their way through it all.

"My job is unique," Robinson said. "If a player tests positive, he is either fined or suspended. He has a right to an appeal, however, and I will try to help him in that process. I am present at the appeals to make sure that the policy is being interpreted the way that we negotiated. A lot of the violations that we see today are with players who unknowingly take supplements that have unapproved substances in them. They are taking them not to enhance their performance but to stay healthy, and they wind up getting in trouble. For instance, in one recent high-profile case that is currently pending, it was a substance that was on the banned list, but the substance that was on the list wasn't listed on the label of the product.

"It is tough to stay ahead of the curve on this stuff. There are always going to be chemists out there creating new substances for athletes. If there is a steroid out there that is banned and that can be tested for, they will go out and change one little DNA strand so that it won't become detectable. It will still get that athlete the same benefit, but it is now undetectable. This is the constant cat-and-mouse game that we are up against.

"Things have changed, though. The attitude changed about steroids back in the late '80s and early '90s when the players started speaking out. They basically said that they didn't want to deal with the fact that if person A uses them, then they were going to have to use them in order to compete. So they wanted out. That gave the players' association the green light to help bargain on behalf of the majority of the players who wanted

Rich Gannon, 17-Year Quarterback, on Steroids

"In my era, the testing was so tough that as a player, you had to be pretty crazy to try to outsmart those guys. I had testers show up at my house in the off-season a couple of times. It was completely random. If you lived in Europe in the off-season, then the league would send someone over to check up on you when you least expected it. I know a lot of guys who did it and got caught, like Bill Romanowski when I was in Oakland, so it was a big risk. Was it cheating? Yes. It was against the rules, and it was illegal. That was the bottom line."

to get this stuff out of the game. As a result, we have arguably the most comprehensive policy against steroids in all of professional sports."

Several high-profile players have been busted for doping over the years. Among them is three-time Pro Bowl defensive lineman Dana Stubblefield, who was sentenced to two years' probation in 2008 for lying to investigators about his steroid use. According to prosecutors, Stubblefield received notice from the NFL on November 10, 2003, that he had tested positive for THG, a designer steroid that was distributed by Bay Area Laboratory Co-Operative (BALCO) and was known as "the clear." (This was the same drug that Barry Bonds allegedly used in his criminal investigation, along with "the cream.") Stubblefield admitted in court that he lied when he said he never ingested the oxygen-producing drug EPO and he never dealt with BALCO founder Victor Conte, who served three months in prison for steroid dealing. Stubblefield was not suspended by the league for testing positive at the time because THG was not added to the NFL's banned substance list until after the tests were conducted.

Another player who has admitted taking steroids is former Pro Bowl linebacker Bill Romanowski. In 2005, he released an autobiography, *Romo: My Life on the Edge*, that detailed his drug use in the NFL. Still, Romanowski claims that though he used products now banned by the league, he never used a product that was illegal at the time. "I looked at the list as the Bible," Romanowski said of the NFL's list of banned substances. "The biggest regret I have in my 16-year career is at the end of my career taking THG, which when I took it didn't have a name, and they didn't know what it was. I knew I was pushing that line, that integrity line, that moral line of right and wrong."

According to the *Boston Globe*, Romanowski had a long relationship with Victor Conte, the head of BALCO who spent four months in prison for orchestrating an illegal steroid distribution scheme. The athletes implicated in Conte's distribution ring have been mostly track athletes or baseball players. "One thing I do know about Victor is he's an honest guy," Romanowski said. "Some of the real criminals were the investigators... with the different tactics that they would use and the different lies that they would use to try to get information. A lot of the guys that were busting him were guys that had bought steroids from him on a regular basis—and took them. People want to say that the league is really dirty," Romanowski said. "I'm here to tell you it's not."

Tony Mandarich, on Beating Steroid Testing

Tony Mandarich has come clean on his use of steroids back when he played for Michigan State. The use of the roids allowed him to beef up, become super-human, and get drafted second overall by the Green Bay Packers in 1989. Mandarich has written a tell-all book, *My Dirty Little Secrets: Steroids, Alcohol, & God: The Tony Mandarich Story*, to explain his addiction to painkillers and alcohol. He also sat down with *Sports Illustrated* 20 years later to apologize for lying to them about his use of steroids in a cover story. Probably the best part of the article is the blow-by-blow account of how Mandarich passed his urine tests:

"For the Rose Bowl in 1988, we were tested two weeks before on campus, and then we heard there was going to be a second test [in Pasadena]. I'd already gotten back on Anadrol-50, a steroid which makes you significantly stronger within a day or two, and now I'm freaking. I'm in this large 24-hour store, about midnight, brainstorming, thinking how am I going to beat this test?

"In the pet area I see this rubber doggy squeaker toy. I get that, then I go to another area and get a small hose, and in the medical area I get some flesh-colored tape. I'm like the Unabomber getting supplies. Back home I rip the squeakers out of the toy, tape the hose into one end and experiment by filling the thing with water. At the Rose Bowl I taped the toy to my back, ran the hose between my butt cheeks, taped the end to my penis, and covered the hose tip with bubble gum. I had gotten some clean urine from somebody else. The tester stood behind me, couldn't see anything, and when I removed the gum everything worked fine."

At the Gator Bowl the following year, Mandarich customized a squeezable glue bottle to replace the doggy toy. "A quarter twist of the cap, no leak, no moving parts—it was almost too easy."

Ironically, Romanowski today owns and operates a nutritional supplement company called Nutrition53. During his playing days, he was notorious for doing whatever it took to stay healthy enough to play every Sunday and to get that edge, including swallowing upward of 100 assorted pills and supplements a day. During an interview on *60 Minutes*, he even admitted to injecting live cells from Scottish sheep.

"I am just trying to help people live better," Romanowski said of his company. "I stand by my products 100 percent. They were tested by some of the best doctors and scientists in the world. As for my past, it is the past. I am on to bigger and better things. That is what life is all about."

Players will always be on the lookout for that next big thing, whatever it is, that can make them either better or healthier. As long as it isn't illegal—or for some, as long as they won't get caught doing it—they will try it. Sometimes they get lucky. Such was the case for former Oilers and Vikings safety Kurt Knoff, who played back in the 1970s and early '80s.

"I played in the era before steroids, but as players we have all tried to do different things to get ourselves healthy from time to time," Knoff said. "I had some bad knee problems early in my career. I remember one time playing in a game against Green Bay. I was doing some training the day before the game and was really hurting. I figured that there was no way I was going to be able to play on it. Now I wasn't a big fan of getting shot up, so I wound up taking this horse liniment called Dimethyl-Sulfoxide, or DMSO for short, which was well known in veterinary circles. It would relieve swelling and inflammation in a short amount of time. It was this industrial stuff that really stunk and actually left a garlic taste in your mouth, even though you didn't eat it. Anyway, I put it on and the next day I was about 95 percent better. It was amazing. It wasn't illegal or anything, but you had to get it up in Canada. One of the guys had some, and I thought I would give it a try. Maybe it was a mental thing, a placebo, I don't know. Either way, it worked great, and I was able to play in the game."

Another drug that made the rounds in the 1990s was the stimulant ephedra, which was banned by the league in 2001. Before its banishment, it was common for some players to drink what were known as party balls before games. Party balls were a potion concocted of ephedra, Coca-Cola, and Ultimate Orange—a drink used by weightlifters that is said to offer "more explosive power than seven shots of espresso." When mixed, the drink was said to give players superhuman amounts of energy that would last throughout an entire three-hour game. Like most things too good to be true, however, the consequences for guzzling a party ball without being properly hydrated could lead to major health problems. The tragic death of former Minnesota Viking Korey Stringer in 2001 brought even more attention to ephedra. Stringer, a 27-year-old, 335-pound lineman, died from heatstroke during the second day of training camp. Although toxicology reports never revealed that Stringer had ephedra in his system when he died, the team's lawyers did present testimony that he used a supplement laced with the substance before every game during his playing career. Stringer's widow filed a wrongful death lawsuit against the team and doctors. Parts of her lawsuit were later thrown out, but her case against the NFL was settled in January 2009. As part of the settlement, the NFL agreed to support efforts to create a heat illness prevention program in his honor.

While steroids still remain an issue for the NFL, there are other drugs that continue to be problematic. One such drug is human-growth hormone, or HGH, a performance enhancer banned by the NFL and other major sports leagues. It is the supplement of choice for some athletes because it can't be detected by current testing. HGH has been hailed as a miracle drug for its value as a healing agent as well as for its anti-aging benefits. Because of its apparent ability to accelerate healing, many doctors have injected HGH into ailing knees, hips, and elbows. It has also been used to treat rotator-cuff tears, torn biceps and hamstrings, and torn Achilles tendons, and it is even used to stimulate knee cartilage production. The athletes who have used it swear by it. Proponents argue that players recovering from everything ranging from Tommy John elbow surgery to torn knee ligament operations could benefit from being treated with the drug. Opponents, meanwhile, have one simple argument—it is illegal and therefore cheating. There is a reason that the penalty for steroids in the NFL results in suspension, whereas the penalty for cocaine results in treatment. Sure, both are illegal drugs, but steroids give players an "unfair advantage in a particular game."

Yet another high-profile case in 2008 involved several well-known players who tested positive for a diuretic known as Bumetanide, a drug belonging to a group of medicines called loop diuretics or water pills, which treat fluid retention and swelling caused by medical conditions such as congestive heart failure, liver disease, and kidney disease. However,

Bumetanide can also mask the use of other drugs, including steroids, which is why it is on the NFL's banned substances list. Now why would football players want to take water pills? To lose weight. Yeah, huge football players need to stay lean and trim, especially the linemen who have weight clauses in their contracts that dictate a healthy weight range that they must fall into. If they don't make weight, then they may be in breach of their contract, which could ultimately cost them millions of dollars. Even if they unknowingly took the drug, they are responsible for whatever goes into their bodies. Under the NFL's steroid policy, which clearly states just that, a player's first positive test results in a four-game suspension, so it is a big deal.

The bottom line with all of this stuff is that players will do whatever they can to stay healthy, both so that they can be on the field to help their teams win and to make money. If performance-enhancing drugs and steroids help them achieve that, then many players will find a way to cheat the system in order to gain that edge. With today's media scrutiny, however, things have changed somewhat. Players know that if they get busted, they will not only be humiliated publicly, they will also lose big endorsement money, to boot. We need only look to Olympic swimming champion Michael Phelps for that. He was busted smoking pot just months after winning a record eight gold medals at the Summer Olympics in Beijing and stood to make tens of millions of dollars in endorsements from those accomplishments. But his reputation is now tarnished. That decision literally cost him millions of dollars. Drugs are a choice, though, and to each his own. Pot may not be in the same category as steroids or even cocaine, but it is illegal. And maybe more importantly, it is cheating.

10

Playing Hurt

Without question, the biggest aspect of the code was for the players to play hurt. The mentality to suck it up and play is engrained in these men from a very early age. From high school to college and into the professional ranks, they are just expected to play no matter what. The players will tell you over and over that there is a big difference between being hurt and being injured. You can play hurt. Hell, most of them played injured too, but that is the point. They know that they have to play, or else they will be letting their teammates down. They will be letting their coaches down. They will be letting their fans down. And worse yet, they will be letting themselves down. Talk about pressure.

The injuries the players suffer and the pain they go through just to play in this league are nothing short of mind boggling. When you talk to the players, even after they are retired and usually suffering from massive health problems, most of them will all agree that they would do it all over again in a heart beat. The prosthetic knees, hips, ankles, and elbows are just part of the deal. The biggest problem for many of these guys, however, is what is going on in their brains. Like boxers have known for years, repeated blows to the head are generally not a good thing. It is estimated that a typical linebacker in the NFL experiences the impact and head trauma equivalent to dozens of head-on automobile accidents during every game he plays. Take a veteran player who has played for 10 to 15 seasons, and there is going to be some serious residual damage from all of the concussions.

Concussions are caused from jarring blows to the head that temporarily stunned the senses, occasionally leading to unconsciousness. A concussion has long been considered an invisible injury, however, because it is impossible to test for—neither an MRI nor a CT-scan can detect it. As a result, players in years past who got their bells rung would just go back into the game whenever they felt all right, unaware of all of the damage that they were really inflicting. Things are changing on this front, though, thanks to the center for the Study of Traumatic Encephalopathy (CSTE) at the Boston University School of Medicine. By collecting tissue from deceased NFL athletes who suffered multiple concussions, the researchers are shedding light on what concussions look like in the brain. The findings are stunning. Far from innocuous, concussions confer tremendous brain damage, and that damage now has a name: chronic traumatic encephalopathy (CTE). According to a CNN report released about the study, CTE is being found in the brains of six out of six former NFL players tested, many of whom died young, some as early as their 30s or 40s.

Dr. Ann McKee, a neuropathologist and co-director of the CSTE, also studies Alzheimer's disease and says the results closely resemble what might be found in the brain of an 80-year-old person with dementia. "I knew what traumatic brain disease looked like in the very end stages in the most severe cases," McKee said. "To see the kind of changes we're seeing in 45-year-olds is basically unheard of." According to the study, the damage affects the parts of the brain that control emotion, rage, hyper-sexuality, and even breathing. Further, it finds that CTE is a progressive disease that eventually kills brain cells. Among the findings from the CSTE, along with other research institutions, CTE has now been found in the brains of late NFL players Tom McHale, John Grimsley, Mike Webster, Andre Waters, Justin Strzelczyk, and Terry Long. Webster, Long, and Strzelczyk all died after long bouts of depression, while Waters committed suicide in 2006 at age 44. McHale was found dead last year of an apparent drug overdose, and Grimsley died of an accidental gunshot wound to the chest.

So far, approximately 100 athletes have consented to have their brains studied after they die. Among them is former linebacker Ted Johnson, who suffered more than 100 concussions while playing with the Patriots from 1995–2004. For years after his career ended, Johnson could barely muster the energy to leave his house. "I can definitely point to 2002 when I got back-to-back concussions. That's where the problems started [with] depression, the sleep disorders, and the mental fatigue," said Johnson, who retired after that. Johnson said he played through concussions because he, like many other players, did not understand the consequences and has publicly criticized the NFL for not protecting players like him. "They don't want you to know," he said. "It's not like when you get into the NFL there's a handout that says, 'These are the effects of multiple concussions, so beware.'"

In a statement, the NFL indicated its staff takes "a cautious, conservative approach to managing concussions." While the NFL supports research into the impact of concussions, it maintains that "hundreds of thousands of people have played football and other sports without experiencing any problem of this type, and there continues to be considerable debate within the medical community on the precise long-term effects of concussions and how they relate to other risk factors." Meanwhile, the league is planning its own independent medical study of the long-term effects of concussions on its retired players.

"Really my main reason even for talking about this is to help the guys who are already retired," Johnson added. "[They] are getting divorced, going bankrupt, can't work, are depressed, and don't know what's wrong with them. [I want] to give them a name for it so they can go get help."

Another player who has definitely had more than his fair share of head trauma is two-time Pro Bowler and four-time Super Bowl champion Bill Romanowski. In late 2003, the then-Raiders linebacker was driving his car out of the parking lot at McAfee Coliseum in Oakland when he suddenly stopped and pulled over. This was a drive he had made countless times before, but something on this particular day was different. After 16 seasons in the NFL and thousands of bone-crunching hits, he couldn't remember where his house was. He just couldn't remember.

"That was tough," said Romanowski, who speaks slowly and frequently pauses these days to collect his thoughts. "I didn't really talk about all of my concussions because I wanted to get back on the field. The sideline represented failure to me. There was nothing that was going to take me out of a game; that was my attitude. When the fear becomes so great, it is amazing where you can take your body and what you can endure. Pain is just a state of mind; it really is. I remember playing in a game against Arizona one time where I got hurt right before the half. I couldn't run at all. When I went to the locker room at halftime, I had my entire hip injected so I could go out and play the second half. I just did it. It wasn't even an issue for me. I also had a shoulder injury early in my career in San Francisco, and for eight games straight I had to take the needle in the shoulder to numb it up enough so I could play. I didn't realize how much pain my body was in until I got done playing. I didn't realize how violent the sport was. For me it all came to an end after my sixteenth season. It was the third game of the season, it was against the Denver Broncos, and I had suffered yet another really bad concussion. I had gotten concussions in every game up until that point, including the preseason games, and knew after that game that my career was over. I sat out the rest of the season but was able to come back and dress for the last game of the year. It was a Monday night game versus the Packers where Brett Favre threw a bunch of touchdowns right after his father had passed away. Anyway, I watched that game from the sidelines and just sat there thinking to myself, 'I did that for 16 years?' The hits were so incredible. I had never really seen it from that angle before. I was in awe. It was the first time I had ever been to a football game as a fan. It was shocking to me, absolutely shocking."

Quarterbacks are particularly vulnerable to head injuries, especially the guys who played several decades ago and didn't have very protective helmets. They would get knocked unconscious repeatedly, yet still be expected to get back in the game. Such was the case for Hall of Famer Fran Tarkenton, who played in the league for 18 seasons.

"We all played hurt," Tarkenton said. "That was just how it was in those days. Hell, I got knocked out in three different games during my career with concussions. Each time it happened in the first half, and each time I was able to return to the game in the second half. Today that stuff doesn't happen because they understand more medically about that type of thing. Back then we just played. Look, there were some injuries you could play with and others you could not play with, that was just the way it was. I played most of my career with a broken shoulder. I could throw to a certain point but not as well as I would have liked to have been able to. That didn't make me more courageous than the next guy. It was just something I did. I broke my leg in my sixteenth year, and I thought I could come back and play on it, but I couldn't. I missed five games because of that, and I think those were about the only games I really missed over my entire career. You just did what you had to do to get out there. When I separated my shoulder I got shot up and went out there. I tore up the cruciate in my knee, too,

Jack Tatum, Former Raiders Safety,
on the Now-Infamous Hit on Darryl Stingley

During a 1978 preseason game against the Patriots, Raiders safety Jack Tatum tackled wide receiver Darryl Stingley as he was stretched out to catch a pass. As a result of the collision, Stingley was paralyzed from the chest down.

"Of course I felt terrible about what happened," Tatum said. "The press played it the wrong way, and many people blamed me for the hit. If you watch it though, you will see that there was nothing wrong with the hit. It was perfectly clean. It was just one of those things that happens in football. It could have happened to anybody. People are always saying, 'He didn't apologize,' but I don't think I did anything wrong that I needed to apologize for. Again, it was a clean hit."

and I played on it because it was either play or retire. Well, I didn't want to retire. I couldn't run very well at that point but I could still throw, so that is what I did. You adapt and just deal with it. That is football."

Seemingly every player you talk to, regardless of what era he played in or for how long he played, has a story about suffering some sort of head injury somewhere along the line. But some were worse than others.

"I remember getting knocked out cold one time after getting clothes-lined on a kickoff while trying to tackle O.J. Simpson," recalled former Chiefs linebacker Bob Stein. "I came to and couldn't remember a thing. I looked down and saw that I was wearing a white jersey, so I went over to the sideline with the other white jerseys, that's how bad it was. From there I just hung out on the sideline until halftime, when I made it to the locker room, where our crack medical staff evaluated me. I told them what happened and that I had an awful headache and couldn't remember a thing. They diagnosed me with a severe concussion and said I should be just fine to play in the second half. I just shook my head. I was 22 years old at the time and figured what the hell. I knew that I was on all of the special teams, so every time either team was kicking or punting, I would run over to the trainer's table to look on the reminder sheet to see where I was supposed to line up. I would just guess as to what I was supposed to do when I was out there, because I could not remember a damn thing. It is insane to even think about that stuff now, but that was your mentality back when you were a kid trying to make the team. Ironically, years later I got a severe sinus infection and had to go through some pretty extensive testing. As a result, it was revealed that I had suffered a fractured skull in that game. Amazing.

"It was a real badge of honor to play injured, and it was an even bigger badge of honor to play well while you were injured. There was an old expression that we all lived by: 'You can't make the club in the tub.' I mean, that was how you earned the respect of your teammates, to play through pain and put your team first. I even remember seeing guys give themselves injections in the locker room. It was crazy. You had to be out there on the field, no matter what, otherwise someone would take your job. You know, when I played back in the '60s and '70s, most of us had second jobs in the off-season. I had many, many teammates over the years who absolutely hated football. Seriously. Good players, too. They figured it was the best job that they could get, so they just did it. It wasn't quite as romantic as many people would think."

When players bear down and play hurt, that is the ultimate unselfish act that they can do for their teammates. Nothing will earn them more respect than to suck it up and take one for the team. This is nothing new. Take future Hall of Famer Ernie Nevers, who was a two-time All-American halfback at Stanford back in the 1920s. He had been a headliner all through his collegiate career, but he reached superhuman status during the 1925 Rose Bowl against Notre Dame and the vaunted Four Horsemen. Against the better wishes of his doctor, he played through one sprained and one broken ankle. With a pair of tin-snips and a hammer, coach Pop Warner concocted a crude artificial ankle brace out of sheet aluminum and rubber inner tubing, then taped it to Nevers' lower legs. Incredibly, he played the entire 60 minutes, rushed for 114 yards on offense, and even registered half of the team's tackles on defense. He played valiantly, but his team came up short as the Irish won, 27–10.

Or how about former Rams linebacker Jack Youngblood? Many of us can still remember that playoff game in 1979 between the Rams and Cowboys when Youngblood became Superman. In the first half, Youngblood was chop-blocked by two Cowboys, causing his left fibula to snap like a pencil above the ankle. Undeterred, Youngblood had the trainers simply tape him back together at halftime so he could get back out there. He inspired his teammates, even sacking Dallas quarterback Roger Staubach en route to leading his squad to a thrilling 21–19 upset victory. What makes the story even more amazing is the fact that he didn't go in for surgery the next week either, opting instead to use a leg brace as the Rams won the NFC title the next week at Tampa Bay before losing Super Bowl XIV to the Steelers. How tough was Jack Youngblood? The future Hall of Famer even played in the Pro Bowl the next week.

* * *

In addition to head trauma, players suffer through all sorts of ailments, conditions, and injuries. Here are just some of their incredible stories of both courage and flat-out insanity. Some are hilarious, others are poignant, and a few may even make you cry.

"I'm probably able to endure pain better than most guys," said Vikings defensive end Jim Marshall, who set a league record by playing in 302 consecutive regular season and postseason games (combined) from 1960–79. "Really, it's a matter of positive thinking. I've studied the association of mind and body [and] the harmony between the two. There are times when the effect of an injury can be minimized by positive thinking. If you tell yourself, 'My knee hurts and we're playing on artificial turf this week,' you might as well be on crutches. My attitude is, 'I'm going to play because that's what they pay you for.' The streak was not something I thought about. I just went to work every day and did my job. I felt a great responsibility to do my job to the best of my abilities on a day-to-day basis because I had a lot of other people depending on me. I never wanted to let my teammates down; that was the most important thing for me. I also never wanted to let myself down by giving an inferior performance. There were times in my career when I was injured—I had broken bones and many serious injuries along the way, but I tried to play through it and stay focused."

Enduring pain is par for the course in football. "The game is about who can endure the most pain on Sundays and recover the following week for the next Sunday," said 14-year defensive tackle John Randle. "You are going to play hurt; that is just football. Every week you just endured the intense pain and then moved on. You had to learn how to manage your injuries. That is a big part of it. You had to learn how to take care of your body, otherwise you would never make it for 16 or 17 straight games. Sometimes when I see baseball or basketball player on the sidelines with a sprained ankle, I just have to laugh. In football, you didn't come out for a sprained ankle. No way. Maybe if it was broke, but definitely not sprained. Even if it was broke, you might just get it shot up so that you could get back out there. Crazy? Hell yes. But that was football. If you couldn't hack it, then you weren't going to be playing for very long. Look, if you don't have at least one crooked finger that has been all busted up and sticks out crooked, then you are not a defensive lineman. That is just a part of the game."

Years later, players remember every injury and its story. "I remember back in the early '60s when I was with Detroit," said eight-year linebacker Carl Brettschneider. "We played Cleveland in what was called the runner-up bowl. They used to have a game down in Miami for the two teams that finished in second place in each division in those years, and the winner would make an extra $700. Well, midway through the game, the great running back Jim Brown came barreling straight toward me through a hole that was about 12' wide. I knew it was going to hurt, but I stepped up and hit him head on. I brought him down, but he damn near ran me over in the process. We used to wear a single-bar face mask in those days, and after the play that bar was down under my chin because he hit me so hard. My shoulder about exploded from the impact, and that thing gave me trouble for the next 20 years. I used to have to get treatment from a chiropractor every couple of weeks just to put the thing back into place. It still bothers me even to this day. You don't realize it at the time, but those injuries can stick with you for a lifetime. Hey, at least I have a good story about it and can say that the best running back of all time did this to me!"

Former four-year offensive tackle Jon Melander understood the pressures to play while injured. "I have had plenty of injuries over my career, and when you are hurt it is the worst feeling ever," said Melander. "You feel alienated by your teammates and you feel scorned by your coaches, so it is tough. I had knee problems my entire career. [It] was just something I had to deal with. The coaches put so much pressure on you to play through it and to get back on the field. I remember having a defensive coach in college who rode me so much about an injury that I actually switched from defensive line to offensive line, just to get away from him. It was either that or quit football altogether, that was how bad it was. I worked hard and made it to the pros as an offensive lineman though, and that was something I was very proud of. I played for six seasons in the NFL before suffering a career-ending neck injury. As a professional, you do feel that extra pressure to play through pain and injuries, because it is your job. You feel conflicted as to whether or not you want to fully disclose all of your injuries because you know that if you come off the field, somebody is going to take your job. Eventually though, for me, it just got to be too much. I had a degree in finance and had other things I wanted to do in life. It was a great ride, but I wasn't willing to risk paralysis just to play a few more years."

Being known as a tough player translates to playing while hurt. "Injuries are just a part of the game," said Joe Kapp, 12-year NFL and CFL quarterback. "My list of ailments is too long to count: dislocated shoulders, broken noses, concussions, you name it. I hurt my knee one time, and the doctor's remedy was to put it in a cast. Well, I did that for about 10 days, and finally I couldn't handle it anymore, so I went down to a tire store and cut it off so I could play again. Hell, Dave Wilcox knocked the shit out of me in a game against San Francisco one time, and I was out cold for I don't know how long. But somehow I finished the game. So how do you get back at a big linebacker? You play smart and you beat him fair and square, that is how you make him pay. Toughness is a state of mind. Where I came from, you had to be tough. When I was on the cover of *Sports Illustrated* back in 1970 with the caption 'The Toughest Chicano,' that meant a lot to me. I wanted to be known as a tough player both mentally and physically, but most importantly I wanted to earn the respect of my teammates. That was the most important thing for me. It was a pride thing for me, that you didn't run out-of-bounds or that you played every game regardless of being injured. I truly appreciated the opportunity to be out on the field. To me it was so much fun to play quarterback in the National Football League, I should have paid them."

There is a leadership component to playing hurt. "For me, playing hurt was all about leadership," said eight-year defensive tackle Keith Millard. "Your teammates counted on you, and you just couldn't let them down. When I got into the league in the mid-1980s, those old timers were all about, 'If you can play, you gotta be out there no matter what.' There is a difference between pain and being hurt. Guys like Dick Butkus, Dan Hampton, Jack Lambert, Jim Marshall, and Scott Studwell took such pride in being able to be counted on. That was huge. I played with so many injuries in my career, from bad knees to busted bones, you name it. I even played with a grade two-and-a-half shoulder separation the year that I set the league sack record in '89. I could barely hold my arm up for those last two games of the season, but nothing was going to keep me off the field. My teammates were counting on me to play because of the double-team factor that I would draw. That alone was big because it freed up my linemates to go after the quarterback. It was incredible pain, but I was willing to do it in order to help my team win. It is a real badge of honor to play that way, too, because guys know that they can count on you. It is the best way to earn the respect of your coaches, as well. The biggest difference between the game today and when I played is the fact that so many players won't play hurt. I am sure the big money has a lot to do with it, especially with so many agents telling guys what to do. Hey, they want to get paid too and can't afford to have their star players suffering any injuries."

If you can't deal with playing while injured, the NFL isn't the career for you. "As a player, if you are going to play 20 games per year, you are absolutely going to have to play hurt," said six-year linebacker and assistant coach Pete Bercich. "There is a big difference between being hurt and being injured though. You are only going to be withheld due to injury if by playing you are going to exacerbate it or make it worse. If you have an injury that can be tolerated, then you can play at your own discretion. The trainers will be more than happy to give you whatever you need to deal with your pain. They want you back on the field doing your job. That is what it is all about. Every game is so important in the NFL, and the teams want the top players on the field no matter what. They look at you and say, 'Son, we are paying you a hell of a lot of money, and you mean to tell me that you can't play because of this, this, or this?' They put the pressure on you and really put the screws to you to get you to suck it up and get out there. If you need to get shot up, then so be it. They want you out there; the fans want you out there; and your teammates expect you to be out there. That is what life is like in the NFL. If you can't deal with it, get out. There are thousands of guys who would gladly trade places with you in a heartbeat. The only recourse that the players have is the fact that if they do something that is medically not sound and they screw you up somehow, then you will have legal recourse in the form of workman's compensation and that sort of thing after the fact. While some guys are fragile, others are simply tough as hell and want to play no matter what. Take Vikings defensive end Jared Allen, I don't think anybody ever has to talk to that guy about playing hurt. He is just going to do whatever he has to do to get out on the field. That is his mentality."

Career-ending injuries also affect coaches. "Guys in my era played for the love of the game because they loved the competition," said longtime coach Jerry Glanville. "They would play no matter what. That was just how it was in those days. I will never forget one time when I was coaching in Detroit. One of our star players had been Charlie West, who was the best safety in football for many years. Charlie was getting up in years and had suffered a lot of injuries. Well, one day I was watching him in a game against the Eagles, and I could see that he couldn't change direction anymore and he just couldn't twist and turn like he used to. He loved the game though and would do whatever he could to help his team win. One of the toughest things I ever had to do in all my years was to tell Charlie West that he couldn't play football anymore. That was really, really tough. To see the look in his eyes was something I will never forget."

"The worst injury I ever saw happened way up in Bemidji, a small town in northern Minnesota, where one of our players suffered a subdural hematoma during training camp back in the early '60s," recalled 50-year Vikings trainer Fred Zamberletti. "There were no neuro surgeons around, but luckily we were able to find a local doctor who had battlefield experience in the war and was able to use some power tools to relieve the pressure on his brain and save his life until we could get him to a hospital."

"One time in a game against the Bears in '55, our quarterback George Shaw got leveled by a blitzing linebacker by the name of George Connor," said 12-year defensive tackle Art Donovan. "He put his shoulder right in his face and busted George's face mask. He was a mess. They drug him off the field and sat him down on the bench. His nose was bleeding, and he didn't know where the hell he was. He is sitting there, and he leans over to his center, Dick Szymanski, and he says 'Hey, Szyzzie, how do my teeth look?' Szyzzie just looks at him and says, 'I don't know, George, there aren't any there.'"

Earning the respect of your teammates often involves playing while injured and returning to the team earlier than doctors estimate. "I remember breaking my ankle in the first quarter of a Monday night game against the Dolphins in 1992," said 12-year quarterback Bernie Kosar. "I wouldn't take the tape off of my ankle though and let the doctors look at it because I knew that they would take me out of the game. I didn't want to look soft on national TV, so I just gutted it out. I didn't want to let down my teammates either, which was really important to me. So I wound up playing the whole game and even threw for a couple of touchdowns in the

Theisman's Last Stand:
The Hit That No One Who Saw It Can Ever Forget

Washington Redskins quarterback Joe Theismann's career ended during a *Monday Night Football* game on November 18, 1985, when he suffered a gruesome compound fracture of his leg while being sacked by New York Giants linebacker Lawrence Taylor. The tackle was even dubbed, "The Hit That No One Who Saw It Can Ever Forget" by *The Washington Post*.

Theismann had been attempting to run a flea-flicker and was standing in the pocket. Taylor blitzed, however, and sandwiched Theismann into Harry Carson, inadvertently landing on Theismann's lower right leg, fracturing both the tibia and fibula. As Theismann lay on the field, writhing in obvious pain, a horrified Taylor frantically screamed and waved for the medical trainers to rush out onto the field. When the instant replay of the hit was shown on TV, a collective gasp could be heard across the football world. The image of his leg bending and snapping in half has become one of the most infamous football injury images of all time.

"I remember handing the ball to John [Riggins], getting it back and then looking downfield," Theismann recalled. "I couldn't find Art [Monk] deep, and then I looked to my right for [tight end] Donnie Warren. At that point, I was feeling some pressure, and the next thing I knew, I heard what sounded like a shotgun going off—Pow! Pow!—and felt this excruciating pain. Then I was on the ground. It was at that point I also found out what a magnificent machine the human body is. Almost immediately, from the knee down, all the feeling was gone in my right leg. The endorphins had kicked in, and I was not in pain. I remember looking up and seeing Redskins trainer Bubba Tyer on my left side. I looked at him and said, 'Please call my mom and tell her I'm okay.' Joe [Gibbs, the head coach] was kneeling on my right side. He was looking at me and he said, 'You mean so much to this club, and now you've left me in one heck of a mess.'"

fourth quarter. It was an amazing feeling, and my teammates definitely appreciated what I did. The bad part about it though was that I did some damage to it. The doctors told me I would be out up to eight weeks, but I came back after just four weeks—which earned me even more respect from my teammates. But because I came back early, I wound up breaking it again shortly thereafter, which really sucked. I wound up getting four screws in my ankle, and it affected my mobility for my entire career. So you never know. Sometimes you think about the old adage, 'Lose the battle but win the war.' But in the heat of battle, you just want to get back out there and do anything you can to help your team win. That was my mindset. In the end it actually never hurt me that badly because it wasn't like I was very fast anyway!"

Everyone finds his own method for getting through the game. "It is just expected that you are going to play hurt at this level," said Ray Hitchcock, two-year offensive guard. "Guys will do what they need to do in order to be able to play. The coaches and trainers don't really care what you do as long as you can perform on Sunday. I will never forget my rookie year with the Redskins in '87. I got to the game early and was getting ready. I looked over and there was a 13-year veteran lineman having a cigarette right there in the locker room. I was floored. He had one at halftime too, and coach Gibbs didn't say a word to him. Hell, as long as he was playing great, I am sure they wouldn't care if he smoked an entire pack at halftime. To each his own, I suppose."

Veterans often do whatever it takes to play. "I would have to go in and get shot up all the time. It was brutal," said 13-year offensive tackle John Alt. "One season I would go in every Friday and get a nerve blocker put in my back. I literally felt like I was getting filleted because they would have to stick this needle down my back to find the exact spot to put the injection in. I dreaded Fridays. Sometimes it would work, and other times it wouldn't. You never really knew. One time I had my knee drained during halftime of a game, which was no picnic. It is like a pit stop in racing. Guys will roll in, get drained, shot up, and then [they] head back out there like nothing happened. It is insane when you think about it. Another time during a really hot game in Kansas City, I had to get IVs put in both arms during the game. I missed one play, and that was it. That was the way it was, though, and you just did it or else they would find somebody who would. My body is a wreck now, of course. I have issues with my neck, back, knees, hips, elbows, and wrists. My ankles are okay, though, so I guess there is one thing that still works on me! I get asked now if it was worth it, and if I would do it all over again. The answer is yes, I would. The highs are extremely high and the lows are extremely low, but it was a pretty amazing experience to be able to play in the NFL as long as I did."

Dealing with your injuries keeps you playing. "If you want to keep your job in this league, you play. Period," said five-year running back Darrell Thompson. "I remember standing in line to get shot up by our trainers before games. It was insane. Some people can deal with the pain and play through it, while others need to get shot up. The guys who chose to sit out for whatever reason, they don't stick around for very long. That is just the way it is. I got my ankle shot up one time because I could barely move it and I was talking to the team doc about Novocain. He was explaining to me about how all of the drugs in the 'caine' family—Novocain, Lidocaine, and Xylocaine—are all derivatives of cocaine, the ultimate painkiller. No wonder the stuff works so well."

Seven-year linebacker Jim Fahnhorst agreed. "I remember back in 1984, I made the jump from the USFL to the NFL and only had two weeks off during the transition between the two rival leagues," said Fahnhorst. "I was just spent. I played in 37 games that year, which was crazy. Anyway, we were playing down in Atlanta, and I had to get shot up in the ribs, quad, and foot. Then I blew my knee out on top of all of that. I was a mess, but somehow I still kept on playing. You do it because you have to. You are a piece of meat. If you don't play, or if you can't be counted on, then they will go out and get somebody younger, stronger, quicker, and cheaper who can. I understood that. We all do."

Thirteen-year offensive tackle Dan Dierdorf understood as well. "If you could walk—hell, if you could crawl out there, you got out there," said Dierdorf. "None of us knew any different way to approach it. That was the way we had always seen everyone play, those who preceded us, and that was the way we did it. I don't know if I would call it a code, so to speak, but rather a tradition. I never wanted to let my teammates down, so I was going to do whatever I could to be out there."

Players stayed in the game until the coaches removed them. "Playing hurt was just part of the deal," said 12-year linebacker Karl Mecklenburg. "I never came out unless they took me out. If I was hurt, I always felt that it was up to the coaches to decide whether or not I was the most functional guy on the field or if my backup would do better."

Even off-the-field injuries had to be dealt with. "It's funny, but of all the injuries I suffered in my 21-year NFL career, the worst happened one afternoon one season when I accidentally severed my big toe while mowing the lawn," said 21-year quarterback Earl Morrall. "It hurt like heck, but I came back and finished the season. I just put a metal cap in my shoe to protect it from being stepped on. I even joked around about it and told the reporters that it made me lighter afoot."

Sure players could play hurt. But could they play well while hurt? "Some players can play hurt, and others can't," said five-year wide receiver and longtime coach Bud Grant. "It is as simple as that. Take a guy like Jim Marshall. He was indestructible. He just didn't bend, break, or bleed like most other people do. He would turn his ankle over, and it would snap back and not swell up. A big part of it is your physiology, in my opinion. I mean, what happens when you get a bruise? Do you bleed a lot? Does the chemistry in your body disseminate the blood quickly, or does it stay swelled for a week? It is up to the individual's genetics as far as how they react to getting bumped and bruised. This is a hallmark of a lot of great players because you don't achieve greatness unless you play. You can't play half the time and be great. The only way to become great is to play all the time. So you either deal with the injuries in terms of pain, or you heal up quicker and better than others. Playing with an injury is no good, either. You have to be able to play up to your level with the injury. That is the key. Anybody can play hurt, but few could play well hurt. There was a big difference. I think guys were tougher in my day, too. I see guys today with muscle injuries who are sitting out for weeks and weeks, and it boggles my mind. That stuff didn't happen in my day. I mean sure, we all got hurt, and we were all stiff and sore. I remember many, many mornings waking up and barely being able to walk. But then you would loosen up and get the adrenaline going. You just sucked it up and got back out there to help out the team any way you could."

Players never wanted to lose their jobs to injury. "We just did it, no matter what," said 10-year guard Conrad Dobler. "That was the mentality in my day. We were always told, 'You can't make the club in the tub,' so we just shut our mouths and played football. If you were in pain, you played. Period. A lot of the players today don't know the difference between pain and injury. Shit, this is a collision sport. Playing hurt is a part of it. Pain is not injury. Pain is something you have to overcome and play through. They don't do that today. Their agents tell them that if they play hurt and in pain, then they will shorten their careers, which we, as older players, all did. Back in our day, we didn't have the luxury of sitting out because somebody would take our job. We never wanted to leave the field because that meant giving another guy the opportunity to take your livelihood. So it was a macho-type thing, as well as a selfish-type thing too. It was selfish in what you were doing to your body, as well as selfish in that you were not willing to give someone else an opportunity to get any playing time. It was a totally different era back in my day; it truly was. Things have certainly changed.

"You know, losing your job due to an injury was always on guys' minds. But it wasn't the only way to lose it. I remember when I first got into the league as a rookie and found out that I wasn't going to make the starting lineup. I was pretty down about it, but I figured I would just have to work hard and hope for the best. We were at training camp and it was the first play of a scrimmage against the Vikings. Our coach, Don Coryell, yelled out, 'All right, first offensive team get in there!' The starting left guard, Chuck Hutchison, ran out there and came running back to the sideline where he proceeded to yell out, 'Does anyone have an extra chin strap?' The coach was so upset that he had forgotten his chin strap on the first play that he looked over at me and said, 'Hey rookie, get in there,' I ran in there all excited and wound up playing pretty good. Long story short, I wound up taking over as the starting guard from Chuck Hutchison from that point on. I was able to take advantage of that small opportunity and make the most of it. Needless to say for the last 35 years, I have carried an extra chin strap with me in my briefcase as a reminder about how precious life is and how a simple inexpensive chin strap can cost you your job. Opportunities come in all shapes and sizes, and I was in the right place at the right time and was able to capitalize on it."

Injuries lead to exploitable weaknesses on the field. "To be able to play in the NFL, you had to not only have a high tolerance for pain, but you had to be durable," said 11-year defensive end Bob Lurtsema. "Teams needed to know that they could depend on you. That was their main concern. Players had to play hurt; that was just understood. I remember playing with Baltimore as a rookie and getting my sternum cracked in practice by the great Jim Parker. I played the whole season with that thing. It hurt like hell, but there was no way I was going to come out or somebody would have taken my job. You block out the pain and just deal with it. If you were into the game and playing hard, then your adrenaline would carry you.

"I will never forget the time when Jim Marshall, our great defensive tackle with the Vikings who holds the record for the most consecutive starts in NFL history, showed up to a game one time in the back of an ambulance. He was suffering from pneumonia or something and could barely walk. I was supposed to start in his place for him, but he insisted on playing. I figured he would just start and then go to the bench to keep his streak alive. Not Jim Marshall. He played pretty much the entire game. It was incredible. Then after the game, he headed straight back to the hospital. He was so damn tough; he just loved the game. What a throwback.

"You know, one of the gray areas of the code dealt with going up against guys who were injured. Hell, we were all injured and hurt out there, but some of us were worse off than others. Well, if a player had an injury that was well documented, guys would go after that kind of stuff in an attempt to slow them down. They wouldn't try to injure them, especially if a guy had a knee problem or something that could be a career ender, but they would try to re-aggravate the injury so he might have to favor it and not be able to do his job as effectively. Agitating was okay, but injuring was a no-no. You *never* wanted to hurt a guy by injuring him, though. That was a huge violation of the code. And hey, if you could take out the quarterback on a clean, legal hit, that was just a bonus. Again, you didn't want to hurt him, but if you could knock him out of the game, that would give your team a better chance to win.

"The bottom line with football is this: if you have a weakness, smart players will exploit it. And that weakness might not even be injury-related. Take for instance quarterback Daunte Culpepper. Once teams figured out that he had small hands and was susceptible to fumbling, defensive linemen stopped trying to sack him so hard and instead just went for the ball. Hell, the guy was 270 pounds. He was a load. So it was easier to just go for the ball rather than to bring him down. That was why he became known as such a terrible fumbler toward the latter part of his career. Teams picked up on it and exploited it."

Today's serious health issues could have been prevented by smarter decisions in playing days, but that wasn't the thing to do. "We all played hurt," said eight-year running back Chuck Foreman. "But was that a good thing? In hindsight, no way. Now we can see the toll it has taken on our bodies. Playing with all of those injuries was honorable back then because it meant putting the team first. But in retrospect, it probably wasn't the smartest thing to do. So many of the older players have serious health issues today, and much of that probably could have been prevented. If we didn't play, then they would say that you simply weren't tough enough. So then they would want to shoot you up with all those needles. The bottom line was that we played through the pain because we had to. If you didn't, then somebody would take your job."

Keeping your job meant staying on the field. "There was a difference between playing hurt and playing injured, and that all depended on the individual's tolerance to pain," said 15-year quarterback Joe Theismann. "We are in a different era today, though. Players who are injured today are evaluated differently than back in my day. Decisions are made based upon the injury as well as the economic investment. When I played, if you didn't play and your backup performed well, you would probably lose your job. So it was really a necessity more than anything else. You just figured out ways to be on the field, whether that meant getting shot up or getting taped up. You did what you had to do in order to get through those three hours, which would in turn buy you another week of rest and help you heal up a little bit better. That was how it was."

Healthy is often just a state of mind. "As an offensive linemen, our mentality is, 'If you can go, you go,'" said 12-year center Matt Birk. "You are never going to feel 100 percent, ever. We always joke around on the very first day of training camp every year when we are all putting the pads on in the locker room and about to walk out to our first practice. Someone will always say, 'Enjoy it boys, because this is the best you are going to feel for the next six months!' It is true, too, because you are constantly hurt. Every practice, every game, every time you lift weights—you are either creating a new injury or aggravating an old one. Being healthy is just a state of mind. You learn pretty quickly that if you want to survive in this league, you have to learn how to deal with pain and how to play with pain. You just do what you have to do every week to get your body out on that field. That is the bottom line in this business.

"I played 10 games one year with a severe sports hernia. It was brutal. I knew it was bad but didn't say anything. I wasn't going to come out either, until Coach [Mike] Tice saw me hobbling around the practice facility one day. He finally made me see a doctor, and I had surgery shortly thereafter. I literally couldn't walk without pain, it was that bad, but I never would have missed a game unless the coaches told me that I had to go under the knife. I did not want to let my teammates down; that was just my mentality. That is how it is in the NFL—everybody is hurt, but nobody really talks about it. We just deal with it and do what we can to help our teams win. That is the culture we live in.

"I will be honest, when I see the older players who are in such rough shape now, I think about that. We all do. You would have to be crazy not to. But nothing in life is free. I just do the best I can and try to take care of myself all year round. I have aches and pains, sure, but nothing like some of the older guys who can barely walk and are in constant agony. I really feel for those guys. Hopefully I will never be in that kind of pain when I am that old, but it is a distinct possibility. Obviously medical care has come a long way, so that helps me sleep a little better at night, I suppose. It sounds a little sick and demented, but this is the career that I have chosen to do, and I wouldn't trade it for anything else. I feel very blessed and privileged to be able to play football for a living. To be honest, if I had a chance to do it all over again, even with the injuries, the answer would be absolutely. I love this game.

"It is a totally different mentality in football. It really is. I remember one of the guys in the locker room talking one time about one of his buddies who played in the NBA. He was telling him about a knee injury he had suffered and about how he was playing through it, even though it hurt like hell. His buddy, the professional basketball player, was just floored that he would put himself through that. He thought he was crazy. He basically said that if he had a bad head cold that he wouldn't play. It is a different sport, a different culture, and a different world from ours, that is for sure."

Helping the team to win often overrides the pain of injury. "We just did it. That was the way it was in my day," said 12-year running back Dave Osborn. "If you had broken ribs or whatever, you just made the best of it and went out there to do whatever you could to help your team win. Today it is a different story. In fact, if a guy had broken ribs today and wanted to play, they probably wouldn't allow him to for fear that he may puncture a lung or something, which might result in a lawsuit."

"As a coach, I tried to leave that stuff up to the individual players," said longtime coach Jerry Burns. "Some guys have that gene where they can play through pain and perform at a high level. I think of guys like [Vikings tackle] Jim Marshall, who was one of the toughest guys who ever played the game. Other guys won't play if they are hurt. It is a personal choice. For me, I never told guys to play one way or another. That wasn't my place. The coach also has to recognize when a guy wants to play hurt but simply can't perform at a high level. That is when you have to let him sit and get healthy because he won't do your team any good by playing at 50 percent out there. On the other hand, if you let a guy play who is really hurt, you are now sending a loud and clear message to the guy on the bench, his backup, that he is no damn good, either, otherwise he would be out there playing. So you had to be careful of that stuff."

Twelve-year linebacker Bobby Bell never came out of a game, not even when his ribs were cracked. "I don't remember ever coming out of a game. Ever," said Bell. "You just didn't do that in my day. Hell, you would lose your job it you came out. I had broken bones, sprains, cuts, bruises—it didn't matter how bad you were hurting. You didn't come out. I even crushed a vertebrae one time. In the pros, if you get paid, you play. It was damn near the same thing in college though, too. I will never forget getting my ribs broken during a game one time when I was playing at the University of Minnesota. They had to carry me off the field, it was bad. My dad, who had driven up all the way from North Carolina to see me play for the first time, walked into the training room and asked the trainer how I was doing. The trainer told him that I had some busted ribs and that I was in a lot of pain. I was lying there with my shoulder pads off and had ice all over me. I will never forget, my dad then came over to me as I was laying there and said, 'Hey boy, I didn't come all the way up here to see you lay up on this table.' So at halftime, I put my pads back on finished the game. Pain is just a state of mind."

Coming off the field wasn't an option in the past. "You were always expected to play hurt," said 14-year offensive tackle Keith Fahnhorst. "Nowadays you see guys tapping their helmets out there to signal that they are coming off the field. I just watch that and have to laugh. In my day if I would have come out for a breather or if they twisted their pinkie or something, I never would have gone back in. They just never would have put up with that crap. It was stupid that we all did play hurt, and that is why we are all crippled the way we are today."

49ers Hall of Fame offensive tackle Bob St. Clair agrees. "I played in games where [49ers quarterback] John Brodie broke his nose, and I remember him bending over and calling plays in the huddle and he was dripping blood all over the field," said St. Clair. "But he would spend very little time out of the game. We weren't allowed to take time out of the game. The coach would have a fit. Cotton was a big commodity for all of us back then. If something went wrong with John's nose, you'd just shove a wad of cotton in it and go on with the game."

Playing injured has sharp consequences. "Shortly after being released by the Bengals in 2000, I went to see one of the best spinal surgeons in the area," said former Cincinnati Bengals offensive tackle Brian DeMarco. "He then told me how bad it really was and about how my spine had slid forward on my hip and about how I had developed ankylosing spondylitis, and that I had multiple fractures on my back. I think he counted 17 in all. Then they ended up having to pull my spine back up onto my hip, take apart pieces of my hip, remold the bottom of my spine, and fuse it with titanium bolts and rods. I am 35 years old, and I have no quality of life left because I gave it all to the league. I gave it to a dream because that is what I wanted. I guess that is what people will say, that I wanted this and that I did this to myself. It is just really difficult as I look at my young kids now. I can't play with them the same as most dads. I can't walk the same. It is no life. I have just decided that I am not going to let the NFL kill me...anymore."

11

The Gridiron Greats

A byproduct of playing this great game is the fact that injures obviously do happen. For some players, they can play their entire career, stay relatively healthy, and then live a long, comfortable, and normal life. For many others, however, the injuries never really go away. For them, the players who left everything on the field, life is a living hell—complete with a variety of crippling injuries, mental health issues, and chronic pain. For some, with no health insurance, disability pay, or pension, they need help. Enter the Gridiron Greats, which was set up by several former players, including Bears coach Mike Ditka, to not only help out their fallen brothers in need but also to create awareness. The organization focuses on the humanitarian side of post-football-related issues, providing financial support and the coordination of medical assistance and social services to help retired players deal with hardships they may face after football.

The bottom line is that a lot of guys need help. According to the group's website at www.gridirongreats.org, "Many players who helped build the NFL into what it is today ravaged their bodies through years of on-field abuse and are consequently unable to maintain a quality of life and financial security for themselves and their families. Often this is due to severe physical limitations, medical issues and, in some cases, dependency on pain medications used in dealing with football-related injuries or other hardships. The lack of adequate disability, rehabilitation, health insurance, and retirement programs for some players, many who are older, has resulted in many retired football players finding themselves in dire need.

As a result, some of the men who have given so much to the game can't afford to buy medicine or to cover medical expenses to remedy football-related injuries. Some players have even found themselves without a roof over their head. Others live in isolation and loneliness, embarrassed by the condition in which they have found themselves."

At the core of the problem is an ongoing battle between the retired players and the current NFL Players Association. The older players feel disrespected and are upset, not to mention they feel cheated out of millions of dollars in funds that they believe are owed to them. One of the guys on the front lines is Bernie Parrish, a former defensive back with the Cleveland Browns, who, after retiring from a very successful career in hotel construction, is now leading the charge for the thousands of former players who are at odds with the NFL as well as the NFL Players Association over a bevy of issues including health insurance, disability pay, and retirement pensions. In the 1960s, Parrish was one of the men who strengthened the NFLPA and worked hard to make it one of the most powerful unions in sports. The union was never supposed to take it to the owners collectively, but somewhere along the line it instead opted for labor peace as opposed to hostile lockouts.

The final straw came in 2006, when Parrish saw a quote from the NFLPA's executive director Gene Upshaw in the *Charlotte Observer*. "The bottom line is I don't work for [the retired players]; they don't hire me, and they can't fire me." Parrish, who had always thought that the union was supposed to represent all of its players, current and former, was outraged. After he attended a reunion with some of his former Browns teammates, stories of players who were in wheelchairs, along with endless tales of players whose pensions were so small that they could barely survive, finally pushed him over the edge. He was now on a mission to find out why and how this could happen. He was going to demand some answers. Soon after, hundreds of players started calling and writing, wanting to join the movement.

Before long, Parrish came to the conclusion that Upshaw wasn't being straight with the retired players and that he had kept them from millions of dollars they were owed. According to a 2007 article in *The Washington Post*, this happened "because Upshaw has allowed a complicated system that keeps players from getting proper disability payments despite

---

The Gridiron Greats

The mission of the Gridiron Greats fundraising efforts is to increase awareness and to raise money to be immediately dispersed to retired NFL players in dire need while also funding the GGAF programs and services activities. The Gridiron Greats' fundraising activities include ongoing corporate and public donation drives, auctions, autograph sessions, and special events. Check out the Gridiron Greats special-event calendar—a special event may be scheduled in your city. A public donation drive is underway, so you can make a donation today. For more information, or if you would like to make a donation, visit www.gridirongreats.org.

---

evidence of countless debilitating injuries, and the union—more importantly its arm, Players Inc.—did not pay thousands of dollars in royalties they have earned." According to the article, the annual benefit for a retired player from the MLB is $36,700, as compared with the NFL's $12,165. Parrish sees the difference between the two in the way the unions have structured themselves over the past 40 years and in the way money has been distributed. He also points to the fact that the NFLPA spent $5.6 million on legal fees in 2003 and 2004, whereas baseball's union spent $309,726 in that same time.

To his credit, Upshaw vigorously defended the union's dedication to retired players, but said he "can't give retired players the same pension as current players because it would take $1 billion to do so." Parrish and the other retired players applauded Upshaw's comments that he "was going to work with Commissioner Roger Goodell to eliminate the red tape that keeps retirees from getting their disability payments, but simply pointed to the $5.6 million paid in legal fees from 2003 and 2004 as evidence that the NFLPA was helping to fund that very red tape." Meanwhile, the NFLPA maintains that it does not or has not directed the retirement plan. That is up to the league.

In the summer of 2008, frustrated and tired, Parrish and former player Herb Adderley filed a class-action lawsuit in federal court in San Francisco claiming that Players Inc. has denied them tens of millions of dollars in licensing fees since 1994. Sadly and ironically, Upshaw died of pancreatic cancer on August 20, 2008, at the age of 63. The reaction to his passing was mixed. While most acknowledged his greatness as a player with the Oakland Raiders, others were very upset about the way he ran the union. "Gene was making $7 million a year when he died," said one former player who wanted to remain anonymous. "Meanwhile, we've got former players crippled, broke, and sleeping in their cars. Needless to say, most of the older players did not shed a tear. He had been robbing from us for years."

On November 10, 2008, after three weeks of testimony, a jury awarded more than 2,000 retired NFL players $28.1 million in a lawsuit regarding the licensing of their images. The jury said the union breached its fiduciary duty to the retired players and violated the terms of the players' group licensing agreements. Specifically, $7.1 million was awarded in actual damages, and an award of $21 million was given for punitive damages. The purpose of a jury awarding punitive damages is to punish a defendant and to deter a defendant and others from committing similar acts in the future. Punitive damages may be awarded only if a defendant's conduct was malicious or in reckless disregard of plaintiff's rights. A jury comprised of eight women and two men listened to three weeks of detailed testimony regarding the operations of the NFLPA and Players Inc. NFL Hall of Famer Herb Adderley served as the plaintiffs' class representative and sat through five-and-a-half hours of testimony each day wearing his yellow NFL Hall of Fame coat. He is 69 years old. Adderley's teammate and fellow NFL Hall of Famer Bart Starr made the trip from his home in Alabama to hear closing arguments in the case. Many other retired players attended court sessions to lend support to the plaintiffs. "I won three Super Bowls, and this feels better than all of them combined," Adderley said immediately after the verdict was announced. "I always felt I had one big play left."

Meanwhile, Jeffrey Kessler, a lawyer for the union, said, "The decision is contrary to the law, and it's an unjust verdict and we are confident it will be overturned." NFLPA Interim Executive Director Richard Berthelsen said the union will first ask the judge to reverse the verdict and will appeal the decision if that request is unsuccessful.

The reaction from the players was swift. "Thank you for all your support in this victory for retired players," wrote former Buccaneers linebacker Dave Pear. "The language in the courts found the union [NFLPA] to be guilty of such phrases as 'malicious and oppressive conduct with evil motive' and 'conduct that was outrageous and grossly fraudulent.' Please keep in mind this is our union the NFLPA. Gene Upshaw has been referred to as a 'benevolent shepherd' by some of the press. In light of this recent conviction of fraud, they might want to kindly rethink their statements. His legacy will be contrary to a benevolent shepherd. He proved himself by his actions to be a ruthless enemy of retired and disabled players."

The older retired players feel at odds with the younger current players, blaming them as the voting members of the union who, as one player put it, "simply aren't willing to share a tiny percentage of the income they generate to care for their predecessors; who can't be convinced of any obligation, of any reason to sacrifice a portion of their paycheck."

There are a handful of current players who have stepped up, though, including former Vikings center Matt Birk, now with the Ravens. In 2008, Birk donated $50,000 to the Gridiron Greats program and also sent a letter to every NFL player encouraging them to donate a portion of their December 21 game check. Of the nearly 1,700 active players in the league, only about 20 players (or 1 percent) donated to the cause. That included eight of Birk's Vikings teammates. Birk was surprised but vowed to just work harder to raise awareness for the cause.

"It's not going to deter me from getting the message out there," said Birk, who was honored at the Super Bowl as a finalist for the Walter Payton NFL Man of the Year Award. "I'm going to fight for this cause. It's in the best interests of everybody involved in this league. We're going to pick it apart and figure out how we can do better.

"This is obviously a topic that is very near and dear to me, and I am proud to be a part of it," he added. "To be able to give back in a small way to all of these guys who have made the game what it is today is a real privilege. It is heartbreaking to see so many of these older players suffering now, in such poor health physically and mentally, and it doesn't have to be that way. There is something that could be very easily done with the amount of money in the game today. That is where the real tragedy is, and hopefully we can keep pushing forward to be able to help these guys out. We owe it to them. We, the current players, need to do a better job of honoring their legacy. We really do. I just want to lead by example with this, and hopefully the guys will just get in line to do the right thing."

* * *

Many of the retired players feel disenfranchised with the union and with the league. Their stories of pain and suffering are sad, but they want to

---

Gridiron Greats: Dave Pear

Former Buccaneers defensive tackle Dave Pear's personal blog lists his employment as "Professional Patient - Social Security Disability" and as of 2008 he lists his ailments as:

1. 1981: Neck: Posterior Cervical Laminectomy at C6-7 with Removal of Hard Disc Compressing C-7 Nerve Root

2. 1984: Neck: Anterior cervical discectomy and fusion at C6-7 and C7-1, utilizing bone-bank bone

3. 1987: Lower back: Bilateral L4-5 disc removal followed by mini Knodt rod fusion at the L4-5 level

4. 1989: Lower back: Exploration, Removal of Knodt's rods. Laminectomy, Discectomy at L5-S1. Right L5-S1 Foraminotomy.

5. 1989: Bilateral Lateral L4-5, L5-S1 Fusion. Left Iliac crest Cortical Cancellous Bone Grafting.

6. 1989: Insertion of EBI Bone Stimulator.

7. 1989: Lower back: Removal of Retained EBI Bone Stimulator and Battery

8. 1993: Lower back: Microsurgical Extensive Decompressive Hemilaminectomy, Mesiofacetectomy, Foraminotomy L1/2

9. 2007: Lower back: Decompressive Lumbar Laminectomy of L3-4 with interbody fusion L3-4 (Four screws inserted into lower back.)

10. 2008: Left hip: Left Primary cementless total hip arthroplasty

11. 2009: Lower back: I am scheduled to have the four screws removed and other additional clean-up work in 2009)

12. 2010: Right hip: Right Primary cementless total hip arthroplasty

13. 2011: Neck: Cervical discectomy at C4-5

---

be heard. This is their legacy. They have many suggestions and opinions about what should be done. Here are a few of them to ponder.

Some retired players are in worse shape than others. "I recently attended a reunion out in Baltimore for the 1958 world championship game between the Colts and Giants, widely considered as the 'Greatest Game Ever Played,'" said Colts tackle Frank Youso. "I wound up playing both ways in that game because Roosevelt Grier got hurt, and I had to fill in for him. I had never even played defense before, but they didn't care. They just said to get in there and raise some hell. I will never forget getting spiked in the hand on the first play of the second half. It ripped my two fingers wide open right to the bone. I came off and the trainer put tongue depressors on each finger and then taped them up. They just said, 'Get back out there!' Blood was squirting out all over the place, but I ran back in and did the best I could. It was tough, but what a ballgame that was. It is hard to believe it was 50 years ago. Anyway, they were trying to raise money for the Gridiron Greats program, and proudly we raised over a half-million dollars at a banquet we had. It was a marvelous experience; it really was. But I saw a lot of players who were in such poor health, which was very sad to see. I just wish we could do a lot more to help out the older players who are hurting or crippled. We all played hurt in those days. That was just the way it was. I had to get taped from my upper thighs down to my ankles for every game for three years. My knees were totally shot, and I literally had to tape them up so I could play. I didn't complain, though. I was happy as could be to be playing football for a living."

Retired players deserve medical care. "Look, we are all hurting, some more than others," said former Cardinals offensive tackle Dan Dierdorf. "I have two new hips and two new knees. I am fairly bionic. When I go through airport security, I am like the one-millionth customer. I am greeted with lights and bells and whistles. It is pretty wild stuff. I keep waiting for someone to run out and give me the key to the city. Seriously though, I am delighted that there is an awareness now that is being created

---

New NFLPA Union Executive

New NFLPA union executive director DeMaurice Smith elected in March of 2009. Smith, 45, is a Washington attorney with connections to President Barack Obama and new Attorney General Eric Holder. He was the outsider among the candidates to replace Upshaw, but Smith impressed the player reps when he presented the union with a comprehensive plan and assembling roughly a dozen advisers, including Wall Street financiers, labor lawyers, and sports licensing experts. His stated goals for the union include increasing health care and opportunities for former and current players. He says the union has "both a moral and business obligation to retired players."

about the plight of a lot of the older players, but we have so far to go. It is very difficult, as a lot of the older players are finding out, to gather that horse after it has already left the barn. The game is so prosperous now and there is so much money involved that it is just unconscionable to think that there are men whose shoulders were the foundation of this game that don't have medical care. They are not looking for sympathy. They are not looking for people to take to the streets to demand justice or anything like that, either. We all knew what we were doing. I think it is just a question of what is fair and not fair. The fact that so many players don't have access to medical care is really bothersome, and we need to fix that. There are some things that are so transparent and so obvious that need to be fixed, and this is certainly one of those issues."

Former Vikings defensive end Carl Eller agrees. "The fact that the league has not done enough to help out the older players is a very difficult and controversial issue," said Eller. "Taking care of the older players was not part of their jurisdiction the way that things were originally set up, so it is not something that they have done illegally or anything like that. It comes down to a question of ethics and about doing the right thing. That is where we need to begin to take a look at this issue and to decide where the responsibility lies and what should be done in the future. I think that more things can be done and should be done, and hopefully as we move forward, a dialogue can be opened to achieve just that."

Their legacy deserves respect. "Those guys are the ones who made this game what it is today, and I think it is our job as younger players to try to make sure that we take care of them," said former Steelers running back Jerome Bettis. "It is important for any group of people to take care of their elders because they provided the path for you to take. So if we don't step up and do that, we are doing a disservice to their legacies and what they created."

Support should be available to retired players. "I am lucky," said former Browns defensive end and Chiefs head coach Paul Wiggin. "I don't need the money. But there are plenty of guys who do, guys who have had to deal with some horrific medical conditions as a result of years of bumps and bruises out on the gridiron. I remember a few years ago going to the 40th anniversary reunion of our 1964 Cleveland Browns championship team, and it was an exercise in spare parts. There were guys there with artificial hips, knees, shoulders, elbows—you name it. Luckily, I have been pretty healthy, so I haven't had to deal with all of that stuff. Some guys got hurt a lot worse than others, though, and they are really struggling out there. They need support, both medically and financially, and there should be some programs in place to help them."

The league and its younger members need to help out. "We need to recognize and take care of the older players who made this game what it is today," said former Vikings long snapper Mike Morris. "It is a very lucrative and prestigious game today because of all of their hard work and sacrifice. I personally think that the older players should be grandfathered into this new day and age of serious money. We should take care of our own. This is a very small fraternity, and the fact that so many of our brethren are hurting so badly is completely wrong. They are the walking wounded, and we need to do the right thing to take better care of these guys. Some of these men can't walk; some of them can't hold down a job; and some of them have serious emotional problems. The younger guys need to help out, and the league needs to help out. That is the right thing to do."

Former Falcons coach Jerry Glanville agrees. "The older players were the ones who built this league," said Glanville. "Sadly, we live in a world where we are all interested in what is happening now. As a result, we sometimes forget about all those people who made this league what it really is. We need to do a better job of taking care of those guys. I don't know how, but we need to."

"Has the NFL done enough to take care of the older players? Absolutely not," said Colts defensive tackle Art Donovan. "There are some fellas out there today who are really destitute. You would think that the players today would want to take care of their own, but it looks to me that the present-day players could care less. But you know what? Everybody who goes up the ladder will come down the ladder—and a lot of them will be in the same position that these other fellas are who are in such poor health."

Mounting medical ailments cause more than just financial difficulties. "Here is a scary statistic," said former Cardinals guard Conrad Dobler. "My offensive line in St. Louis consisted of myself, Dan Dierdorf, Tom Banks, and Bob Young. As of today, I have had seven artificial knee transplants and am going to need two new hips; Banks' has got two new hips and one new knee; Dierdorf's got two hips and one knee; and Bob Young is dead. That is just one offensive line. Come on! Do you want to tell me that is just a coincidence? Every other industry that is out there where you have individuals that work for you and they get hurt, they are taken care of with workman's comp. The NFL owners are just greedy sons of bitches as far as I am concerned, and they don't want to do it. You gotta hand it to them in one aspect—they totally screwed us players back in 1993. They were smarter than we were when they negotiated our labor deal, I will give them that. What they did was basically say that they would up the salary-cap rate, but in turn the players have to take care of funding the pensions and disability plans out of that. So now they can say that they gave the union the money to take care of this, [and] it is not their fault. Don't blame us for all of the players who are now crippled—blame the union for negotiating a shitty deal. So we as retired players, with no voice in the union, can't do anything about it. We got screwed. When you look around at all of these beautiful new stadiums and you see the rings of honor, those are the guys who made this game what it is. These are also the same guys who they are throwing under the bus. They are not compensating us, and that is wrong. It is totally ridiculous. Look, this game beats you up. So many of us older players have been through hell and back. All of the health problems lead to financial problems, which in turn lead to family problems and divorces, which can then even lead to drug and alcohol problems. A lot of guys are hurting out there now and they need help. They feel totally abandoned by a league that generates $7 billion a year. It is a mess."

The existing pension plan just isn't enough. "So many of us, practically every one of us older players, has long-lasting injuries from football that have affected our health as we have gotten older," said former Philadelphia cornerback Irv Cross. "I have had both of my knees replaced and all kinds of other surgeries over the years. Luckily, I have always had health insurance to help with the medical costs, but so many of the older players don't, and that is really unfortunate. We didn't make the kind of money the players make today, and that is a problem for many of the older guys. The pension plan and disability program that the league has just hasn't kept pace with the needs of the retired players. That is the big issue right now. It has to be addressed right away. Guys with no health benefits are getting wiped out financially. Other players have gotten into financial trouble or gotten divorced, which can be devastating. Hopefully, some things will change in the future.

"The crime of the whole thing is that there is so much that could be done with the NFL easily and not hurt anybody, which would help close those gaps. There are so many issues facing these guys. So many of the benefits that the players enjoy today are the result of the sacrifices of the guys who came before them. Nobody is asking for any handouts; they are just asking for the pie to be distributed in an equitable way. It is a mess. It seems like every time I pick up the newspaper I read about guys I played with and against who are dying, and that is such a shame. To see some of these players, who gave so much to the game [and are now] left with so little, is truly sad. With regard to the Gridiron Greats program, I salute Mike Ditka for what he is doing. I really appreciate it—Mike Birk, too. What a great guy. I wish there were more players like him playing today who really get it. It would be so easy for the brotherhood of professional football to just get together and resolve our own issues. We are all the same—we just played at a different time."

It's time for a change. "The younger players don't have a clue about this stuff," said former Vikings running back Chuck Foreman. "I think that disability and health insurance should be paid for, at least partially, for the older players. There are so many health issues that arise years after you retire from the game. All of us players who started that union feel betrayed. The union was started so that we could make sure that every former player, when they were done playing, would have an opportunity to at least have disability and health insurance. We didn't have any opportunities to contribute to any 401Ks or retirement funds or anything like that in those years. We have guys who can't even walk, and yet they can't collect a disability check, either. I have talked to several young players in the game today who don't even have a clue, and that is so disrespectful in my eyes. They don't understand. We were the ones who built this league, and they are the ones benefiting from our sacrifices. It is extremely personal to me, and I get very emotional even thinking about it. The league needs to change its stance on this stuff. The league spends about $13 million a year just to fight all of our guys who try to get disability. Something has got to change. It really does. Come on!"

Former Vikings defensive tackle Doug Sutherland agrees. "I don't want to take a shot at the NFL," said Sutherland, "but how do you file for workman's comp 15 years later? From my understanding, there were actually teams that used to file workman's comp claims on their players

Jennifer Smith on the Gridiron Greats

"I feel very privileged to have had the opportunity to be a part of such an amazing group that has provided help and hope to so many retired players" said Jennifer Smith, co-founder and former executive director of the Gridiron Greats Assistance Fund. "The genesis of the Gridiron Greats goes back to former Packers lineman Jerry Kramer, who wanted to help some of his teammates who were in crisis as a result of their injuries, lack of disability support, and sub par pensions, some as low a $179.00 per month. The organization was started when Jerry auctioned off his replica Super Bowl I ring after the original that was missing for 25 years was found; the funds were used to start the organization. Jerry then reached out to other players he knew who deeply cared about the issues facing retried players such as Mike Ditka. Mike's involvement not only took Gridiron Greats to the next level, but his participation and willingness to utilize his notoriety to call attention to the plight of retired players and publicly call for the NFL and NFLPA to 'Do The Right Thing' was extremely significant. Several other former players and men of great character also joined the group from there, including: Gayle Sayers, Harry Carson, and Joe DeLamielleure—all of whom were on the original board of directors.

"We all saw an injustice and witnessed many retired players suffering needlessly in silence—without receiving any help from their union or the league—often times being turned down multiple times for disability benefits, financial aid, and assistance. Mike spent countless hours working with the organization, donating not only an extraordinary amount of time, money, and resources, but also his heart; he deeply cares about the suffering so many former players have to endure. Mike did not choose to assume the role of becoming the face of this issue. Rather, it evolved that way, and the retired players who were suffering and in need finally felt that they had a voice—it was a loud one. I think Mike is aware of this fact and feels a great responsibility to these players. I think this together with his genuine concern for these men and their families is why he is involved in this issue.

"Initially, the organization decided that it was going to be about more than just writing checks to players in need. We hired an employee whose job was to be available to speak to players 24/7 and work with their families in assessing their needs and finding solutions. Financial aid and pro bono medical programs were then developed. It was all about doing whatever we could from a humanitarian perspective with a very hands-on personal approach. It was remarkable to see what impact a few hours on the phone with a player in crisis or a family member could have or what a few thousand dollars would do for some of these guys. The appreciation expressed by the players and their families was both inspiring and motivating.

"The main focus the first year was to be all about raising awareness and calling attention to the suffering and how the union and league were treating many of the men who made this game what it is today. The media attention we created brought these issues to the forefront and may very well have put some pressure on the NFL and NFLPA. The NFL went on create the NFL Alliance and the NFL Cares Foundation, and even the PAT seemed to have stepped up its grant giving. So much noise was made that with the work of people like Bernie Parish and his Retired Players For Justice Group, the issues were heard in the U.S. Congress and Senate. The exposure also resulted in many other players forming advocacy groups and other organizations for retired players such as Fourth & Goal, Dignity Without Football, and Heroes of Texas. Individual players like Daryl Johnston and Mercury Morris got involved lending their expertise and knowledge.

"I particularly want to acknowledge the hard work and contributions of Bernie Parish and Herb Adderley, who have truly made an enormous impact. In 2009 they won a class-action lawsuit against the NFLPA on behalf of more than 2,000 retired players which resulted in a settlement worth nearly $26 million. This was a classic case of *David vs. Goliath*. The case involved the misrepresentation of retired players with regards to compensation for the licensing of video games, trading cards, and other sports products. In the end, for Bernie and Herb, as well as all of the players, it was their code of honor that truly prevailed.

"The stories of the players in crisis even touched a few active players who provided financial support and public awareness. It started with Kyle Turley who donated a game check and created Gridiron Guardian Sunday. Matt Birk immediately signed on to participate then went on to spearhead the program after Kyle retired. Now, as of 2009, the NFL Players Association has a new executive director in DeMaurice Smith, who appears to be putting the issues that face retired players high on his agenda and there also seems to be the desire to improve the way in which the NFLPA treats retired players.

"From a humanitarian perspective there are a lot of resources out there. There are a lot of people from many walks of life who care, and there are many organizations out there that are willing to help as well. Medical, pain management, drug and alcohol rehabilitation facilities, pharmaceutical companies, and various social services agencies are all stepping up and making pro-bono resources available to players in crisis. While I know many retired players and family members feel they are alone, they truly are not. There are many people who care and want to lend support. I am one of those people. I have since left the Gridiron Greats and have developed a vast resource group for retired players. Through my Retired Players Resource Group I am now able to help players in crisis interface with a wide variety of groups and agencies. We are assisting them in securing financial aid, medical care, and social services while also guiding them through the process of applying for aid and other benefits.

"With regard to the future, it will be a long and winding road for retired players as they work to fix a completely dysfunctional and likely corrupt disability system, and also deal with the issues of sub par pensions, but I am cautiously optimistic. There are now a lot more people involved with many other advocates, individuals, and groups all working together to secure the benefits and assistance these retired players deserve. If people want more information, or if they want to help out, they can learn more at: www. retirednflplayersresources.com."

and then keep the money instead of giving it to the hurt player. How crazy is that? We heard of teams having injured guys sign disclaimers that they wouldn't sue them if they got hurt in lieu of big contracts, and then cutting the guys a short while later just to protect themselves. Guys were literally signing their lives away. Who knows what was true and what wasn't, but there was a lot of stuff that went down in those days that was not on the up-and-up, that was for sure. And good luck trying to fight them—it was like David vs. Goliath. The players would lose those battles every time. The bottom line now is that a lot of us are hurting. I am walking around on a fused ankle and a fused big toe, and I am way better off than most guys of my era. Hopefully, we can change some things around to get some guys the help that they need."

There are two sides to this story, and compromise is the key to a solution. "I work with an attorney as a financial advisor now and deal with both ends of the spectrum on this issue," said former Vikings linebacker Pete Bercich. "In defense of the NFL, a lot of players took early pensions and knew what they were doing. Right or wrong, they signed off on it. They knew what they were doing, and they did it anyway and now they are complaining about it. They complained about what I made, just like I complain about what the guys are making today. I made $62,500 my rookie year. Today, a rookie undrafted free agent makes $279,000 a year. To me that is unfair, but it is what it is. There is nothing you can do about it. Ten years from now, who knows what that number will be? Now, as for the other side of the issue, I feel terrible for a lot of these guys who are crippled and struggling financially. They are the ones who built this league. The NFL is what it is today because of their hard work and sacrifices. Period.

"Technology has grown the game exponentially. Look at the popularity of fantasy football. You can sit down in a bar with your laptop and watch your fantasy team while watching all eight games on big screen TVs. It is crazy. You couldn't do that in 1960. There are big bucks driving all of this stuff these days. It is a totally different animal. Football is so popular and the corporate dollars are astronomical today, whereas they just weren't available thirty or forty years ago. Plus, football is the only sport that is maybe even better to watch on TV, whereas baseball it is way better to be there in person. Baseball sucks on TV. Even basketball, when you are there in person, you are in awe of how athletic these seven-foot guys are flying down the court. It boggles the mind. On TV, though, they all look proportioned. They are all tall, so they all blend in as a bunch of big guys squeaking their shoes. Football, meanwhile, with the replays and the high-def, is awesome.

"The TV revenue is where all the money comes from, and that is the bottom line. The game has grown. But we should do a hell of a lot more to help out the older guys. Personally, I am grateful for what they did. Those guys played for the love of the game, and I really appreciate that. They need our help and the league should figure out a way to be there for them. The league needs to make sure that the financial integrity of the game maintains itself, though. That way the sport will stay healthy and continue to grow. It will be interesting to see how they tackle these issues of medical costs, disability benefits, and pensions. They are going to require some significant revenue, and the money has to come from somewhere. Both sides are going to have to compromise, otherwise nothing will ever get done."

12

Sub-Codes to the Code

The Long Snapper Code

"I can tell you without a doubt that there was a sub-code to the code that dealt specifically with us," said 12-year long snapper Mike Morris. "If an opposing player tipped me over or dunked me and forced me to screw up a snap, then it was game on. As a long-snapper, you are in an awkward position with your head down, particularly for punt formation. So if a nose tackle wants to get you, it is a pretty easy thing to do. If they chose to do that, however, it was just understood that we were going to do the same thing to their long snapper. It would escalate. And our guys would make sure it would happen, too. We would retaliate by lining up a huge guy on top of their long snapper the next time they had to punt and just make his life miserable. You had to send a message for that stuff or guys would take liberties with you all day. Things have changed today with regard to this, too. Now teams have to wait a full second before they touch the long snapper, otherwise it is a penalty. Back in my day, you could dump him as soon as the ball moved. It was tough, but you just had to deal with it."

"Back in my day there were no long snappers, just centers," said 17-year center Mick Tingelhoff. "There was a code, or unwritten rule, about that though, where guys knew not to mess with you when you were in that position. You were vulnerable when you were long-snapping for punts and kicks, absolutely. You could be knocked over pretty easily, and defensive linemen knew that. They could and it was legal, but they knew that if they did then we were going to do the same to their long snapper, which may or may not result in a botched punt or kick. So we just left each other alone."

Not all defensive players adhered to this code, however.

"I will never forget playing the Bears one time and seeing our poor center, Mick Tingelhoff, have to deal with Dick Butkus every time he long-snapped the ball on kicks and punts," remembered 15-year Vikings kicker Fred Cox. "Butkus would get a five-yard head start and then just tee off on him every time. Mick used to end up at my feet after he hiked the ball from having rolled backwards after getting drilled. I felt awful for him, but that was just the way it was back then."

The Kneel-Down Code

"There is definitely a code that deals with when you are lined up to do a kneel-down at the end of the game or at the end of the half," said longtime coach Jerry Glanville. "The defense is not supposed to come across the line of scrimmage, and there is not supposed to be any contact when it is assumed there is going to be a kneel-down. Conversely, the offense is supposed to just eat the ball and kneel down or have the quarterback simply take a knee. Well, one time Kansas City violated this code against the Raiders when their quarterback faked a kneel-down and threw a touchdown pass. That is a big no-no. If you really want to piss off your opponent and give them some ammunition to come after you the next time you face them, just do stuff like that."

The Practice Code

"I would say that there is a code when it comes to practicing," said former Packers running back Darrell Thompson. "Getting hurt in a game was understandable, but going down in practice was totally unacceptable in my opinion. Guys who don't go full speed in practice are not respected by their teammates. You see, as a running back, I would try to read guys' tempos while we were practicing. There was nothing worse than getting blown up by some asshole who would come at me going half-speed, which in turn would get me to go half-speed, at which point he would kick it into full-speed and knock me over to impress the coaches. That is how you get hurt when stupid stuff like that happens. Plus, it is disrespectful too, because it is embarrassing to get blown up in front of all of your teammates, especially when you slowed down to avoid contact with the guy. So for me the best way to go was full-speed all the time. I would let my coaches worry about backing me down. Determining the mood of everybody on the team was impossible, so in order to protect myself, I just went 100 percent all the time. This is an internal team code, and that is how you get your respect from your teammates and from your coaches. You need to let people know what you do and how you play the game. Once they know that about you, they will leave you alone and let you do your thing. Practice is a huge deal in football. We practice way more than we play. I mean baseball, basketball, and hockey players, they play several times a week. We play once—that's it. So it is important that you establish yourself in practice so that you don't get hurt. Football practices are not physical; they are extremely violent. There is a difference."

"I would say that there was a sub-code to the practice code that dealt with guys wanting to prove themselves," said former Buccaneers linebacker Pete Najarian. "I remember getting into a brawl during practice one time when I was with Minnesota. They had a big tackle, Tim Irwin, who looked at me as the lowly backup linebacker. Well, I was trying to become a starter and was doing everything I could to make that happen. Anyway, he was trying to intimidate me, and he wanted me to kind of give in to him in practice so that he didn't have to work quite as hard. Well, I wanted no part of that. As a result, however, he cheap-shotted me at the end of a play. I took offense and used the ensuing play to let him know that I wasn't going to be intimidated by him. Things escalated, and a pretty good melee erupted from there. We went at it, and the guys let us go. I remember my defensive coaches all screaming and yelling at me in front of the entire team, but then back in the huddle they all patted me on the butt and told me good job and that he deserved what he got. The offensive and defensive units were teams unto themselves and stuck together. In many regards they had their own codes separate of one another. Anyway, tempers flared all the time in practice, and sometimes you just had to blow off some steam by pounding on somebody."

The Pretending-Not-To-Hear-The-Whistle Code

Occasionally, when a player knows that he has cheap-shotted a guy a good second or two after the whistle, he will pretend he was not able to hear it. He will use his hands to convey this by pointing to his ears frantically so that the fans can see he didn't hear anything because of all the crowd noise.

Joe Theismann, 15-Year Quarterback, on Momentum

"Momentum is a huge part of football," Theismann said. "As the quarterback, you could dictate things by calling certain plays that were momentum-changers. You had to use the crowd to your advantage; that was so important. Either you are working to wake up your home crowd or to silence the crowd when you were on the road. You had to be conscious of that stuff at all times because you didn't want tens of thousands of fans sitting around on their hands. You wanted them out of their seats, getting excited, and cheering for you. You wanted to channel that excitement and make it contagious. But you had to give them a reason to get excited. It didn't just happen. You could do it in a number of different ways, too, from throwing a big pass to going for it on fourth down. Or maybe you would run a reverse or a gadget play. You just wanted to keep them in the game and keep them engaged. Trust me, things went a lot smoother out there when you were winning and the fans were with you."

It is certainly a gray area. A defensive player might gladly take a 15-yard penalty early in the game in exchange for a free shot on the quarterback. Such was the case back in 1976 during a game between the Browns and Steelers when Cleveland defensive end Turkey Jones beat the offensive lineman Larry Brown and wrapped his arms around quarterback Terry Bradshaw. The whistle blew, but he just kept on going, lifting Bradshaw off of the ground and then slamming him violently on to the turf head-first. The flags came flying, at which point Jones claimed that he never heard the whistle. The Steelers were awarded a 15-yard penalty for roughing but lost Bradshaw, who had to leave the game with a concussion. As for what happened to Jones? He ended up with a $3,000 fine, but his Browns wound up winning the game, 18–16.

The Wide Receiver Code

"There was an unwritten rule that we as receivers didn't cut opposing defensive backs at the knees," said former Giants wide receiver Stacy Robinson. "I remember many plays where I would be running stride for stride with a cornerback, maybe on the opposite side of the field from where the play was, and telling him, 'Don't worry man, I am not going to cut you as long as you stay up on me.' They did not like to be cut, and if you did cut them on a block, they would really take offense to it. It was legal, but it was an unwritten rule that you just didn't do it. It was especially prevalent with the older veteran corners when I was around, the guys like Mike Haynes and Darrell Green. Now if he was giving me a forearm to the face and trying to jack me up, then he was fair game. So we had that respect back and forth with each other. If he played me straight, then I would play him straight. That was our code."

The Team Trainer Code

"As a trainer, we did whatever we could to help our teams win," said 50-year NFL trainer Fred Zamberletti. "If that meant buying a little extra time for our guys, then that was what we tried to do. For instance, if our quarterback went down and I had to go out there to check on him, I might just have him lie there for a few extra minutes to sort of stall. That would give our backup some extra time to warm up, which might be a big deal, especially if it was going to be a third-down play where he was going to have to throw the ball deep. Quarterbacks need to get the blood flowing a little bit into their arms before they can really air it out, so that would help them get ready. Little things like that, little tricks of the trade, that was our code."

The Pro Bowl Code

There is a code that the player adhere to while playing in the Pro Bowl that basically says don't go too hard out there and don't play tough defense— just give the fans a show. The bottom line is that nobody wants to get hurt at the Pro Bowl. As one player put it, "You don't blow somebody up on a slant route at the Pro Bowl. You take it easy on them and try to have fun." In 2007, Drew Brees lived every player's Pro Bowl nightmare when he dislocated his elbow as the NFC's starting quarterback. The threat of injury exists in any football game—even a low-key, halfhearted affair such as the NFL's version of the All-Star Game.

"You can't go into any football game worrying about an injury because that's when you get hurt," said San Diego Chargers tight end Antonio Gates. "You've just got to go out there and play your game and hope for the best." Perhaps the most notorious Pro Bowl injury didn't even occur during the game, but rather the day before on the white sands of Waikiki beach in Honolulu. It happened back in 1998, when Patriots running back Robert Edwards' career was shattered when he blew out his knee during a rookie beach flag-football game. Many players today just use the time in Hawaii to relax and bond with other players. In fact, many of them now prefer to just watch from the sideline and enjoy the festivities, knowing they can't get injured just soaking up the sun.

The Injured Reserve Code

Occasionally, teams will violate league rules by allowing players on the injured reserve list to practice. According to Ross Tucker, a former offensive lineman who played for four teams in a five-year NFL career, New England did just that in 2005. In an article published on SI.com, Tucker wrote, "I had heard the Patriots did this before I signed with them, and I saw it firsthand during my time there. I asked veteran receiver Troy Brown about it one time and he responded, 'Every team in the league does that.' I quickly let him know none of the three teams I played for previously had done so. Basically, the Patriots would put a player on IR, knowing it meant he couldn't play in a game or practice with the team for the remainder of the season. By skirting the rules and practicing him anyway, it allowed them to develop his skills during the year. A side benefit is that they were also able to give some of the older players less repetitions and therefore additional rest."

The Using-Your-Helmet-As-A-Weapon Code

Every now and then in the 1950s, '60s, and '70s, when a big melee would break out, a guy would take off his helmet and use it as a weapon. This was a big no-no.

"I remember one time when I was playing with the 49ers, and we got into a huge brawl with the Rams," recalled former San Francisco guard Howard Mudd. "We had a pretty intense rivalry in those days, and fights would break out between our two teams from time to time. Well, on this particular brawl, there must have been at least 15 players all mixed up in this big pile of bodies. It was pretty ugly. Anyway, I was standing next to Merlin Olsen at the time, and we both just stood back and watched. All of a sudden one of our running backs, a kid by the name of Gary Lewis, took his helmet off and started beating guys with the thing. He was swinging it all over the place, it was really scary. Just then, we see this huge lineman rise from the pile and he is pissed. It is Rams defensive end Deacon Jones, who was one of the toughest guys of our era, and he was so upset about

---

Bob Lurtsema, 11-Year Defensive End, on the Difference Between Offensive and Defensive Players

"It is actually pretty funny, but the offensive players are polar opposites from the defensive players," Lurtsema said. "The offensive guys are more passive, while the defensive guys are more aggressive. In fact, you can walk through any NFL locker room and immediately be able to pick out the offensive guys versus the defensive guys without even looking at their names on the lockers. The defensive guys will have shit all over the place, while the offensive guys will have their things neat and orderly, with their clothes all hung up perfectly. It is night and day. The offensive guys are introverts, and the defensive guys are extroverts."

---

this kid using his helmet as a weapon, a clear violation of the honor code, that he just picked him up and threw him out of the scrum. I mean he literally went flying. Merlin and I were like, 'Holy shit!' Needless to say, the pile broke up pretty quickly after that. Gary learned a valuable lesson that afternoon though—keep your damn helmet on.'"

The Scab Code

In the spring of 1987, the NFL owners and players sat down to negotiate a new collective bargaining agreement. Upset about the owners' refusal to listen to their free-agency demands, the players went on strike. The owners, fresh off of seeing the rival USFL go out of business just a year earlier and feeling good about their monopoly-like status, decided to call their bluff. They were going to field teams with or without them. You see, the owners had a big financial stake with the TV networks in seeing to it that the games were televised, even it if meant using scab players. Unlike the labor dispute of 1982, when the networks paid the owners in advance, the agreements this time between networks and the owners dictated that the only way the owners could receive TV revenue was to make sure games were played.

With that, the team started putting together scab rosters consisting mainly of players already cut in the 1987 preseason, along with some guys from Canada, a handful of semi pros, and even a few free agents off the streets. The fans were horrified of what had become of their teams and stayed away in droves, with some games drawing fewer than 5,000 spectators. The teams wound up playing several games that actually counted in the record books. The whole fiasco turned out to be a huge union labor dispute, with Pro Bowlers and quarterbacks alike picketing team offices in front of stadiums. Every time a replacement player would enter a stadium, the veteran players would scream, "Scab! Scab!" Rocks were thrown, scuffles broke out, and things got intense. In St. Louis, a big union town, they even surrounded the stadium with semi trucks that they had commandeered and refused to let the opposing team buses into the stadium.

Many of the scab players were torn. On one hand, they were living their dreams by being able to play in the NFL. On the other hand, they were breaking the player code of honor by siding with the owners. In so doing, they knew that would be blackballed when the labor dispute had finally came to an end. For most of the scabs, they didn't care. They just wanted to play. They were making $4,000 a week, way more than whatever else they were doing at the time, and their moms could see them on TV. Eventually, a handful of veteran players cried uncle and started to trickle back to work. By the third replacement game, more than 150 of them had crossed the picket line. Their reasons varied. Some said they needed the money; others said that they didn't care about free agency and just wanted to get back to work. Many others said that they just wanted to help out their teams after realizing each outcome counted toward which squads made the playoffs.

When it was all said and done, the Washington Redskins, with no one crossing picket lines, went 3–0 in replacement games and won the Super Bowl. As for the players, of the nearly 1,500 replacement players, only 61 (approximately 4 percent) remained on NFL rosters one month after the strike ended. One of those players was linebacker Peter Najarian, who played for the Minnesota Vikings. Najarian had played in that same Metrodome stadium as a member of the University of Minnesota just months earlier and was thrilled to run out of the tunnel as a member of his beloved Vikings. His struggle to gain acceptance after that was challenging, to say the least.

"I was brought in to play on the scab team and yeah, it was tough," Najarian said. "I felt a little bit like I was betraying the guys, but I looked at it as an opportunity to showcase my talents. I had been with Minnesota during training camp and got released, so this was my chance to prove what I could do. How can you blame a guy for taking his shot? Sure, there were threats and this and that about how you were going to be blackballed once a deal was struck between the players and the league, but it was a choice that every player had to make for himself. For me, I just said go for it, and that is what I did. I talked to a lot of guys prior to doing it though, because I didn't want to kill my chances of making another team down the road. All of the guys I spoke with told me the same thing—publicly they wouldn't support me, but privately they would do exactly the same thing I was doing. I was one of the lucky ones. I was actually retained by the Vikings and was able to stick around. I got some flack from some of the veteran players afterward though, absolutely. I represented a guy who was trying to take one of their jobs. This was a union thing, and I was one of the guys who broke with the union. So I just sucked it up and worked hard, and everything worked itself out. I ended up playing for several years in the NFL after that, which was something that clearly wouldn't have happened had I not taken that leap of faith. So yes, I broke that code, but I was able to make amends and fulfill my dream of playing in the National Football League. I would do it again in a heartbeat, too."

The Wrong Way Code

One should never razz a man who has mistakenly taken the ball into his own end zone. Such a thing has happened only twice in football history—once in the collegiate ranks and once in the pros. The first time it happened was all the way back in 1929, during the Rose Bowl between the University of California and Georgia Tech, when Cal center Roy "Wrong Way" Riegels ran 65 yards in the wrong direction in what turned out to be an 8–7 loss. The other incident occurred on October 25, 1964, at Kezar Stadium in San Francisco during a game between the Vikings and 49ers. It all started with a lob pass from 49ers quarterback George Mira to Billy Kilmer, then a halfback, out of the backfield. Marshall, who was charging in on a blitz, saw the ball pop out of Kilmer's hands and immediately scooped it up. He then mistakenly ran 66 yards with the ball into his own end zone. Thinking that he had scored a touchdown for the Vikings, Marshall threw the ball into the air to celebrate. The ball then landed out of bounds, resulting in a two-point safety for the 49ers. It was immediately tabbed as the Wrong Way Play.

Cheating in College Football

Cheating and corruption scandals in college football, both on the field and in the classroom, are almost as much a part of the sport's culture as tailgating and mascots. Programs have been skirting the system for more than 150 years, ever since college kids started throwing around the pigskin on the gridiron. From coaches committing recruiting violations to the age-old tradition of handing out cash under the table, sports fans from coast to coast have seemingly seen it all. Boosters have always found ways to help entice prospective blue-chip recruits into attending their alma maters. Tales of shiny new cars, wadded-up $100 bills, and even new houses for mom and dad have all been a part of the lore associated with big-time friends of the program.

Let's face it—college football is big business. Really big. The top programs pay their coaches millions of dollars a year, and the television revenues that flow into their respective universities can reach into the tens of millions of dollars. The penalty for teams that get caught doing filthy things can range from probation to the dreaded death penalty, which can end a school's athletics program. Such was the case for SMU back in the '80s, which even had to shut down its football program for two years. SMU wasn't alone, though—after all, seven of the nine schools in the old Southwest Conference had been placed on probation that decade for various recruiting violations.

Perhaps the most egregious offense, however, is something that doesn't go on so much today but certainly occurred in decades past—the systematic fraud of academic cheating. The lengths some schools would go to in order to qualify certain students as eligible was beyond shameful. Everything from placing students in football-friendly classrooms and in front of football-friendly professors to getting extra help from football-friendly tutors has been alleged and uncovered for years. According to a 2007 *Sports Illustrated* article, former Cincinnati Bengals running back James Brooks revealed that he had never fully learned how to read. When asked how he made it through four years at Auburn University, Brooks replied, "I never had to go to class."

And Brooks wasn't the only one. Take Washington Redskins All-Pro defensive end Dexter Manley, who tearfully admitted his illiteracy in 1988 before a televised Senate committee hearing. Manley had problems learning as a child. In his second year in the second grade, he body-slammed a teacher against the blackboard in frustration. Manley, despite obtaining a score of 6 on the ACT test, went on to receive a full-ride football scholarship to attend Oklahoma State University. According to *The New York Times*, he also got a new car, to boot. Manley stayed for four years, entering and leaving with reading skills no better than a second-grade level before being drafted in 1981 by the Redskins. Manley, to his credit, got help and returned to a school where was able to learn to read and write.

"They were asking me to do something I just had no capability of doing," Manley said. "But I would always go to class. I would sit in the middle of the class or on the front row and try to get sympathy because I gave a tremendous amount of effort. I always made myself known, always befriended the teachers." Ironically, it was football, he said, that kept him out of trouble. "If I hadn't had [football], I don't know what would have happened to me. People like me are either dead, in jail, or insane because when you can't read, you have no knowledge of anything. So what do you do? You're frustrated, and the next thing you know you turn to drinking and drugging or stealing and robbing." As a pro, Manley lived a life of lies. At practice, he'd sit quietly in the locker room pretending to read the newspaper, and when he went out to dinner with the guys, he'd order last and just parrot their selection.

One player who vowed to do something about the problem was Vikings All-Pro defensive end Alan Page, who anchored the vaunted Purple People Eaters defense from 1967–78. Today Page sits on the Minnesota Supreme Court. In 1988, when he was inducted into the Pro Football Hall of Fame, he decided to use that national media platform to do some good. Declining the opportunity to swap gridiron gossip, as most of the football brethren do at their inductions, he instead shocked the pro football establishment by choosing Willarene Beasley, the principal at Minneapolis North High School, as his presenter. Never in the Hall of Fame's history had a person not in the football fraternity made an induction speech. Page selected her because of the fact that she was an educator and, as a black woman, represented minorities. Page's speech was about the values of education, not football; about learning to tackle issues, not quarterbacks; and about ABCs, not Xs and Os.

"I wanted to take advantage of that recognition and use the day as a mechanism for something meaningful," said Page who, following her introduction speech, launched the Page Education Foundation from the steps of the Hall of Fame. On why he decided to use that forum to speak of education rather than football, Page recalled a preseason afternoon practice some years ago when, during a defensive meeting, one of the coaches asked some of the players to read aloud from the playbook. It was at that moment that Page realized that several of his teammates couldn't read, while several others were struggling to just get by.

"In that moment, listening to my teammates unable to read a simple playbook, everything crystallized for me," Page said. "I don't know why it took me so long to realize it, but at that moment it became clear that this wasn't a dumb-jock problem or an athletic problem. These men were supposed to learn to read in first, second, or third grade, long before they were football players. You think about something, and you think about it again, but you can't point your finger at it. Well, that day I realized the problem I wanted to try to address was education, pure and simple."

"It was very simple in my mind," Marshall recalled. "It was one of those things where I just got all turned around. I picked up the ball and thought I was going the right way. Of course I wouldn't have run at all if I didn't think I was going the right way. So I crossed the goal line and threw the ball out-of-bounds to celebrate. That's when Bruce Bosley, a 49er offensive tackle, ran up to me and said, 'Thanks Jim!' He was giving me the razz, and then it hit me. Uh-oh. I had really done something bad."

The Vikings held on to win the game, however, with a final score of 27–22. The big play of the game came early in the fourth quarter, thanks to—you guessed it—Jim Marshall. The Captain caused a key fumble that was picked up by Carl Eller, who then took it 45 yards into the end zone to give Minnesota a ten-point lead. Incidentally, the Wrong Way Play has lived on in infamy, even being voted as the hands-down No. 1 pick of NFL Films' list of 100 Greatest Follies. Incidentally, Marshall later received a letter from Riegels that read, "Welcome to the club."

The Equipment Code

In the 1950s and '60s, the players were responsible for lugging their own equipment around. It is not like today, where they have valets and chauffeurs that take care of everything for them. If a player lost his cleats, for instance, then he would have to suffer the consequences. Such was the case back in 1958 with New York Giants offensive tackle Frank Youso.

"I will never forget the time I lost my cleats. That was tough," Youso recalled. "I had just played in the All-Star Game and my teammate, Phil King, and I flew out to San Francisco to meet up with our team for a game. We got to the airport and quickly realized that the airline had lost our cleats. So right away when we got to the stadium we told our coach, Jim Lee Howell, that we didn't have any shoes. He told us to just suit up and to wear our street shoes, they were nice leather overshoes that you would wear with a suit, basically saying that we could have the day off. Well, Phil and I were sitting on the bench early in the first quarter, enjoying the game and the sunny afternoon, when all of sudden coach Howell screams, 'Youso and King, get in the game!' I said, 'We don't have any shoes,' to which he said, 'I don't care what the hell you've got, just get in there!' So we ran out there and wound up playing the entire game, slipping on that wet grass all day. I even had to go up against Hall of Famer Leo Nomellini, which wasn't very fun without any traction, let me tell you. Needless to say, we learned a tough lesson that day, and we never packed our cleats again—we would tie them together by the laces and carry them around our necks on the airplanes."

NFL Fan Code of Conduct

In 2008, the NFL unveiled its first Fan Code of Conduct. According to a copy of the code, drunk and disruptive fans can be ejected from stadiums or parking lots without refund—and stripped of their season tickets. The same goes for fans who verbally or physically harass other fans, use obscene language or gestures, or interfere with the game by throwing objects onto the field. Fans who become drunk or unruly during pregame tailgating will not be allowed into stadiums. The policy evolved from a growing number of fans complaining to the league and its teams about their experiences at games. The NFL, which attracted 17.3 million fans to regular-season games during the 2007 season, began looking at a code of behavior after hearing a growing number of fan complaints about their experience at games. The rules say season-ticket holders and others fans are not only responsible for their own behavior but for that of guests or anybody else occupying their seats. "Event patrons and guests who violate these provisions will be subject to ejection without refund and loss of ticket privileges for future games," stated the code. Patrons can now lose their season tickets for the remainder of a given season and be barred from purchasing them again "depending on the severity of their actions."

"I commend the league for taking a stance to protect the right of paid spectators," said Lou Marciani, director of the center for Spectator Sports Security Management at the University of Southern Mississippi. "The hard part will be implementing it. As for the process of deciding who's intoxicated and who's not…good luck."

Afterword by Mike Ditka
Hall of Fame Player and Coach

There *is* an honor code in football, absolutely. It is about respect for your fellow players and about respect for the game. When we look at the honor code nowadays though, we need to start by talking about the obligation that the league has to its retired players. *They* were the ones who made the game what it is today. *They* were the ones who blazed the trail for today's players and laid the groundwork. So, we can't turn our backs on these guys, no way. And sadly that is what has happened over the years. There is a big problem with disability and with the pension programs, and we need to get the word out. Many of the former players are suffering from a wide range of health problems, including early-onset dementia and Alzheimer's, as a result of repeated head injuries. It is really sad to see.

Football is a tough game played by tough people. Players get injured and that is a part of the game, I get that. They should be taken care of though, like they are in any other business or occupation. That is where the problem is. I saw it first hand for many, many years and I finally decided to do something about it. I wanted to help out and just do something. So, the idea behind the Gridiron Greats organization originated from a Hall of Fame Trust that I put together years ago to help some players who I knew that had been going downhill in a hurry. Players like Jim Ringo, John Mackey, Willie Wood, Bill Forester, and Pete Pihos, to name a few. I saw these guys starting to deteriorate and it broke my heart. I wanted to help out so we put this group together to raise some money. Former Packer Jerry Kramer actually came up with the name Gridiron Greats, and he has been a big part of this whole movement. He had been doing essentially the same thing that I was, trying to help his former teammates, so we decided to combine forces and make a go of it. Since then we have really helped out a lot of people, and that has been extremely gratifying.

We have generated a lot of awareness and publicity to our cause, which has been good to see, too. As a result, we have made some wonderful friends and corporate partners, as well as several strategic alliances with medical facilities that have donated millions of dollars in pro bono services to retired players who need help and simply can't afford it. Those contributions are making a significant impact. We need more of those types of people, who want to give back and help us out. We can't do this without them.

I wish more of the current players would step up too, the way Matt Birk and Kyle Turley and some of the other guys have done. The players today are making a hell of a lot more money than we did in our day, and I feel that they have an obligation to help out those who paved the way for them. I really do. They don't understand that 20 or 30 years from now, they are going to be in the same situation if they have serious injuries and try to get disability coverage. What if they don't have insurance or can't get it? They will be right there too, and that is sad.

There are programs that should be put into place right now that could prevent all of that and in a sense take care of not only the current players, but also the retired ones. They need to take the steps to put a program into place that would insure the fact that when today's players retire, they won't ever have to pay a medical bill for an injury suffered on the football field. They have got the money to put those programs into place today, but they won't. Why? Is that important to them? Apparently not. That is sad, really sad. What is important to them is what is current. I understand that, but I don't agree with it. If you forget about what helped make the game what it is, the game will never be as great as it could be. I wholeheartedly believe that. We have all made contributions—all of us. The game is not about the people in the game today, however, it is about the whole accumulation of people throughout time who have made the game what it is today.

I am not sure what the future holds for Gridiron Greats to be perfectly honest. We have done some tremendous things, and I would like to think that we are making a difference. In 2009, we moved our headquarters from Green Bay to Chicago and also hired a new president to run the organization, Ken Valdiserri. Ken worked for me when I was with the Bears, and he is a really sharp guy. We had to bring in some new blood and put forth a new business plan. It was time. We now have some plans in place on how we are going to raise some money and I am hopeful that we can keep it all going. It seems like a never ending process, but it is something that I firmly believe in and am committed to. It is not easy raising money in this economy but between golf events and social gatherings we are trying our best to get some things done. We just keep plugging away.

There is also new leadership with the player's union and that is good to see as well. DeMaurice Smith was named as the new head of the union in 2009 and we, the older players, are hopeful that he can get some things done for us. Anything he can do would be terrific because his predecessor, Gene Upshaw, did nothing. In fact, in my opinion Upshaw was a determent to not only all of the retired players but to everything the game stands for. He set it all totally backwards. So, Smith represents a step in a new direction. We are anxious for him to get in there and show us what he can do.

As for the challenges that lie ahead, there are many. Gridiron Greats is just a band-aid, we are not the answer to the problem. We need change starting at the top with the league and with the union. You look at so many other unions and what they have been able to do and you just shake your head. Take the Screen Actor's Guild for instance, what they have been able to do with their pension program is just tremendous. It is a very strong union, and it represents its members well, both young and old. The people in it are taken care of forever.

I think that overall Gridiron Greats is very sound, very fair, and we were trying to help people. When you do that, however, sometimes you get a lot of criticism. As a result, a handful of frustrated retired players have started take action on their own. Several new coalitions have been formed and a Pandora's Box has been open up. Guys want to see things get done, they are hurting. I understand that and am sympathetic towards them. I wish we could all be on the same page, but that is not the reality of where we are at right now. Some of these new groups that have been formed are like loose cannons. Everybody seems to be jockeying for position right now, and that is troubling. Sometimes I wonder—where does common sense come in? Where do right and wrong come in? Look, nobody is trying to steal money from the NFL or from the Player's Association. We just feel that they have an obligation to take care of these former players. There are not that many of them, and it is not like they are going to go broke doing it either. Come on!

The more I think about it, the more aggravated I get. Maybe the NFL is *that* big and *that* powerful that they don't give a darn. Sometimes I get so frustrated that I want to bang my head against the wall, yet I am still determined. The bottom line is that you can form all the coalitions you want to and you can have all the dialogue you want to, but unless something concrete is set up and is administrated by a group outside of the NFL as well as outside of the Player's Association, nothing will ever get done.

At the end of the day I guess that I am an idealist. I finally came to the realization that there is no loyalty in sports. None. Nobody is loyal to anybody. Owners aren't loyal to the players, and the players aren't loyal to the owners. It is what it is. It is a dog-eat-dog world out there. This is an age where the players have power-agents who are only interested in getting paid upfront money and are not interested in the consequences. It is a flawed system. Look, I am not out to get the NFL. Hell, I love the NFL, it is a huge part of my life. There is just this one aspect, however, that has really got me upset. And it is not just me, it is a whole bunch of retired players who feel betrayed and disrespected. So, we need to all come together and represent a united front. We need to make sure we hold people accountable and make sure they do what is right. That is what the honor code is all about in my opinion, doing what is right.

Sources

Chapter 1
1. "Spying Isn't New; Neither is Paranoia." *The Sporting News*, Sept. 13, 2007.

Chapter 2
2. "Carl Eller: No More Days Off," by Ralph Reeve, *Pro Quarterback*, January 1972.
3. Neil Reynolds, *Pain Gang*, (Potomic Books, Washington DC, 2006).
4. "He Does What He Wants Out There," by Roy Blount Jr., *Sports Illustrated*, September 22, 1975.

Chapter 4
5. "Spying Isn't New; Neither is Paranoia," *The Sporting News*, September 13, 2007.
6. "Videogate Just Latest Chapter in Long History of NFL Spying," by Jerry Magee, *Union-Tribune*, September 13, 2007.
7. Ibid.
8. "Spying Isn't New; Neither is Paranoia," *The Sporting News*, September 13, 2007.
9. "Patriots Won't Be Hit Harder," by Mike Reiss, *Boston Globe*, September 21, 2007.
10. "Report: Belichick Earns New Deal," by Christopher Gasper and Mike Reiss, *Boston Globe*, September 17, 2007.

11. "Patriots' Players Dismiss Shula's Comments," by Robert Lee, *The Providence Journal*, November 7, 2008.
12. "Spying Isn't New; Neither is Paranoia," *The Sporting News*, September 13, 2007.
13. "Specter Calls for Independent Investigation," by Christopher L. Gasper, *Boston Globe*, May 14, 2008.
14. "Former Videographer Details Patriots' Spying," by Greg Bishop, *The New York Times*, May 15, 2008.
15. "Kennedy on Patriots Issue," by Mike Reiss, *Boston Globe*, May 15, 2008.
16. "Stealing Signals Isn't Just a Sign of the Times," by Les Carpenter, *The Washington Post*, September 17, 2007.
17. "Eli Tipped Giants' Play Call to Steelers on Goal-Line Stand," *USA Today*, October 27, 2008.
18. "NFL Players Look for Any Edge They Can Get," by Jeffri Chadiha, ESPN.com, August 1, 2007.

Chapter 5

19. "Notorious Image Sticks with These Raiders," by Jeffri Chadiha, ESPN.com, August 1, 2007.
20. Ibid.
21. "What Separates Cheating from Strategy?" ESPN SportsNation, August 10, 2007.
22. "Notorious Image Sticks with these Raiders," by Jeffri Chadiha, ESPN.com, August 1, 2007.
23. "NFL Players Look for Any Edge They Can Get," by Jeffri Chadiha, ESPN.com, August 9, 2007.
24. "After a Long Rain Delay, Tarp Finds Patriots' Field," by Damon Hack, *New York Times*, January 14, 2005.
25. "What Separates Cheating from Strategy?" ESPN SportsNation, August 10, 2007.

Chapter 7

26. "Fighting for Your Cause: Players, Coaches are Split on Camp Quarrels," Don Banks, CNNSI, August 12, 2008.
27. Ibid.
28. "Fighting for Your Cause: Players, Coaches are Split on Camp Quarrels," Don Banks, CNNSI, August 12, 2008.

29. Ibid.
30. Ibid.

Chapter 8

31. "McNabb on Offensive" by John Gonzalez, *Philadelphia Inquirer*, February 4, 2009.
32. Ibid.

Chapter 9

33. "Ex-NFL Player Stubblefield Gets Two Years' Probation in Steroid Case," Associated Press, February 6, 2009.
34. "Romanowski Marketing Healing Supplements," by Daniel Malloy, *Boston Globe*, June 26, 2007.
35. "Romanowski Marketing Healing Supplements," by Daniel Malloy, *Boston Globe*, June 26, 2007.
42. "Tony Mandarich Explains How to Pass an NCAA Urine Test," LarryBrownsports.com, By Larry Brown, March 6, 2009.

Chapter 10

36. "Dead Athletes' Brains Show Damage from Concussions," by Stephanie Smith, http://www.cnn.com/2009/HEALTH/01/26/athlete.brains/index.html, January 26, 2009.
37. Ibid.
38. "Dead Athletes' Brains Show Damage from Concussions," by Stephanie Smith, http://www.cnn.com/2009/HEALTH/01/26/athlete.brains/index.html, January 26, 2009.
39. *Pain Gang*, by Neil Reynolds, Potomic Books, Washington, D.C., 2006.
40. http://www.nytimes.com/packages/html/sports/20070612_NFL_FEATURE/index.html
41. "The Hit That Changed a Career," by Leonard Shapiro, *The Washington Post*, November 18, 2005.

Chapter 11

43. "Parrish Tackles NFLPA Head-On Seeking Better Pensions for Retirees," by Les Carpenter, *The Washington Post*, June 17, 2007.
44. Ibid.

45. Ibid.
46. "Parrish Tackles NFLPA Head-On Seeking Better Pensions for Retirees," by Les Carpenter, *The Washington Post*, June 17, 2007.
47. Ibid.
48. http://retiredplayers.org/2008/11/10/jury-awards-retired-players-281-million/
49. Ibid.
50. Ibid.
51. "Birk Committed to Cause," by Chip Scoggins, *Star Tribune*, February 3, 2009.

Chapter 12

52. "Saints QB Brees Dislocates Elbow in Pro Bowl," by Ronen Zilberman, Associated Press, February 11, 2007.
53. "Tucker Agrees With Walsh: Patriots Practiced with IR Players," ESPN.com, May 22, 2008.
54. "NFL Unveils New Code of Conduct for its Fans," by Michael McCarthy, *USA Today*, August 6, 2008.
55. "Breaking the Rules: College Football," by Stewart Mandel, SI.com, July 25, 2007.
56. "Why Manley? Why Now?" by Ira Berkow, *The New York Times*, November 22, 1989.
57. "Dexter Manley's Incredible Story," by Laura B. Randolph, *Ebony*, October 1989.